IN THE NAME
OF GOD
WHY?

EX-CATHOLIC NUNS SPEAK OUT
ABOUT SEXUAL REPRESSION, ABUSE &
ULTIMATE LIBERATION

BY DR. FRAN FISHER

D1453163

Griffin Publishing
8850 Auburn Folsom Road
Granite Bay, CA 95746

www.improveintimacy.com

Printed in the United States of America

Book cover design by Caren Halvorsen

Published by Griffin Publishing

1st Edition August, 2010
2nd Edition March, 2012
First Edition published by BAEB Publishing 2010

For more information regarding Dr. Fran Fisher and her services,
email: drfran@improveintimacy.com
To order copies of book, visit www.improveintimacy.com

In the Name of God Why? / Dr. Fran Fisher

ISBN-13: 978-0615612225
ISBN-10: 0615612229

1. Religion / Sexuality & Gender Studies. 2. Religion / Religion, Politics & State. 3. Religion / General. 4. Religion / Christian Church / General. 5. Religion / Christian Church /Leadership. 6. Religion / History. 7. Religion / Ethics. 8. Religion / Christian Life / Love & Marriage. 9. Religion / Christian Life / Spiritual Warfare 10. Religion/Christian Life/ Spiritual Growth. 11. Religion/Christian Life / Relationships. 12. Religion / Christian Life / Women's Issues. 13. Religion / Christian Life / Personal Growth.

Also, by Dr. Fisher:
Keep It Simple Sweetheart ~ Relationship Love & Romance Handbook
ISBN-13: 978-0615612249
ISBN-10: 0615612245
BISAC: Family & Relationships / Love & Romance

Fran as Postulant.

My sister, Helen and I.

My wedding ceremony as the Bride of Christ, family celebration.

CONTENTS

Sister Jane Frances de Chantal, circa 1968.

PROLOGUE:
A LONG ROAD TRAVELED

In the interest of intellectual honesty, it is fitting that I begin this work with my story. As a sexologist and former Franciscan nun, I have made dramatic changes in the way I perceive and now honor my sexuality. As I moved into my middle years and reflected on the changes I had gone through, I became conscious of a profound lack of understanding of my sexuality. There appeared to be little self- knowledge and comprehension of why I had, as I saw it, repressed such a vital life force. This awareness led me to study human sexuality at a graduate school devoted to this subject. It also led me to wonder how many other former nuns shared experiences similar to my own.

I was raised in Northern England in a tight-knit Irish Catholic family. My father provided well for his family. He worked as a coal miner; a hard, thankless job. We were always well-fed, well-clothed, and I feel, to the best of his ability, well-loved. Unfortunately, his generation of Irish men had little love to copy and even less example of gentleness. The contradictions one feels in this situation is in itself an interesting phenomenon. He was a heavy drinker and would regularly binge on weekends. At these times, my two sisters and I would be fearful since he was capable of becoming violent. He usually shouted and broke furniture, but he was generally not more physically violent than that. It was a very unusual event when he would hit any of us. My mother and I were the only ones to experience this. It is not an understatement, however, to say we lived in fear when he went out to drink and was in a bad mood. Because I was the tallest and strongest (both of my sisters had health problems), I would be the one to "take him on"

1

and defend my mother from his threats.

My mother was left motherless at a very young age. She once shared with me her story of being dragged from under a bed, along with many of her sisters, to the convent orphanage. Her father could only keep a few of his nine children. The decision was very hard on her and the others not chosen. She never spoke about her orphanage experience. It is not surprising to me that she lacked tenderness: she probably had experienced very little. Being brought up in an Irish Catholic convent would almost certainly have meant severe suppression and condemnation of all forms of intimacy, sensuality and sexuality. What she gave was total dedication to her family in the best way she knew: strict, merciless discipline, a high degree of self-worth and a blind observation of Catholic doctrine. A big treat for me was to sleep in her bed when my father worked the night shift, because it felt warm and good to be close to her. I don't ever remember any snuggles at this time. As a mother myself, I know the pleasure I received from snuggling with my two children when they were young. My mother would make me lie on my back with my arms across my chest and pray "If I should die before I wake, I pray the Lord my soul to take," so that if God took me in the night I would be in a state of grace.

I give this brief account of their background as backdrop to the following. I am sure there was no cruelty intended by my parents. Nevertheless, the effects of my history have led me to this point where I can look back without acrimony and examine why I have repressed and suppressed my sexuality for so long. It has been a struggle to confront my past and myself. Questions needed to be asked.

I really believe my background prepared me to live in fear of sex. Never to allow myself to see the sexual act as pleasurable and if I had to do it, then to endure it as a duty to my husband. But where did it start, this mental block toward sex? I have no conscious memory of sexual thoughts or feelings in my early childhood. It was as if sexuality did not exist for me until the day I began to menstruate. On that day of fear and mystery, my mother and her friend sat having tea when I came in from school and told Mum of the "event." She immediately shared the news, and her friend said to me, "Well now Frances, you're going to have to be careful of the boys from now on." I did not know what she meant, but I heeded her words and the kernel of sexual repression sown so much earlier in my childhood flourished. It was fertile ground, richly manured with years of Irish Catholic indoctrination.

In my home, sex was variously described by my mother as dangerous, bad, dirty, vile, nasty or filthy. The injunctions to see sex and human bodies in this light created massive conflict for me. From my early teen years onwards, I was a very sensual person. I was tall for my age and also rather outgoing. I developed an active, if clandestine, interest in the opposite sex (due to my mother's watchful eye). When I was fourteen I met a young man of eighteen. We had a "relationship." Dating was not allowed (and certainly not with an eighteen year old), so trying to see him and not let my mother catch me was spice to my life. One evening, a few weeks into our secret dating, while we were petting in an alley, he took his penis out and coaxed me to touch him. I believe I had never seen a penis before, let alone touched one. At that moment, the silhouette of my mother appeared at the top of the alley and her voice calling to me stopped the further development of my sex education. The ramifications of this evening bring both sad and warm memories to me. The Catholic Irish mentality takes caring one step beyond what could be called healthy parenting. The day after this event I remember the fear of what I had done eating away at me. I remember sitting in front of an enormous coal fire at my mother's feet, crying and telling her that I might be pregnant. Without asking me for any details, she sat and stroked my head and cried with me, saying, "Oh God, the only one out of the nine of us to have this shame." I have no other recollection of having been held or touched by her so this was a special moment, warm and safe, regardless of the words. Then she asked to see my panties from the previous day. When I brought them to her she looked at them and said, "Yes, that looks like the filthy stuff." When I heard her say those words my fear intensified; we both thought I was pregnant! I think she intended to fill me with fear (or perhaps in her ignorance her own greatest fear prevailed, that her girls would bring her that shame). She succeeded. I never saw that man again. In actuality, he had never touched me and no ejaculation had taken place. But those were inconsequential points for the "lesson" I was being taught. Now I knew for sure that sex would ruin my life. My mother did not explain pregnancy to me; I did not know about intercourse then. I must have menstruated as normal later that month, yet I don't remember her using the relief of that event to talk to me nor did she try to explain anything about sexuality. All I knew was I never wanted to play with another penis and I still, to this day, have a problem seeing semen as anything but a distasteful body fluid. This experience in retrospect had another consequence. When I came to realize that what was on my panties could not have been semen but my own juices, then they too came to be "the filthy stuff."

If my mother was sex negative, my father was sex prurient. Rarely did we hear anything spoken about sex; mostly it was in the form of off-color jokes. He almost always spoke of women in pejorative terms. They were variously described as "cunts" or "whores" depending on whether they were displaying independence or sexuality. One summer he visited Amsterdam with the coal miners' social club. He brought home lots of magazines and kept them under the cushion of "his" chair. I remember looking at them once and being curious, but he caught me and I never looked again even though they were there for years.

There was a lot of social drinking within my extended family. At these times all the children would be included in the revelries. I remember quite vividly as a budding adolescent, my drunken uncles coming up behind me and groping my breasts. The memory makes me shudder.

My interest in boys lessened after the pregnancy scare and my interest in school heightened. I attended a Franciscan Monastery high school. A contingent from this order came to recruit when I was fifteen. Two of my friends and I became very interested. At that time I was going to Mass every morning on my way to school. I felt it started my day out calmly and with peace. Into my sixteenth year, the three of us girls would spend a lot of our free weekends at the lovely convent in Belper, Derbyshire. This time of my life is still one of the happiest in memory. The big feather bed, the clean, peaceful, loving atmosphere. The mystery which surrounded the nuns was captivating. I loved being in an atmosphere of quiet, alcohol-free thoughtfulness and spirituality. It was in direct contrast to the atmosphere of my home.

My father refused to allow a girl to continue school past seventeen. He thought we should work in the local factory, be a hairdresser or a machinist, in order to pass the time until we were married and then have a trade that would help out our husbands. From an early age I saw and detested the life of most of the women around me. Upon graduating from high school, there were three 'professions' open to me, nursing, teaching or secretarial. I chose nursing because it allowed me to leave home immediately. Reflecting upon that decision, I do not recall even thinking about how close proximity to human bodies would affect me. The important thing for me was that I would be paid a small salary which freed me from dependency. I began my course of study just before my eighteenth birthday.

Although the pregnancy scare had dampened my interest in boys, I did have fun running around with a gang of young people, but they were considered lowly in my mother's eyes. She would stop me from going out with them whenever she could. My sister and I went to dances together and met men, but I was really very prudish with them. Although I would allow kissing, any other form of petting would scare me. During the initial months of my nursing training, the other girls cut my skirts outlandishly short and changed my name from Frances to the more 'hip' Fran. We had a blast. It was great fun being with them. I was always upset when boys would come and split up our group; we were having so much fun just on our own. Then when it was my turn to be 'picked' I would go through agonies because it seemed to me that their only interest was in "the part of me below my belt." It became intolerable for me (and, on reflection, for them too). Nine times out of ten I would freeze them out after a couple of dates. I recognize now that my actions could have been misconstrued as teasing, because I would be very turned on to some of the boys but equally conflicted about how to follow through with actions that my conscience would not allow.

Surprisingly, although the boy issue was a major problem for me, I do not believe it was, at least consciously, the stimulus to enter the convent when I did. The catalyst came six months into my nursing training when the schedule for the next six months was posted and there was my name on the roster for night duty. I still remember the panic...me on night duty, alone on the ward with forty sick people. Perhaps that was the last straw, which I took to 'prove' that I didn't belong in the secular world. I wrote to the Mother Superior requesting that I enter as soon as possible. To renounce sexual desire (which I did not allow myself to experience) and to live a life of poverty, chastity, and obedience was one to which I felt ideally suited. I was frightened of responsibility. The life in the convent was only marginally more austere than the nurses' home, so I thought. My world, the one I felt was truly meant for me, was the cloister...God's world. To be a "virgin bride of Christ" allowed my lively brain free range with romantic imagery (as my letters home would attest) without any physical contact; I felt happy with my choice.

The day I entered was terrifying. My sister and her fiancé took me to the convent. As I said good-bye to them and we kissed. My sister said, "We'll see you in a couple of weeks." We both thought I would be able to have visitors if anyone was in the vicinity of the convent. "Oh no," said the novice mistress, "Frances isn't allowed visitors for the first six months!" Suddenly the "good-byes" took on a whole new meaning, and I realized maybe there had been a few gaps in my preparation. My next surprise was my "bedroom." The poverty and austerity of the dormitory was stark. My mattress was filled with straw. I remember the terror of the first night, putting on my strange big white gown and climbing onto the hard surface. I lay most of the night with tears blinding me, while wondering what was going to happen to me next, and being acutely aware of the others behind the curtains in beds just like mine. There was no talking. The "grand silence" was to prove one of my greatest trials. One that I failed many times: after all, wasn't I the one at school from my earliest recollections who had had their legs slapped the most often for talking? No humming, no singing as I scrubbed floors. I was constantly being shown the sign to "shush." Oh, what had I done to myself?

I was a "postulant" (introductory period) for six months, and a "novice" (after receiving the habit) for about a year. It was not very long, yet the teaching and the indoctrination of those few months are indelible. I agree with Karen Armstrong in her autobiography, *Beginning the World*, when she says that it is difficult to confront those years "because they never die."

Sexuality was never mentioned in the convent. In fact, not only was it never mentioned, it was deliberately excluded, expunged from the life around me. At home I used to love to watch a TV program called "Top of the Pops." It was a disco style production with young people dancing to the top music of the week. I managed to convince my novice mistress that I should write a paper on this program for one of my classes. She, not having ever seen the program, gave permission for us to watch it the next time the show was on, as part of our one-hour recreation. I shall never forget her face as she saw scantily dressed young people writhing to the strains and sights of The Rolling Stones. The undiluted eroticism, was from her perspective, shocking and she immediately switched off the television with a very deliberate, stunned silence following the action. She gave me a look that spoke volumes: Where had I come from to watch such wanton "entertainment?"

We rarely saw men other than the elderly priest, our chaplain, who said daily Mass and heard our confessions. However, as a novice, I had a young priest for my spiritual advisor. He was a student at a university not too far from the Mother House. We talked for hours about books and world issues. He was the first man who I can genuinely say was a platonic friend. The novice mistress on many occasions made it quite clear that she did not approve of the time we spent together in the parlor. We didn't tell her about the books: *The Lion, the Witch and the Wardrobe* or *The Gospel According to Charlie Brown*; she would definitely not have approved. What joy it was to talk to him, he provided a male perspective in a disciplined, narrow, female world.

If I was unaware of any sexual attraction to my spiritual adviser, that was not the case for a young visiting priest who came to relieve our aging chaplain for a time. This man was young dark, slightly balding, and gorgeous. I was nineteen and still, under that dark brown habit, sensually alert. Although hardly a word was spoken between us (we were definitely kept well away from him), I do remember the attraction. The silent dropped eyelids in chapel, staring at his face from the safe distance of my pew. How strange to feel sensual in rough serge and tough cotton. I think I was so dissociated from my sexuality that I have no recollection of dreams or fantasies about him. It was all in the present tense; that is, when he was in front of me at Mass or passing in a corridor my senses would jump, but otherwise sexuality was sublimated by spiritual practices. It was easy to suppress sexual feelings because I knew they had no place in my life and should not be there. More importantly, if the novice mistress ever noted any outward display of pride or sensuality, one would soon be told about it and have to do penance. In retrospect I question why I didn't talk about my feelings to my fellow novices. There were three of us in the novitiate and nobody ever addressed the subject of sexuality. I was unaware of sexual feelings toward any of the women I lived with or sexual activity within the convent on any level. The professed nuns lived in another house. I certainly remember having feelings of arousal upon leaving the convent when I went back into nursing training. I remember being what I would now call infatuated with one of my female fellow students, although we never acted out sexually. But my time in the convent was spent in sexual dormancy.

I never masturbated, never touched myself. I do, however, remember tightening the cord around my waist to try and emphasize the small size. This was fruitless, of course, because the habit is designed to sabotage any such pride. The body was supposed to be ignored, depreciated, submissive and totally controlled. Bodily functions such as menstruation were treated (particularly by our novice mistress) as a time for deliberate sacrifice. On entering the convent we were required to bring two yards of terry cloth. This

8

was made up into sanitary napkins with our number on each. Our novice mistress took the new ones and distributed them to the older nuns, giving the novices older, harder ones. To add insult to injury, after laundering, she would not allow us to use our own piece of cloth the next month, a practice that is grossly unhealthy because she also had a practice of not allowing us to use enough soap powder to wash properly. Additionally she did not like us to use "too much." hot water. There was another nurse in the Novitiate, and this "discipline" caused much mumbling (and chafing). When we complained we were told it was part of the "discipline" and we had to endure, to cure our pride.

In my imagination, I thought my habit the most beautiful dress I had ever worn. It set me above all other women. I was pure, untouched, and untouchable, protected by God, my only lover, my perfect soul-mate. No decision was mine. No money was mine. No clothes, feelings, expectations. Nothing. Nothing for the foreseeable future was in my control.

In my letter home each week I portrayed God as a real lover to me. I felt I was in a personal, intimate relationship with "Him." Spiritually, I was fulfilled; yet sexually completely dormant.

After a year and a half, I began to feel emotionally drained and intellectually stunted. No matter how badly one wishes to be successful and live life with pure intentions, personal reality is not always how we would like it to be. I experienced two bouts of pneumonia and coughing fits that forced the novice mistress to ask me to leave the chapel because I was making so much noise. Theology classes became a time for disciplining my mouth not to ask the questions that provoked the good Sister to chastise me for impudence. In class, questioning Mary's virginity after she bore Jesus was considered, according to our aged theology teacher, doubly sinful for it brought sexuality and marriage into the classroom and also challenged the very tenets of the Church's doctrines.

My novice mistress was a very disturbed woman (I heard many years later she had a nervous breakdown and was released from her vows). She eventually created in me such turmoil that I had to recognize my vocation was questionable. I could not accept everything I saw around me and submit my mind and soul to what, for me, became abuse. The older sisters told the other novices and me that these things were our trial and we had to submit unquestioningly. I wondered why God would give me such a strong personality and then expect me to deny it for his sake. In retrospect, I am thankful for having this novice mistress to test my vocation at such an early stage. If it had been someone else with more warmth and compassion, I think I would have stayed a long time before coming to the realization that life in community was not my path.

It was clear the life of a celibate ascetic was not for me. I left quietly, inconspicuously one Saturday morning while all my Sisters were in chapel. It was a black day. I was filled with a sense of failure. Only one dear fellow Sister knew I was leaving, and we cried and gave each other a hug after Grand Silence on my last night. No one else said good-bye and I did not hear from anyone again until nineteen years later when I made contact with the nun who recruited me.

The skirt my sister had brought for me to wear home was above the knee. I squirmed when my knees showed because they had become big and squishy from so much kneeling. My hands were huge from so much cleaning. I had lost a lot of weight. So the clothes hung on what could pass for a skeleton. We stopped at a gas station and as I was walking back to the car, some young man whistled at me: My legs felt like jelly, I felt sick and exposed. If this was what it was like again, how would I cope back in the world? I returned to my parents' home. In my memory the failure of my religious vocation remains a source of shame. I was once a Bride of Christ, now divorced after only eighteen months and returned to my parents with twenty pounds in my pocket (my dowry upon entering) and ruined hands and knees. The hands mended and to this day I have a passion for nice nails and I don't care to look too closely at my knees.

I was like a lunatic escaped from the asylum. I was twenty years old but must have acted like fourteen. My old friends were still around for me. We went out as much as possible. It was as if I was trying to get back, in fun, the year and a half I had lost. One particular night my old friend from junior school asked if I'd like to go ice-skating. The reason this event is even noteworthy is because of the frantic way I threw myself into it. To this day, the pleasure of feeling my body skimming the ice, the freedom of racing across the surface, and even the spectacular falls and the abandoned laughter, are indicative of the release I felt from no longer being trapped, incarcerated, my personality buried in the convent. If only experiencing sexual abandon could have been so easily achieved.

Finally the time came to make a decision. It was clear to me my parents' generosity in keeping me at home gratis could not go on forever. After a couple of attempts to avoid the night duty issue in different jobs, I bit the bullet and went back to my old hospital to resume my tuition. They were very good and put me back to the point I was at in my training before I left. I was on the roster for the next set of night duty! It was fun. The other student nurses were just as nervous and, together with the girls I'd known prior to entering who were now almost through school, night duty was a breeze: a great relief.

I was making good progress in my life. In retrospect, however, my sexuality was still highly conflicted. I had found a sure way to protect myself. In the convent I needed to wear glasses, issued free by the National Health. All the nuns who needed spectacles wore a similar frame and it didn't seem odd there. I continued to wear them when I got out but they were very ugly. One day I fell off my bike and broke the arm off one side of the glasses. As a temporary measure my father mended them by fastening the arm back on with a straight pin. It looked ridiculous. I carried on wearing them like that for some months. Of course, I had very short hair in the convent, which I continued cutting myself with the expected result--hideous! As I see it now, my deliberate attempt to make myself look odd was intended to find a man who could see through all that and care for me on a deeper level, almost like my dear friend and spiritual advisor had done.

My old nursing friends were my best support team. They helped me get back into life. We shopped, trimmed my hair, curled it and let it grow, bought new glasses and went to discos, but I still hardly ever got a date. Now I was twenty-one. I was concerned because I had never had a relationship and thought there must be something very wrong with me. I remember a terrific urgency to meet someone and form a relationship. Yet I'm sure my demeanor was still telegraphing "get lost" signals.

One of the student medics asked me out and we went for a drink to the "Doctors' Bar." I left my glasses in my room in an attempt to improve my appearance. He pointed to an object on the bar and asked what I thought of the work of art. I squinted and strained my eyes and said it was a good representation of two eyes and a big nose. Someone from behind us laughed out loud and said to my date, "Where did you pick her up, a convent tea party?" With knees buckling under me we walked out. As I passed the art work I still couldn't make it out, even up close. "It's two balls and a penis," said my date. That relationship didn't last long!

At a disco one night I met John. He worked for the airlines. He was blond, tall and quite stunning. I was proud to be with him, but he made me nervous because it was as if he had a perpetual hard-on. With a man like him I had to ask myself why I imagined a weekend in his cottage alone would be anything but a sexual trial for me. I insisted on sleeping in the twin bed. If I had thought of it, I would have brought my flannel pajamas. However, a little blue nightdress with capped sleeves had to suffice. I slept with my rosary beads under the pillow to protect me and jumped out of my skin every time he came near me. When he walked into the kitchen in the morning with a hard-on proudly marching before him out of his dressing gown I thought I would faint! This definitely was not the man for me! His sexuality was too unbridled for my taste. Why did I accept an invitation for the weekend? To this day no answer comes to me, other than to remember that every time I got close to what I wanted I would run away. I also re-live the terrible fear of my teenage years and recognize the dangerous naiveté I lived by. I have to say I think it was at this stage in my life that I developed a wicked sense of humor. It was said that my tongue could bring down the biggest ego or the hardest erection. I realize now what a disservice I did to myself by engaging in this vicious self-defense.

I had several platonic male friends. One of them introduced me to Richard. He was intelligent, quiet and reserved. We were good friends before ever I realized he felt anything more for me. The relationship became sexual in a wonderfully casual, non-threatening way, with me being the initiator! (So I thought.) Laughter was the emotion most memorable throughout those early months, when we began to pull down the walls of my self-doubt and ignorance. The first time we attempted to have intercourse, I looked at the challenge very coolly and laughed. "It's impossible: That will never fit in there!!" It did and we were married fifteen months later. We now have two adult children and our marriage has survived twenty five-years.

As I view my sexuality from the vantage point of my youthful forties, I see that when I was in situations where, sex and or intimacy were offered (I could not differentiate between the two), I wanted more than anything to engage in the activity. Yet most times when the moment of decision arrived, I would turn my back and walk away. I always felt that, morally, I had taken the higher ground. We are taught in the Catholic Church, from a very early age that our bodies are the Temple of Christ. Therefore, if you violate your body in any way, you violate Christ's "space." Since I accepted this philosophy completely and went to communion daily, I felt my body was truly special, so special that sex would contaminate it. I therefore wanted an impossible relationship, one that fulfilled all my romantic fantasies for warm sex but on the other hand was celibate.

The indoctrination is still there in the depth of my mind today. I understand now that no matter how hard I tried to overcome it, the act of walking away left me with a feeling of superiority—of good over evil. As I reflect on it now, it is of course a fallacy and one of which I am not proud. What it actually did was to deprive me of personal pleasure and intimacy, which I craved. Now I relish intimacy in many areas of my life with lots of different close friends. Sexuality is something very different and I enjoy the freedom to choose for myself when to be intimate or when to be sexual.

The issues surrounding personal choice versus pleasing people went unsettled throughout my adult life. I did not have the tools to view and address sex and intimacy as different. Fourteen years ago I met a sexologist. The result of our conversation was that I decided to study human sexuality. It was clear to me by this time that my husband thought there was something "wrong" with the way I thought about sex and in many ways I agreed with him. I would rarely speak about the subject and never watched erotic films. Although our friends were sexually open people, I felt myself on the periphery of relationships with them. I never allowed myself to become too close, although I was every man's "buddy." I enjoyed being with open-minded, free spirits, but what concerned me more importantly, was the fear that if I allowed intimacy with any of these people it may lead to sex and so there could be no physical contact at all. There was still no appreciation that it was under my control.

My first weekend workshop at the Institute for Advanced Study of Human Sexuality was quite probably the most traumatic experience of my adult life. As I have said, I had never seen a "porn" movie all the way through. I had never discussed sex openly with anyone except my husband. Retrospectively, I understand how guarded I was even in this limited interaction. The young students from the junior college appeared so much more sexually experienced than I. There was no escaping it; I had to address my sexual history. I spent the first evening of the workshop alone in a hotel room. That was the first time in my whole life I had spent the night alone. I didn't sleep a wink, I had a vicious headache and my mind played back images of the day's events. The second day I was a wreck. I drove home at the end of my "baptism of fire" in silent confusion. It took me a month to assimilate all that had transpired during that short weekend. I would find myself sobbing while driving down the freeway, and I did not know why I was crying. The tragedy of my innocent ignorance took me a long time to process. It was three months before I was able to go back and join any more classes. I remember an exercise where I stood naked in front of a full-length mirror and was hit by a tremendous feeling of shame. Tears came to my eyes when they looked down at my knees. But the disclosure and understanding were memorable, freeing and thoroughly remarkable.

After more than three years of studying the subject, I was finally at a stage that I could address and begin to understand the conflicts and their genesis. The faculty at the Institute advised me not to worry about a dissertation topic: "through the course of time, it will find you." Eventually enough questions surrounding those formative years were posed to force me to look at the conflicts of my religious principles regarding sexuality. This is a topic I had diligently tried to ignore for twenty-seven years. I was forty-five years old before I admitted I loved sex. This was a milestone in my life. I had finally crossed the chasm, joyfully, from consecrated virginity to the open acknowledgment of my passionate sexuality. I could move on from being the child, permitting everyone else to control my sexuality, and finally own it, enjoy it, and grow.

Sexual freedom is more encompassing than anyone could ever have explained to me. Recognizing that I have control over my body has mysteriously given me a whole new outlook on my life in general. Never again would I subjugate myself in any manner for the comfort or convenience of anyone else. I was truly unaware of the damage being done to my own sense of self, let alone the disrespect drawn to me by always putting myself in an inferior position. I didn't need to wait for someone to put me down. I would feed them the ammunition and help them load the gun to fire at me. Understanding my sexuality has freed me from that misery, forever!

I no longer attend services in the Catholic Church unless it is to support family or friends. The ambiance of the Church is still restful and nostalgic if my mind and soul need a peaceful place, as long as there is no service going on. My personal connection with God needs no mediators.

In formulating a hypothesis for the work I embark on, I hope the findings will be a source of discovery to the participants but also to the wider field of sexology. Investigating how other women have made the transitions in their life, how they have released themselves from their vow of chastity and how they have discovered themselves as sexual beings will be a rewarding challenge to me. Perhaps the cumulative stories of many women's struggles

15

with spirituality and sexuality hold answers to the questions that still confound us. Conflicted as I was between what it meant to be a "good Catholic girl" and at the same time be a "good wife" to a sexually aware man, left me little time on my life journey to take stock of my personal sexual wants and needs. Trained from birth to be submissive, the road to discovering myself has been long and sometimes tortuous, but all the searching for understanding has paid dividends. Attending intimacy workshops, plus three and a half years of immersion in sexuality education has given me the promise of pleasures to come. I have often heard "the power of women" being talked about, and made a mental connection to explain it as "women using their sexuality as a power tool." To follow that road was an anathema to me. I always wanted to be judged by the quality of my mind, my character and integrity, not by the quality of the sex games I was capable of playing. Now I realize what a dreadful mistake that thinking was. By hiding behind such high-minded thinking, the very fundamentals of my womanhood were being denied. I could never become truly who I was until I recognized and honored that part of me; that lusty, sexual part that was buried in my childhood.

Of course I recognize that there are many more dimensions to this subject than can be covered in this short prologue. However, the stories to follow will perhaps fill in some of the gaps and add an element of enlightenment to the study of former ascetic women and how they perceive their sexuality.

Since this is a revised version of the original work from 1998 a lot has happened in the ensuing years. It seems only right to acknowledge that my husband was diagnosed with Alzheimer's disease in 2001 and passed away on July 2nd 2009. We would have celebrated our 37th wedding anniversary on the 24th of that month.

The tremendous irony here is that because of the challenges of living with him, I was forced to explore and grow. Almost simultaneously to my success I lost the partner to share my joy.

I now joke, with a pain in my heart, that I am the only celibate sexologist in California; an eerie throw back to my memories of the ability to go dormant.

16

CHAPTER ONE
THE POWER OF STORY TELLING

Finding the most appropriate research method to understand this study group was not an easy task. Charting the sexual transitions of women who had chosen a life of strict asceticism and then left had not been done to the best of my knowledge. Given that, to formulate a research procedure based on hypothesis testing was very difficult, since we know so little about the population. I therefore chose exploration as the basic objective in this study. Because I was studying an unexplored area, the research design had to be chosen to suit my requirements of eliciting the most information possible surrounding sexual perceptions in one's life passage from childhood to present day. This was a large project and one, which I decided, was best suited to multiple case study analyses of a small number of women. This method proved to be very powerful and sensitive, one that I felt particularly lent itself to self-report on sexuality and allowed for in-depth self-analysis. Using a statistical method alone to elicit this information would make less sense out of human desire, goals and social conduct as it related to such a group of women.

Therefore, the emphasis was not on standardized objective information, but rather subjective, expressive, reflective data, from which a thematic analysis emerged, without priority being given to deductive hypothesis testing or statistical treatment. Such data can be elicited from a questionnaire I distributed to a further 20 former nuns is available to amplify my findings. My expectation was that my work would add to the field of sexological knowledge and eventually yield insights from which wider statistically-based testing would emerge.

This research therefore is a sexological study utilizing a life-narrative method. This approach has been used for some time and is by no means novel. Psychologists, sociologists, anthropologists, and literary students have utilized autobiographies in order to more closely explore the lives, social conditions, and experiences of their informants. It is also recognized by researchers that especially in the area of self-reporting on sexual abuses in childhood, lower estimates are received when using questionnaires than when face-to-face interviews are conducted. This type of interview facilitates recall, helps clarify questions for the interviewee and also assists in determining causal relationships.

E. N. Evasdaughter, in her book *Catholic Girlhood Narratives The Church And Self Denial*, argues that by examining the writings of these women she offers insights into shared experiences of Catholic women as a group. She illuminates the ways in which the girls' choices, behavior and development were deeply affected by the repressive gender training and the Church's ideal of a "Catholic woman." In studying the narratives of a group of women with a Catholic childhood in common, Evasdaughter is able to construct similarities in women's personal histories and concludes that resemblances are demonstrated among all the writers. Their life stories have been represented in autobiographies which are truly valuable in understanding and making sense out of the influence of the Catholic Church in all facets of their lives, without concentrating on causality of the childhood influence. Rather, she thinks that by taking a look at the whole life in retrospect, one can recognize life choices as a bundle of potentials of which several might have been developed. Evasdaughter feels this method communicates a more accurate idea of Catholic women and, above other influences on them, how the Catholic Church dominates over all.

I wanted to examine the motivation and integral nature of how people saw themselves or what motivated them in the interpretive manner of this method. Once they became the storytellers, people translated for themselves events and circumstances, which up to that time have evaded deductive self-analysis. Listening to a life story gives us a glimpse through the teller's lens to motivations and feelings that would be hard to elicit through statistical study. Objective analysis of these stories allowed us further understanding.

Rosenwald and Ochberg say in the introduction to their book, *Storied Lives*, the way people construct the stories of their lives, what they leave in and what they choose to delete, is often as interesting as the story itself. "Personal stories are not merely a way of telling someone (or oneself) about one's life; they are the means by which identities may be fashioned. It is this formative and sometimes deformative power of life stories that makes them important." Sociologist John Dollard, argued that a "biographical account, when carefully interpreted by the investigator alert to the mirroring of society in the individual life, stands as a deliberate attempt to define the growth of a person in a cultural milieu to make theoretical sense of it."

Another approach to narrative research is a multiple-case strategy. K.J & M.M Gergenworks on the assumption that "persons are members of society and each member constructs knowledge about society from a slightly - but not completely - different perspective." Expanding on this theory, D.P. McAdam proposes that, through multiple case research, examining any particular aspect of life sheds light on that subject, which can inform and enlighten the reader. The women in my study had all been intimately involved with a sex-negative institution, the Roman Catholic Church. As G.C. Rosenwald et al., say, "That institutions have enormous power over the behavior and life chances of the individuals has long been recognized...social influence shapes not only public action but also private self understanding...the strictures of social control can in turn limit personal emancipation." In the case of women who had made the transition into and out of strict religious orders, the way they have constructed their life stories draws a connection between the present and the past; allowing us to interpret and thus understand a little more clearly how they perceived their sexuality. We learn from these stories whether sexuality was indeed an indomitable force that strove to express itself beyond the confines of the societal script that was written for them. The interviews offered them an opportunity to reflect on how their personal lives had changed and to speculate about the future as well as offering insights into the ways in which sheltered childlike nuns became responsible adult women. This is a tantalizing adjunct to this methodology. Women who have made such major life changes have a rich and diverse history. Only through their own words can we share a glimpse into how they have translated their experiences.

FINDING THE STORY TELLERS

In selecting the women for this book I wanted to expand on the limited information already available. Others had addressed Lesbian nuns and former nuns, (Curby and Manahan). My emphasis was inclusive rather than exclusive of any gender preference.

Lucinda San Giovanni had studied role passage out of religious life. My intention was to recruit as diverse a group as possible and follow their stories from childhood to present day. Therefore I followed-up on any contact I heard of from many different areas of my own life which turned out to give me 28 former nuns from 12 different orders as my core interview group. I deliberately tried to select from as wide a geographical area as possible and as diverse an ethnic composition, in order to see if these diversities had any impact on my findings.

I was concerned that few former nuns would be willing to share their intimate stories with me and so I was thrilled to meet "Kate," a vivacious, vibrant, 50-year-old who had been in the convent for 30 years and only left two years before our meeting. She gave me great encouragement and several suggestions as to how to contact other women. I met a former missionary nun whilst on vacation and friends from across the country introduced me to other former nuns. In this way my group grew and the 12 to 20 participants I was hoping to find for intensive interviews turned out to be 61 possibilities.

I worked from the standpoint that I wanted to understand the sexual component in each of the transitions. That is entering, leaving their communities, and how they handled their sexuality afterward. Therefore, no exclusionary criterion was given to length of stay in the convent, age on entry, age on leaving or relationship status at time of interviews. Again I was hoping for diversity, as I looked for change in sexual patterning.

In order to augment the findings from my interviews and also include all respondents, I designed a modified sexual questionnaire which was distributed to all 61 women. I contacted each of them by telephone and had extended conversations to confirm their status as former nuns and also to explain my study. Oral permission to participate in the study was received prior to sending a letter of explanation of the study. A letter to give permission to use the material was also included. A self addressed stamped envelope was sent with each package to 61 former nuns.

The response rate to the questionnaire was 80%, giving me a final sample of 49 former nuns, 28 of whom were interviewed.

Once permission was received an interview was arranged. I traveled to various parts of the United States to conduct the interviews. This was an ideal group from a researcher's perspective, because they were so sensitive to the questions and motivated to participate. Since the questionnaire had been sent prior to our meeting, the participants were aware of the areas I was interested in exploring. They had obviously given a lot of thought to their answers and were enthusiastic and personally concerned with the issues. All expressed their belief in the inherent importance of the study, and told me it was overdue. They were articulate, introspective and intelligent. Many said that they had never before put into words their thoughts on the subject of their sexuality, and were happy to have the medium to do so.

Questionnaire data collection was terminated at the time of the final interview. All questionnaires were coded with a numeric identification number that corresponded to the person's name in the database. The purpose of the identification number was to track responses. Anonymity was assured to participants and therefore all identifying details were taken out, names changed, no religious names were used. Nor in the report did I identify the communities these women came from, or where in the country they lived.

There were certain areas on which I wished to have the women focus and explore. Only in that sense was there any formal structure to the interviews. These areas were to reflect on what was happening in their lives from a sexual perspective, before they entered, during, and after they left convent life. Beyond those guidelines it was unstructured since I wanted to elicit how they construed and organized the meanings of the particular events they were describing, and therefore what was happening in their lives around the transitions. I was looking for themes to emerge. The interviews were from two to four hours in duration and usually took place in the participant's home. They were audiotaped and transcribed by myself. Access to the material was restricted to my research associates. I made follow-up telephone calls after each interview to ensure that nothing had come up for the women of a troubling nature and also to ensure they had nothing more to add to their stories. In the event one of the women did want to add to her story, I had the ability to add to their tape by recording our telephone conversation (with their permission). Further telephone calls were made where appropriate to assure myself that there were no unresolved issues that may have called for professional intervention. Dr. Barnaby B. Barratt, a psychoanalyst with two decades of clinical experience, who was at the time a Professor of Family Medicine, Psychology and Behavioral Neuroscience at Wayne State University School of Medicine, agreed to be available for telephone counseling if needed.

A copy of the findings from this research was sent to the interview participants in gratitude for their time and participation. Further copies were sent to current nuns who have given their time and assistance in referring contacts and giving me guidance with my literature search. They have also indicated that my work would be of interest to other convents and the general public.

In conclusion, I feel very strongly that this methodology is the only one which I could have used to develop a rapport with these women, to allow them the space and trust to speak about their most intimate feelings. For women with this background to share their sexuality took a great deal of courage. As will be seen in the body of this thesis, the stories are open, candid and full of detail. I was surprised to have reached so many former nuns willing to partici-pate in this study and to divulge their intimate private memories and aspirations for their sexual future.

Chapter Two
Voices from the Cloisters

From a historical perspective, Heinemann says that in early days of Christianity, women were actively involved preaching and had official offices. One woman who represented the best historically and is now gaining renewed notoriety is Hildegard of Bingen. Several authors, Craine, Fox, Lachman and Newman, among others, have written about her astonishing life. Her talents were many and varied and she was famous for her scholarship, musical talent, art, theology and holistic medical knowledge. McNamara cites Hildegard on twenty-two occasions, as she gives an in-depth historical account of Catholic nuns through 200 years. She documents the gradual lessening of power experienced by women in religious life. As centuries passed, they lost many of their rights and their position became more and more oppressive. Heinemann writes, "At the root of the defamation of women in the Church lies the notion that women are unclean and, as such, stand in opposition to the holy." In the assessment of clerics, women were second-class human beings. Clement of Alexandria writes about women, "The very consciousness of their own nature must evoke feeling of shame." Though Clement does not explain to women the reason for this intrinsic shamefulness, he does make it clear how they should dress, "Women should be completely veiled, except when they are in the house. Veiling their faces assures that they will lure no one into sin." McNamara, says ascetic women became an embarrassment to the male clerics, "peer pressure, slander, seduction, and rape have been mobilized to neutralize women who choose a life without sex." A glance at the art from this period will demonstrate the veracity of that statement, since much of it depicts nuns and monks cavorting. It is this imagery that Ruether refers to when she says that religion has historically been highly political and highly sexual. Further historical accounts of Christianity and the Catholic Church in particular among many others are by Green and Bokenkotter.

Woman is generally seen as the temptress. In multiple references throughout the literature women are described in this way. Heinemann, says, "to this day the Church's celibates believe that danger has a female face, and this belief has been taken into account in the formation of priests." In her autobiography, Mary Wong, says that she went to Mass every day and saw a young seminarian, her own age, that she knew well,

> Michael has already been taught the dangers of too
> much contact with the female of the species and has
> heard story after story of seminarians and priests who
> have been led astray by the wiles of a woman. Never
> forget boys that women are like bees: they'll make
> honey of you, but they'll sting you if you get too close.
> Michael never gets too close.

McNamara's first chapter entitled, "Chastity and Female Identity" states,

> Chastity combined with celibacy, the renunciation of
> biological sex and of social coupling, was virtually
> unknown to the family-centered societies of antiq-
> uity...Few women with desirable assets in property or
> beauty ever succeeded in reserving their bodies from
> the domination, protection and even the love of men.

It took centuries to change this thinking. "Women became the metaphor for the meek and humble destined to inherit the earth" (McNamara). To gain control of the masses, the Church attempted to control their sexuality and procreative abilities. The shift in paradigm from women as equal, to women as subordinate was the price paid along with the degradation of sexuality. Richard Sipe says,

"Women became increasingly associated with sin intrinsically and with witchcraft lustfully. It is hard to overestimate the importance of antifeminism in the formation of celibate consciousness and priestly development for over two centuries when the discipline of celibacy was being solidified." Others writing on the topic of feminism, antifeminism and women's place in the Church and society in general are: Daly, Elizonado & Greinacher, Eller, Friedman, Goldenberg, Greer, Griffin, Hammington, Henry, Lund, Murry, Murphy, Murphy, Pomeroy, Ohanneson, Quinn, Sanday and Welldon.

According to Sipe, others look at the origins of celibacy in the Catholic Church and agree, "The notion that sacrifice offerers must remain untainted by sexual encounters goes back to ancient civilizations." He gives examples of sects and religious groups from antiquity which practiced celibacy. More specifically, McNamara traces the history of women and their particular place in Christianity from the beginning. She feels that in those early days living in chaste celibacy allowed women to join men as equals because they were seen to prove themselves by the same discipline and training as male ascetics used to judge themselves. "Virginity wiped out gender differences and turned women into men by giving them independence and the authority to pursue a lofty spiritual calling."

Historically then, monasticism for women was seen as a way to circumvent the traditional role mapped for them. My study will show that although time marched on, this truth still held true for many and that the "foremothers" in religious orders were the role models they wished to emulate, rather than their biological parent.

Sipe attributes the foundation for present day Catholic Church views on celibacy to be based on two quotations from the New Testament. In Matthew 19:12, Jesus says "...and there are eunuchs who have made themselves eunuchs for the sake of the kingdom of heaven." Sipe continues "He who is able to receive this, let him receive it." Sipe denies that either of these quotes is a demand for celibacy but he does feel that they give permission to practice it. Heinemann thinks the whole debate about celibacy began because of a misinterpretation from translations of the words of Jesus. She thinks the discourse of Jesus, when taken in full context, actually had nothing to do with celibacy but was rather a condemnation of divorce and adultery. In recognizing that some men would not be willing to accept the change in the law, Jesus says,

> Not all men can receive this saying...need we say that
> the whole institution of celibacy was based - and still
> is today, practically speaking--on a foolish objection
> by the disciples? Their protest boils down to the idea
> that it would be better not to marry at all *because* that
> way one loses one's sexual freedom, and the possibil-
> ity of getting rid of one's wife.

In repudiating adultery and divorce, Heinemann feels Jesus was in conflict with his disciples who were "polygamously minded."

> Jesus, as we have seen, did not say anything at all about
> celibacy. He simply corrected, to his disciples' horror,
> the biases of a polygamous society contemptuous of
> women, and sketched an ideal image of marital unity.
> But celibate theologians in a call to renounce marriage
> later reinterpreted his teaching. While his words on
> becoming one flesh were transformed into praise of
> celibates as the eunuchs for the Kingdom of Heaven.

According to Sipe, there is no current operational definition of celibacy. In the past celibacy has been viewed from the vantage point of what has to be given up (as in the dictionary definition). Sipe quotes from the avowed celibate, Donald Goergen's book, *The Sexual Celibate*, in which the topic of celibacy was dealt with from a sexual premise rather than an abstinence starting point. Goergen describes true celibacy as "an ideal like perfect beauty to which many aspire but few if any attain."

A synopsis taken from Sipe asks the question

> Where does the nonessential practice as difficult as and
> unique as celibacy derive its power and persistence? In
> the Roman priesthood, there are three sources: spiritual,

political, and economic…if political power and economic questions had been absent, I doubt that celibate practice would have been legislated beyond monastic walls.
What makes celibacy a tempting broker of political and
economic power is its simplicity. Marital, family, and
sexual ties are complicated, engendering obligations,
bonds, and alliances of marvelous intricacy. They form
the kind of net that can entwine nations together and
ensnare the mightiest.

In his second book, Sipe examines the contemporary quan-
dary of institutionally enforced celibacy. He himself is a former
Catholic priest who married and had a son. His perspective is to
honor and value celibacy but to see it as something that must be a
personal individual life choice as valuable on an intrinsic level as
marriage, but different not better or worse. "If we can see that both
Christian marriage and Christian celibacy are expressions of love
for the Risen Lord, then both states become immensely meaning-
ful." Thomas, in his book, *Desire and Denial*, asks three poignant
questions, "is celibacy compatible with human intimacy and sexual
fulfillment? Is celibacy rooted in an anti-sexual asceticism that can
be emotionally repressive?" Finally, "above all, is the dichotomy
between sexuality and spirituality not only wrong but destructive?"

Wong, in her memoir spoke of a young priest's disillusionment
with celibacy. She had gone to him for counseling on her own concerns with celibacy, only to be told that he had had a female lover
for some time,

I'm afraid I've become rather cynical about the
Church. Like most priests, I'd like to marry and still
be able to continue my ministry, but I'm afraid it won't
come to that in my lifetime. The Church changes, but
it changes slowly. The problem is that I have only one
lifetime. I can just picture myself sitting in a wheel-
chair at 95 in some dismal retirement home for priests,

hearing the news that the pope had just made celibacy optional for priests. No, thanks...*The thing is, I know how convenient it is for the Church to repress sexuality: there's no more powerful way to control people. Sexuality is life force, energy: control that and you've got them by the balls* (my Italics).

The literature specifically related to female celibacy is scarce. However frequent references were found in the autobiographies of former nuns. Marcelle Bernstein collected the stories of 500 nuns and former nuns from California to Zambia. This is a valuable reference, one that I shall utilize here with several quotes to illustrate 20th Century thinking of many women in religious orders. She refers to an American novice mistress who viewed the vow of chastity as if

> It attempts to flee from the realities of sex and rigidly
> exclude the physical from thought and conduct. Sisters
> must be taught that they are dedicated to God's service
> as women, rather than as individual angels uneasily
> enclosed in a body. But that, of course, is exactly what
> they have been taught.

Bernstein also says that much is written and said about the vow of chastity that must worry a great many people. "It is not celibacy that is the cause of nervous troubles," snaps an Italian master of novices, "but a lack of sense of total dedication." Many of the women spoke to her candidly admitting they feel real losses. One only needs to read the descriptions of physical and mental torment experienced by Armstrong to understand the intensity with which this rule was followed in those days. It is a modern phenomenon in society in general to recognize a woman's sexuality; convents never allowed nuns to acknowledge their sexual drive. Religious orders dealt with the problem by refusing to admit it existed and any reference to the physical was repressed.

References to controlling the body and making it submissive

abound in all of the autobiographies. "Such nuns regard their sex as something attached to themselves that they don't use, like a spare tank of petrol on a car." Bernstein further comments that, as late as 1975, evidence that celibacy and chastity cause difficulties was ignored by Pope Paul VI when he called the celibacy and virginity of Catholic priests and nuns "happy and easy sacrifices." Another quote from Bernstein addresses the issues of silence around sexuality within convent life,

> I still don't think anyone I've met in religious life, admits there is a problem in suppressed sexuality [said one young nun]. It's obscene the way we haven't talked about sex in an open fashion. Says another: We weren't given any education with regard to the facts of life. Some sisters entered when in their teens without knowing them, and they never came to grips with them in a realistic way. How could a girl with that background truly choose to be celibate? The young girl who went from school into the even more restricted and protective convent environment, who met men rarely and formally, if at all, and who had no chance to experience any attitudes or life-styles other than her own - this girl cannot have known what she was sacrificing. She did not choose sexual renunciation; it was a piously motivated manipulation.

Wong relates in more poetic language the poignancy of the day she received the habit despite the nuptial imagery, this is not a wedding like any other, full of orange blossoms and honeymoon dreams. I am going to join my crucified bridegroom; like Him, I too must die. On His altar I will lay the life I might have lived, the children I might have had. Merciful numbness moves in to deaden the pain. I will do it.

The opinion of the Catholic Church has historically been sex negative. This is an ironic twist for a religion that acknowledges that

God became man. In his chapter entitled "Carnal Love," Fox, writes,

> Of all the world religions, Christianity has the biggest
> bias against the body. This is a disastrous theology.
> If I were Satan, and if I wanted to destroy Christian-
> ity, I would work overtime to tempt Christians to hate
> the flesh. Because we are the only religion that ever
> believed that God became flesh...It is an extraordi-
> nary leap to believe that God entered this world. And
> yet, as I have traveled the earth and seen different
> religions, I found we have the most negative attitude
> toward our body. Our bodies carry the most shame
> and guilt just for being a body.

By adolescence most young Catholics have received the message loud and clear that sex is bad. Sipe says that the official Church
teaching has not changed. Every sexual thought, word, desire and
action outside of marriage is mortally sinful. Procreation has to be
the intent behind every sexual act within marriage otherwise it is a
mortal sin. In the area of sexuality there are no venial sins. "Sex,
not greed or cruelty (where some minor violations could be toler-
ated), was the fast track to hell." The way the Church controls its
masses is through placing this heavy burden of shame and guilt
upon its members. Miller's psychoanalytic work titled *The Shame
Experience*, examines the effects of shame and guilt in a phenom-
enological study.

We have seen from the brief highlights of the literature, the tremendous pressure asserted upon women historically in the Catholic
Church to be submissive and pure. The reasons for entering convents are many and complex. In the very early days of Christianity,
ascetic women had parity with men. As times and politics changed
convents became prisons for some. It was common practice among
the royalty of the early European kingdoms that their daughters
remain in convents in preference to contracting matrimonial alliances that might involve their relatives in political difficulties.
Numerous princesses of ruling dynasties remained unmarried in

their convents. Other reasons women were sent into convents included those who were politically inconvenient. There are several examples given by Bernstein of Russian royal families depositing unwanted female family members in convents. Widows too, particularly royal ones ended up in convents, thus stripped of their lands and wealth. Mistresses' illegitimate offspring of bishops and princes are documented to have ended up in convents. The Diderot novel *The Nun* is a translation of the well known French work originally entitled *La Religieuse*. Diderot wrote about a young girl who was put in a convent to assuage her mother's conscience. She supposedly escapes from the convent and recounts her experience, among which was her seduction by the abbess (which is described in detail). V.L. Bullough refers to this work and says it reflects Diderot's concern with the effects of celibacy on women. He says Havelock Ellis believed the role of the Abbess was modeled on a true character of the time. This book is described as a "landmark in female sex variance."

Lest we should think these days are over and done with and the influence of the ancient church is passed, Chibnall, Wolf & Duckro found that nuns were no strangers to sexual trauma and the extent to which women in formation were exploited by both spiritual directors (priests) or religious superiors (women) was significant. Of particular interest when relating to all aspects of sexual trauma was that the women kept their experience secret for an average of 54 years. The previously mentioned research by Chibnall, Wolf and Duckro at the University of St. Louis School of Medicine resulted in a paper, "Women Religious and Sexual Trauma," to be published in1998. This paper is based on their extensive research "A National Survey of the Sexual Trauma Experiences of Catholic Nuns,*"* which appeared in the Spring of 1998. This is a unique piece of research that sheds much new light on the subject of religious women. Ritter & O'Neill carefully examine the effects of patriarchal religions on those subjected to them. Doehring in her published dissertation examines the way images of God change in those who have suffered abuse. Flaherty wrote from the perspective of children who have been sexually abused and the recovery process of spirituality in one's life. For further extensive references on this subject, I refer the interested reader to Chibnall, Wolf and Duckro. Wilson writes articles for and counsels nuns and former nuns who are survivors of incest and child sexual abuse.

Heinemann concluded that women were trained to be silent by the education they received. The Church silenced women, covered them up as much as possible, and took them out of the public eye. "The woman preacher disappeared from the ecclesiastical scene. From the Church's standpoint the best woman is the one least talked about, least looked at, and least heard from. Daughters of this world marry and are given in marriage, but the daughter of the Kingdom of Heaven refrains from all fleshly lust."

History remains of great relevance for today's Catholic women. Wong, writes about socializing with a group which included a Catholic priest,

> I pray for grace never to do anything to endanger his commitment to celibacy. I would never forgive myself if I did anything to draw his focus away from his important work. Although a man, he is also a priest. Catholic tradition from the time of the Fathers of the Church had always seen women as the source of man's problem's-Eve enticing Adam to taste the forbidden apple--and as a Catholic woman I carry that image of myself and of all women in my very bones. As a nun I had set myself off from all that, disconnecting myself from the rest of women, denouncing the part of me that caused men problems...I know that sex is bad, that for a nun it is even worse, that for a nun in the company of a priest-well it is almost unmentionable.

Although this story sounds archaic, it reflects the tone of one that will follow in this study, in which the woman in question would consider herself to be modern.

In her book, *Catholic Girlhood Narratives,* Evasdaughter defines the situation Catholic girls grow up in as a specific variety of oppression, "for the ideal presented to them has been that of 'the Catholic Woman' a term used frequently by clerical writers... and roughly definable as a kind of idealized domestic not given to female pleasures or intellectual pursuits, and not willing to participate seriously in the working world."

Memoirs and autobiographies from current and former nuns tell similar stories of struggle and personal pain. On a broad level, I related to many of the stories because they could have been my own. Bernstein discusses several women's reasons for entering the convent in relationship to sexuality, marriage, and family. San Giovanni, explored the role passage of nuns from religious to secular life.

Catholic educated women have had a very long and tortuous road to travel to release themselves from their history. Evasdaughter says,

> For Catholic women asserting their rights to sexual
> pleasure often has less to do with what other people
> think of as gender rules, such as the rule against adul-
> tery for women, and more to do with whether the sexu-
> ality of women is corrupt and wrong on all occasions.

There are many works on the subjects of celibacy, sexuality, and the Catholic Church. A representative view of these topics is given by the following authors, from both the historical to current perspectives: Bullough, Frein , Sipe, Heinemann, Thomas. Sergio specifically relates to women and their spiritual relationship with Jesus. The vows nuns make involve much more than a simple vow of chastity. Celibacy is only one of its components. Celibacy is defined as "abstention from sexual relations, and abstention by vow from marriage" (Webster's). This definition is too narrow to incorporate the complexities to which women submit themselves on entering religious life. The concept of asceticism encapsulates better the lifestyle and sacrifices made. The definition of an ascetic is, "a person who practices self-denial and self-mortification for religious reasons, a person who leads an austerely simple, non-materialistic life, and very strict or severe in religious exercises or self-mortification" (Webster's). Asceticism, as the total denial of all bodily pleasure required by religious orders, has a long history. "The rigoristic preference of celibacy and abstinence to marriage was already outlined in Stoicism and came to fulfillment in the Christian ideal of virginity" Heinemann. Stoicism is considered a foundation of Christianity (Bullough). Heinemann feels that from ancient times this idealization of virginity is based on body-hating pessimistic misinterpretation, rather than on the true teachings of Jesus.

Masturbation was a particularly contentious issue for all subjects in my study. Theories, facts, myths and beliefs about this particular practice abound in the literature, as do records of the effects of bogus beliefs: DeMartino, Ellis, Fox, Haeberle, Hite, Kelly, Kinsey et al., Lightfoot- Klein, Marcus & Francis, Masters, Masters & Johnson, McNeill, Nevid, and Szasz. Ellison and Zilbergeld developed and nationally distributed a 16-page survey entitled "Sexuality of Women Survey." Details specifically related to the masturbation issue have been useful in this current study. The impact of the teachings of the Church and society in general with regard to masturbation has had worldwide ramifications which ultimately showed in my study as an almost universal difficulty.

The Second Vatican Council was an international conference of theologians and clerics assembled in Rome by the Pontiff John XXIII. It was in session from 1962 through 1965. Few practicing Catholics and even fewer religious men and women could fail to be affected by the call for fundamental changes in the way the Church was to look at all its institutional practices and sexuality was included in that investigation. For the first time in centuries the attitude of docility began to change for Catholic women. Recent research by Bender, Kane, and Liftin focus primarily around the changes that occurred in women's religious orders during the initial influence of Vatican II. Borromeo, Garibaldi, Chittister et al. and Harrison, focus on the changing life and religious patterns in convents post-Vatican II. To many it was a release of pressure, giving them freedoms they had longed for. For other traditionalists it was a tragedy and sent turmoil into their ordered existences. Most of

35

the women in my study left their religious orders in the above time-frame. All left amid the conflict of change. The Second Vatican Council began the revolution but unfortunately in the intervening years the more traditional Pope John Paul II has worked assidu-ously to set the clock back and re-establish the old Catholic teach-ing on morality, "especially in regards to matters of sexuality." In a study, *Human Sexuality, New Directions in American Catholic Thought*, commissioned by the Catholic Theological Society of America, I feel an honest attempt was made to move forward if in no other way than to gather empirical evidence and present it for public analyses.

In the decade between 1960 and 1970 approximately 50,000 women left religious life (San Giovanni). At the same time there was a considerable change in women's political awakening and sex-ual freedom worldwide. Feminist writers such as Daly, Greer, and Friedan led the change. A Catholic woman herself, San Giovanni saw the impact of so many women leaving their convents in these years and wrote a sociological inquiry about members of one par-ticular religious order who all left in the 60's. She looks at these ex-nuns and their emergent sex roles as they prepared to leave their orders. Some nuns remaining in their convents became outspo-ken proponents for social change and the phenomenon called the "activist nun" was coined. Ferraro & Hussey continue to defend a woman's right to choose [conception].

There has been relatively little written in the press about the large numbers of women who left their convents during those tu-multuous years following Vatican II. Profiles appear occasionally in Catholic newspapers such as pieces by Szews and Hedrick. Eb-ough, Lawrence & Chaftz collaborated on the study, *The Growth and Decline of the Population of Catholic Nuns Cross-Nationally*. They attribute the declining numbers of women entering religious life to be due in part to the greater availability of education and the increased opportunity in the workplace for women in industrial-ized nations in the West. D. Fisher critiqued Hendricks-Rauch's research on married priests and their wives, and found "nine out of 10 resigned priests and 95 percent of resigned nuns in the study are very satisfied with their decision to resign. One in every two married priests in this study group married a nun. Nearly nine priests in 10 had met their future wives while they were still in active ministry." Calaianni also wrote on the subject of married priests and married nuns.

Schwarz wrote a two-volume psychoanalytical dissertation on the sexuality of women and the Catholic Church. She states that before the late 1960s most women in the Catholic Church were "obedient and unquestioning." Attitudes changed after Vatican II, according to Schwarz, particularly around the issue of contraception. Although she does not specifically relate her findings to nuns, I found her dissertation to relate fairly accurately to the attitudes of my participants. Curb and Manahan's *Lesbian Nuns: Breaking Silence* was a groundbreaking work in which a group of women "came out" about their sexual orientation. It was not a scientific study. Curb and Manahan edited the autobiographies of a group of current and former lesbian nuns who responded to a call to break the silence surrounding their very existence. No critical analysis or conclusions are made in the book; however, the great value of this work is to allow the diversity and sexuality of this group of nuns and former nuns to be made public for the first time. The enthusiasm for this work was in direct response to the euphoria of the women's movement at that time.

To the best of my knowledge there are no specific works dealing solely with former nuns and how they view their sexuality. This is a gap which I intend to remedy. There is an abundance of literature written about the sexuality of priests both current and former. Their celibacy and sexual practices have had both serious study and media attention in increasing amounts over the past two decades, due in part to the extraordinary publicity surrounding some of the abuse charges leveled at members of the clergy. The same is not true with regard to women in religious life. There have been several autobiographies, with detailed descriptions of life behind convent walls, and stories of abandoning the life. They are cathartic memories of women putting their lives back together. Where sexuality is mentioned at all, it is generally only briefly as for example, in Armstrong, Baldwin, Bernstein, Hulme and Wong. Bernstein interviewed 500 nuns and former nuns about the many facets of lives in the convent but failed to address sexuality except in a very rudimentary fashion.

The public has probably learned more about nuns and religious life through Hollywood than by serious study. Films such as *The Nun Story, Sound of Music*, and *Agnes of God*, have greatly influenced and affected the way the world and indeed young women themselves viewed the life of a nun. *Sister Act* is only one of several newer films proving the mystery of the convent can still sell at the box office. The romanticized picture was a lure to many whose stories are to follow; 66% responded yes to the question asking did they have an idealized, romantic view of religious life prior to entering? The narratives illustrate poignantly, their journey.

Chapter Three
Finding Common Ground

As indicated in my prologue, my interest in conducting this research was very personal. The fundamental stimulus for choosing the topic was to examine, on a scientific level, what the driving forces were in the lives of women who would voluntarily deny their right to be sexual, and the impact of that decision on their sexual development.

My primary concern when I first chose this topic was to locate and convince enough women to participate in the research to make it a viable addition to the field. I had anticipated difficulty in finding subjects. Another concern was that they would so censor their stories that it would be difficult to elicit a true understanding of their sexuality. My own bias and reticence to talk about sexual issues in the not too distant past, was the reason for my concerns. I thought that if I felt like this then perhaps it might be a common trait amongst former nuns.

Sexuality plays a major role in everyone's life, whether people recognize it and have awareness of it, or not. In particular, when looking at a group of women who have made religious commitments that shift them in and out of the possibility and legitimacy of sexual expression, the hope was that these people would share some personal understanding about the way sexuality impacted other aspects of their lives. In analyzing these stories, I hoped to uncover first, what the family of origin's influence was on the burgeoning sexuality of the participants as young Catholic girls. Second, I wanted to trace their sexual growth or regression as they made their transition from secular life into religious life and back.

Finally, my hope was to learn how they had developed since their departure from their convents, how they viewed their sexuality currently and their aspirations for the future. When collecting data on their life in religious communities, I hoped for a frank and candid assessment of their feelings round their sexual development. I expected this to be an area where the sample may have censored their responses. Since my own experience was limited to the novitiate, I had no expectation of the sexual growth or pattern that I would uncover when looking at those who had professed vows and been in religious life for many years.

Given the historical background of enforced celibacy, coupled with the notorious antifeminism of the Church, I was looking for changes in attitudes and in ideologies, particularly those surrounding sexual patterning. It would be possible to go into the convent as a sexually repressed adolescent and find, as the years passed and hormone levels changed, that celibacy may become difficult to endure. If fear of sex were the major reason for entering, it would now not be an issue and one may leave at this point. There are many types of relationships and reasons for both entering and leaving. I was not looking for causality; as stated, I was looking for patterns to emerge. Sexuality may be one of the major reasons that motivate some women to go into the convent, as in the case of the woman who recognizes her lesbianism and wishes to spend her life in an all female environment. Fear of sexuality on all levels may prompt a woman to enter into an asexual environment. Alternatively, sexuality may be what makes a woman leave. For instance the nun who falls in love with the priest or the layman with whom she works. Or she may become aware of her "biological clock ticking," and not be able or willing to deny her right to experience childbirth. However, the real issue as stated was how patterns seem to work, how people make sense of their sexuality in light of their commitment or make sense of why they made religious commitments in context of their sexuality.

Another aspect of this study which interested me greatly, was to explore whether these women had an understanding of how, or indeed if, sexuality and spirituality were integrated in any way during the transitions.

I hoped to attract a diverse group who had been in religious communities for various lengths of time. I anticipated finding women still deeply religious and still very connected to their Catholic faith. Alternatively, there could be those like myself who were disillusioned and in disdain of the patriarchal empire, which is my current view of the Catholic Church today. I am very much aware of my personal set of anticipations, or biases. I am hoping to dispel these biases with reasoned, analytical study.

In, *Lesbian Nuns: Breaking Silence*, Curb and Manahan found "many common threads" in the stories of the respondents. This publication was not an academic thesis, but it did deal with the sexuality of current and former Catholic nuns. I too was looking for the "common threads" in my research group.

At the time these women were in religious life, there were approximately 400 different religious orders in the United States. These included contemplative, diocesan, nursing, teaching, social workers and missionary orders. My initial intent was to gather as diverse a group as possible in order to reach a comprehensive, cosmopolitan total. I was unable to put together a thoroughly mixed cultural group. There were no African Americans or Asians in either the interview group or the wider survey. However, they were self-selected from no single type of order, from all over the country. Given these limitations I hoped to find similarities of attitudes that showed the power cultural background had on the sexuality of these women.

Another basic limitation of this study was of course that it was limited to those women willing to talk to me about their sexuality. When I began this work I thought it would be difficult to get former religious women to speak about this subject matter. That presumption proved to be an incorrect bias. All the women who agreed to speak to me appeared to have been open, and in the majority of cases, eager to participate. A certain amount of self-editing undoubtedly occurred, as was the case in my own story. The richness of the material gathered, however, was evidence of the complex lives of the subjects. No claim is being made that this is a representative or random sampling of all former nuns.

Chapter Four
"In the Beginning..."

I am worth celebrating.
I am worth everything,
I am unique.
In the whole world there is only one me
There is only one person with my talents,
experience and gifts
No one can take my place
God created only one me, precious in his
sight.
I have immense potential to love, care,
create, grow and sacrifice
If I believe in myself.
It doesn't matter my age, color, or
whether my parents loved me or not
maybe they wanted to, but couldn't.
Yes, I have made mistakes
I have hurt people,
but I am forgiven.
I am accepted, I am Okay.
I am loved in spite of everything.
So I love myself and nourish the seeds
within me.
I celebrate me.
I begin now, I start anew.
I give myself new birth today.
I am me and that is all I need to be.
Now is a new beginning.
A new life, given freely
So I celebrate the miracle
And I Celebrate Me.

— Ruth 1997

This was the poem given to me by Ruth, one of the first women to be interviewed. It reflects the magnitude of perceived change and heroic efforts the women whose stories follow have made, and their feelings of accomplishment in the end. The stories that follow are verbatim and have been only slightly edited by myself in very few cases for clarity of sentence structure.

I wrote my prologue prior to the first interview in order to maintain my own truth and to avoid any possible influence by the subsequent stories. It became eerily apparent to me as I sat listening to the women relate their life histories that in several areas we had similar experiences growing up in Catholic homes. I became quite adept at listening for the first clues about problems in their homes as children, because almost universally the initial opening statements when addressing the issue of parents was that they came from good Catholic homes with hard working parents. I remember myself as a child in school; if anyone ever asked about my parents I would always paint a perfect picture of my home life. The line from Disney's "Bambi" comes to mind when Thumper is told "If you can't say something nice, don't say anything at all." When questioned a little more closely about their parents later in the interview process, many times statements, tone and demeanor changed. It felt as if, once the women were comfortable, they allowed themselves to elaborate on the deeper memories of childhood. Other times the injustice meted out to them as children was the first thing on their minds and became uppermost in the story.

Ruth was the ninth of ten children. One brother was a priest and the sister with whom she most closely bonded entered the convent when Ruth was two years old. She stated she was very lonely as a child and felt abandoned when her sister entered. The only photograph her mother put on the mantle of any of her 10 children was the one of her priest son flanked by her two nun daughters. Her father was alcoholic and according to Ruth, her mother hated sex. She told me she was in her early 50s before she ever addressed or spoke about sexual issues and abuses which occurred early in her childhood. She said,

> The sexual repression didn't come from nowhere, and
> it didn't just come from the convent. When I was four
> I was abused by an uncle of mine. I repressed it until
> a few years ago. I found out later that he did the same
> to my other two sisters, and this was never talked
> about. One sister is seven years older, and the other is
> 14 years older than I.

Ruth went on to tell me that when she was in eighth grade a janitor at her school grabbed her and French kissed her. She said, "It scared the shit out of me. Those things made it a no, no and kind of reinforced, I believe, that going into the convent was the safest place to be."

The names have been changed for all the nuns interviewed for this story. For personal concerns, some of the narrative from the original study has been excluded Most of the findings, however, are inclusive of the entire sampling of women interviewed and included in unidentifiable aggregate discussions.

Out of 28 interviews, six women did not recall issues of sexual or psychological abuse in their childhood. One of the six, in retrospect saw her parents' obsessive religious behavior as psychologically harmful. Two felt they suffered cruelty from their mothers upon leaving religious life. Three had experienced incest, one at the hands of her brothers and their friends, two by fathers. Two were raped, the first by a friend of the father, and the second by a paid assailant at the behest of the mother, who had physically and mentally abused her severely throughout her childhood. A grandfather sexually traumatized one, two were sexually molested by uncles, one of these was also abused by an ex-priest and further psychologically and physically traumatized by her mother. A further 13 considered that they had suffered some varying levels of psychological abuse as children, seven of those had alcoholic fathers. This was a significant discovery and with the benefit of hindsight shows a gap in my research that did not address issues of abuse and alcoholism in the family of origin. After the third interview if the subject was not addressed or I felt the issue was being avoided, I added questions on this topic. My questionnaire lacked any direct reference to incest, sexual or psychological abuse.

The Chibnall, Wolf & Duckro study is the first empirical research on the issue of sexual abuse among religious women [nuns] but did not assess childhood psychological trauma. Their overall findings showed two out of five (40%) of the respondents had reported some type of sexual trauma in their lifetime. About 19% of the nuns in their study reported sexual abuse in childhood; 13% reported sexual exploitation; and 9% reported sexual harassment. A further 11% of respondents reported sexual harassment within the community. The Chibnall et al. report states that their findings were generally consistent with scientific literature on sexual abuse of children. "The percentage of Sisters reporting sexual abuse was clearly at odds with any argument that religious life has served as a particular haven for women who have been sexually abused. If that argument were true, one would expect that women religious would report much higher rates of sexual abuse than women in general. In fact, the best available estimates suggest that 25 - 30% of women in general report sexual abuse in childhood." In the current study statistics based on the informants above found 27½% had suffered sexual abuse as children. This number concurs with the general public according to Chibnall et al. but is considerably higher than their findings for religious women. The sample in this study was too small to draw any significant conclusions. In this group, however, escaping from sexual trauma into a safe place was a statement often made.

Further information from Chibnal et al., state the average age for disclosure of sexual abuse was 54 years. In a newsletter entitled "Breaking Open the Silence - Healing the Woundedness" distributed by the Sisters of Charity of the Blessed Virgin Mary, Wilson found the average years of silence after sexual assault was 33 to 47. As previously noted, Ruth told me she was in her early 50s when she first talked about the incidents from her childhood.

In this study, 10 out the total 28 women interviewed were from Irish Catholic homes, two were from Italian backgrounds, two were French and one had a Latino family. The remainder considered themselves American with no strong ethnic influences. Alcoholism was reported in eight specified Irish homes and in a further five non-Irish families. The mothers in these homes were either strictly disciplinarian, passive aggressive or extremely passive to the point of being described by the women as "beaten" physically or mentally, by their husbands. In these families conflicted by religion and alcohol, the mothers often seem to take refuge in religion and the children along with them.

It seems appropriate in this first chapter of stories to address why these women chose the route that led them into religious life. As their memories unfolded the decision to go to the convent was made quite early in life, at grade school age in most cases, and was very closely connected to their home life issues.

For example, Grace told me she had thought of entering the convent from her middle years of high school. She further told me

> I'm pretty sure the reason I entered was because it was counter-cultural, you know it was the 70s, the days of cults and communes and flower-power. This was a socially acceptable way to be in a commune and get a chance to do something different from your peers in terms of going to college. I definitely entered for the community, not in terms of some personal relationship with God, which is something I was pretty sure I didn't have, although I knew it was something I was supposed to have, so I tried to be as authentic as possible.

Elizabeth said her father was a bright, brilliant man who couldn't show his feelings. Her mother was outgoing, very sexy, it was "okay" for her mother to be sexy but not "okay" for the children. "I was aware that babies came from Mom and Dad, Mom let me touch her tummy when she was pregnant." Elizabeth was three years old at this time. There were seven children in the family. She never remembered being given any negative messages regarding sexuality during her childhood and the only related situation she could recall was the following,

> When I was seven I was in a grove of trees with my
> sister and brothers when a group of adolescents asked
> us to take down our panties if they took off their pants.
> I remember peeking through my fingers at them but
> didn't take mine off. What I remember is my father
> was so angry, my sister ran home to get my father. The
> next day we saw one of the boys in the grocery store
> and I whispered to my father, that's one of the boys
> who took their pants down. My father was so angry at
> that little boy. I never quite knew what it was about,
> but that was my first memory. Of course growing up
> Catholic we had all the teachings of the catechism; it
> was so rigid, so that would color everything. We all
> went to Catholic schools, through high school. It was
> an all-girls high school. I had wanted to become a
> nun ever since first grade. Now I believe in past lives
> and I've done it so often in the past it was deep in
> my psyche. The convent I entered was in the grounds
> of my high school. I was pretty wild in high school,
> so they kept back my acceptance letter three weeks
> longer than the others and I was told by the Superior
> General of the Community that she had watched me
> every day coming down the hill. I didn't do anything
> wrong I was just loud and had fun, I enjoyed life. She
> said to me, "Now you're not going to boarding school
> and you can't be like you were when you enter, you
> have to leave all that behind."

Both of Caroline's parents were first generation Italian American Catholics. She was the eldest of six children. Her memories of childhood are vivid.

I think what formed me most was being the oldest girl in an Italian American family where the boy child is the most prized first one. I know I felt it all my life and dealt with it in therapy but never really knew it was real. It honestly didn't hit me until a nephew was born 21 years ago that would make me 30 years old at the time. I was standing in the kitchen and my father was on the phone, he was talking to somebody about his son who had just had his first born. His words were "Yes he's healthy, he's doing fine and you know my son he's always had great luck, his first born was a boy." That made it real, it was like being socked in the stomach. I know the history of my sexuality, and who I am, was formed a lot on that relationship with my father, always trying to be the boy for him. I was always trying to be something for him. I couldn't have put that into words. I look back now and I was trying to be that first born boy. I remember when I was young always being by his side and learning how to use tools, how to go fishing. When I was young my father used to take back packing trips up into the Sierras on horseback. I used to watch him prepare and pack all of his camp stuff and I really wanted to go with him someday. I said, "Dad, when can I go?" And he'd say "When you're older." "Well how old do I have to be?" "You have to be 14." During the course of therapy, I realized that trip never came true. I never went backpacking with my father. I remember writing about it in tears that it was the cross over when I became a girl when I started to develop a girl's body my relationship with my father grew further and further

49

apart. I made the connection that I couldn't go on that backpacking trip because I was a girl.

This reluctance to be female was so pervasive for Caroline that she told me her breasts did not develop. She felt that it was "mind over matter." She had willed her body to remain masculine. Her story continued,

> Going back in time a bit I remember having no infor-
> mation about sex or how babies were made, despite
> the fact that I was the oldest of six children and there
> was always someone pregnant around [her parents ran
> a shelter for pregnant teens]. My understanding was
> that Mommy and Daddy prayed really hard and then
> you got a baby. All through Catholic education was
> learning how terrible boys were, I went through coed
> elementary and all-girls high school. All of the mes-
> sages about sex were bad, evil, and negative. I had
> no information. Throughout high school, there was
> no necking, no petting, I didn't have a boyfriend to do
> that with and good girls didn't do that anyway. I was
> Student Body President and I was a good girl. Con-
> gruent with that from an early age I knew I wanted to
> be a nun.

I interviewed Lua Xochitl [self-named meaning Wild Flower Moon] in the garden of her home on a beautiful sunny day in the sum-mer of 1997. She was a born story-teller and the four hours I spent listening to her life history was a tremendous experience for me.

> I am the daughter of a woman who was Irish, Apache,
> born in New Mexico and my father who was Mexican.
> He came to New Mexico and met my mother. Their
> first child died of hunger. My elder sister was born
> then and my parents moved to Los Angeles where I

was born the youngest of five children. My mother passed away when I was six months old, she was 29 years old. My grandmother passed away the same year three months earlier. My oldest sister was nine years old when my mother died so she lost her childhood because she had to be mother to four siblings, me being an infant. She became a nun and was one for 24 years. I came from a very poor family, and I think what happened to my mother is, she saw herself with five children and said, "I can't do this anymore" and left. It's never been very popular to be of mixed blood in this society and I think she lived through a very hostile time. I was born into a Mexican, Catholic family, which is like the Irish Catholic; double shit on your back. Now I understand how enmeshed the Church is in Ireland, now I understand why it's taken me so long to shed all that shit. My father remarried, I was six years old and they went on to have five more children. I got lost in the mix, so I think I can say to you, I pretty much raised myself. All that, I think, affected how I related to myself and my own body and my deservedness or my non-deservedness. So I was raised a good Catholic girl. Being raised in the Church, the youngest and losing our mother, I was inculcated with a great deal of fear to do with sex and men and the world. The Church and priests and nuns were a sanctuary for me to escape into in my head. It wasn't surprising to me in my senior year to say to my Dad that I was entering the convent. Also I have an aunt and an older sister who entered the same order. But as far as I was concerned at the time I was making a very independent decision, which is not really true as you look back at the layers in your life. I entered essentially to escape. The strongest force in my life was my father he was a very political figure. As I grew up I looked more and more like my mother so he distanced me I think. He felt a lot of pain and guilt for my mother's death. He lived with the fact that he hadn't been able to provide for her as well as do his work for his people; my father was a man who worked for the Latinos. He was very strict. I had two older sisters but they never went out on a date. He didn't have to say anything we just knew we couldn't cause him any worry, that he had enough worry just trying to support us. I think it's one of the hardest burdens to put on kids, to make them responsible for raising themselves. So naturally that curtailed any necessary wildness that has to happen in your teenage youth. It curtailed any kind of self-absorption that needs to happen at that time so you're not doing it at 40 and 50 years old. My pleasure as a kid came from being in school and being away from the house.

Hazel, a gently spoken homemaker addresses the family dynamic issues fairly representative of those women who came from an Irish Catholic background,

I am the third of four children. There was a troubling aspect to my growing up. Much as I knew I was loved, my father was an alcoholic, and as the third in the family I was the youngest for a number of years. I've tried to figure out what was going on in those years with a father who was alcoholic. I see in some ways I was conflicted by it. I thought I was responsible. I thought I could do something about the trauma that he was

52

responsible for, but I never could; obviously there was
no way that I could have. I can't help but think that it
affected me, perhaps even my thought to enter the religious life. I don't know if there is an answer, but I do
hold the question in my heart. Was that part of my reason for seeking the religious life? Mom was a staunch
Catholic and Daddy would go to Church Christmas,
Easter that sort of thing. He would make fun of her;
she was the object of ridicule for him. In a number of
ways she was a battered wife. We go back and revisit
our childhood when someone close to us is experiencing a similar thing. It was as an adult that I realized
this about my parents. It was a typical, if there is such a
thing, alcoholic household. The silence that engulfed us
about this behavior I think influenced me in a number of ways such as sexuality. I wouldn't talk about it,
because that was how we handled serious matters in
our family. Looking back, my sister and I marvel at
the fact that no one talked about the chaos that this was
causing in our family. Now I find freedom in being
able to talk about things that as a child I wouldn't even
think about discussing. Some of it was my mom. She
was not born in Ireland but the Irish, and I don't mean
to stereotype people, but there is a cultural characteris-
tic; perhaps with that generation especially, even using
the word pregnant was not said. I chuckle at the verbal
gymnastics that went on rather than name reality,
which I know influenced my appreciation of sexuality.
My father was more married to his job than to his wife,
their relationship was more like an armed camp. That
had a powerful influence on me. When I got married I
decided I would not fight because I'd seen how destruc-

tive that was between my Mom and Dad. Well that was not the answer either; the pendulum had swung the other way as we have come to realize. To squash feelings is not the answer. When I look back on my family, I loved my Mom and Dad dearly, but I couldn't go to them with things that were troubling me. Especially as a teenager when so much of our personality is starting to come forth and you're not quite sure how to deal with it. For example, I saw the word rape in the newspaper and asked my Mom what the word meant, she couldn't answer. Right away I thought, oh, you don't talk about those things. It's obvious what happened as a result of that; if I can't talk about that, there's a lot of things I can't talk about and I didn't quite know what to do with all of those questions. One of the dimensions of that is a continuing sense of responsibility for people and issues in my life, a feeling of always having to fix things for everybody. I think it had its genesis in those early years when I couldn't talk about those issues and felt responsible in some ways. My father was a binge drinker. He would start to drink as soon as he came home on Friday afternoon. He would quickly become inebriated and would stay like that for the rest of the weekend. Monday morning he would get up and go to work. He became less violent over the years but more emotionally battering, first to Mom and then to the rest of us. And yet there were such contradictions. My Dad sensed that my older sister and brother had a bond of high school kids and my younger brother had a lot of attention because he was a little guy. My Dad said to me something about whenever you're feeling sad or alone I'll give you the signal. The signal was that he'd

54

put his finger beside his nose and that would show me that he knew how I felt. Isn't that such a contradiction? It's enough to make a young person wonder what the hell's going on here? How can he be so sensitive to my needs and be so abusive first to my Mom and then to us? I wouldn't know how he would be to us. It was always that on-edge experience.

I used to do a lot of babysitting. I remember the house I lived in was high on a hill and I would wait at the dining room window for my ride to pick me up to go babysit, usually the father of the house. Dad would storm through and be angry at me for something, because he was drunk and I was just a focus. Mom would probably be in Church. He would call me lots of names, "you whore" or whatever. Again I'd wonder now what did I do? I'm waiting here to go babysit-ting, a sense of not knowing what was going to happen brings the tears to my eyes even now. I can say from the position of safety, I loved you Daddy.

Yesterday would have been his birthday. Sexuality was just not a part of my life. I think if I was really honest with myself, I just wonder if I just plain didn't think about it, in light of my style that I had learned early on; well you just blow that off and you don't think about it. I don't remember talking to my sister or anyone about sex. It just didn't matter. Entering the convent, although I did long for it, offered my Dad an opportunity for ridicule. He just made more fun. I look back on that with affection. One of the things I learned from that, I would let him go so far and then I'd say,

In the Name of God Why?

> "that's enough," and he knew when I set the limits,
> whereas Clare [her sister] would let him go beyond her
> limits. This is an example of what he would do. My
> sister and I had both gone back home. She was work-
> ing on her Masters. I was waiting to enter the convent.
> Daddy would grab Clare and try to feel her breasts.
> He tried that on me once and I said "you're not trying
> that again" and he never did. Clare never set boundar-
> ies and that was her right but I thought I'm not going
> to let him manhandle me. I think that served me well.

When I asked if this kind of behavior was common in her teenage years she answered in the affirmative and said it had the effect
on her sexuality of putting it into neutral.

> It was in neutral, it wasn't disgusting, it was just-I
> don't want to talk about that. Which I guess is in
> keeping with that mindset. Whatever is painful, deep,
> challenging, difficult, except for certain academic
> areas where I felt quite comfortable about probing and
> going further, it's just some areas that I would say no,
> I don't need to talk about that. However, [There was
> a significant pause here and a rueful laugh] I think--I
> know, there's a very high cost we pay for that think-
> ing, and I think I began to pay that price in the con-
> vent.

This was an extremely important area of Hazel's story, one that
will be enlarged and expanded upon when we follow her life into
the convent. As her interview progressed, Hazel discovered areas
of her own life story that she previously had never given thought or
shape to. The fact that she remarked on her mother probably being
in Church whilst her father was attempting to molest her and ac-
complishing it with her sister, was an interesting observation.

Kate's story varied somewhat in that, although she was from an Irish Catholic family, her father was the peacemaker. Her mother was the disciplinarian who laid down the rules although Kate said, she wasn't very strict.

We would go to our Dad to try and change the rules, and he'd try. They weren't very together in bringing us up. My Dad was very generous and very sweet, very loving. He was also an alcoholic and a compulsive gambler. That was really scary for me because I was the oldest. I became the gatekeeper in my family and would try and protect the younger children. I would answer the door or the telephone because I'd want to know if he was slurring his words. My Mom would be very upset because he'd be drinking and I would try and keep the little ones out of the way. I don't think their marriage was very happy, mostly because of his drinking and gambling. I realize now that I grew up in a pretty sexually repressed family, not just my own family but my extended family also. I think the Irish in general have very repressed feelings as well as talking about sexuality. Many of my cousins never married or married very late in life, some in their forties. Many of them never had children. Sex also was an unspoken topic; I remember when I was very young I saw some caterpillars mating and I thought that it was bad and dirty. Somewhere I got messages that it was bad, but I don't know how because I don't remember anyone talking to me about sexual things. When my mother was pregnant I was six years old, I didn't even know she was pregnant. She didn't talk about it, eventually she said the stork was going to bring a baby and she had to go to the hospital to get the baby. I remember being scared because I thought she might die or something at the hospital. I had no idea how she got the baby, I never noticed her body change or anything. I didn't have a very good image of what marriage was. Sometimes they would kiss when my father came home from work but they weren't usually very affectionate at all. I think my Mom, in her anger at my father, took her anger out on my younger brother. She would be really critical and negative to my next brother. I have two younger brothers. He really got a lot of the brunt of the screaming and yelling and name calling and now that I'm older I can see it was probably a lot of her anger at my father which she directed at my brother. I think with all of that, when I entered the convent I was really trying to escape from my family. I was always looking for peace. I remember when I was a kid in school I would say, if I could just have some peace. I really did feel as if God was calling me to it. I wanted to be really, really intimate with God, but looking back on it I see it was a way of not developing intimacy with another sexual partner. [This was an interesting use of the word "another," as if Kate was seeing God as her sexual partner.] I did always make friends easily, so I think emotional intimacy was easy for me. I don't like this about myself now but at the time I thought religious life was a higher way of life. The life I saw in my family I thought, I don't want this. I'd look at my aunts and they were married and had kids and I thought this is so boring. They were all house-wives, none of them had jobs or careers, I thought I just can't stand the idea of being in a house all day and

looking after kids and cooking. It just seemed like a
waste of a life. At that point I didn't see a lot of options and religious life was an option that allowed me
to have a career and do something bigger for the world
and not just being trapped in a family, which now I see
as being very dysfunctional.

Several women expressed this same ambivalence about following the life choices of their female family members. The routes
open to them were few and limited in scope. Entering the convent
led to a much wider choice of career paths and the nuns who taught
them were powerful role models as will be illustrated in the stories
to follow.

Maria was the second girl in a family of five girls and one
boy. Her story opened with the statement that they were a strong
Catholic family, all were daily communicants. All the children had
gone to Catholic boarding schools. As her story progressed she
was somewhat conflicted by a considerable amount of, what she
considered, inappropriate behavior from her father. She also had
issues only recently resolved with her mother. She said,

We were from a very religious family, daily communicants. I'm not sure if everyone has a similar experience as mine. I think in your family there's always
an elder who gives you permission around sexuality,
especially who gives you permission to be who you
are; I feel like my Dad did that in a lot of ways. He,
from the very beginning said anything that you want
to accomplish, you can, any field, you can do anything. There was also a playfulness he had and now
today, when I read about a lot of these abuse things,
talk about tickling as a part of power and abuse; he
tickled us a lot. I think that was where maybe some
of us got some arousal or had some connection with
him. But to my knowledge, none of us were abused,

physically. I think a lot of us were abused emotionally or psychologically. Because along with this kind
of strict attitude he had, and fun attitude, and from
my point of view gave me permission to be a sexual
human being, he also had that side that I thought was
abusive because he was a heavy drinker. He was also a
very fearful person. My Mom was pretty closed down
emotionally. Over the years I've satisfied the need to
get rid of some of the anger about her not teaching me
how to be a full human woman. So the two of them
were very difficult for me as a young person to kind of
put together. He was strict and we were afraid of him,
but he was the one who was fun-loving and would go
to the beach and stuff like that, so there's a push-pull
there. Of course sexuality was not mentioned or talked
about. Unless if I go back to when my Dad took my
sister and me and told us the whole facts of life. He
told us we could ask any questions we liked, and that
was when we were in fourth or fifth grade. I'm not
sure how this plays out in my relationships with my
husband or with other men. One time I was sent home
from school because my sweater was too tight, according to one of the nuns. I said to my mom, "Sister
Mary wants me to tell you I need another sweater."
She said "I don't know, ask your Dad," and so I went
in. I was a sophomore, and I said, Dad, what do you
think of the sweater? And he said "I like it, I like it."
So there was some times like that, when he would be
permission giving, but certainly there was rigidity
around sexuality with boyfriends. Although my older
sister and I double-dated a lot and I necked and stuff,
[I] never petted. One boy went to touch my breasts

and I twisted his arm so hard he had a cast on it for
weeks. I don't think any of us screwed around because there was such terror around how that would fit
with my family, with my Dad.

Maria received a lot of attention and generosity from her god-
parents. Her godmother said, in response to Maria's news that she
was entering the convent that she felt she was doing it to get away
from her Dad and his drinking.

I was very angry when she said that, but over the years
I came to realize it was a promise I'd made at one point,
if I go to the convent, just stop my Dad from drinking. I
think before I left for the convent I had started to sever
the relationship with my Dad and mom, I went at 16 and
stayed for 19 years.

Miriam, a bright-eyed Irish descendant told me,

I grew up in an Irish Catholic, no talk family. As
far as there being such a thing as sexuality, we had
no awareness of it. We were a family that dated and
usually married the person. I went into the convent to
escape a very dysfunctional family.

Her father was alcoholic and her mother was a strict disciplinarian. Another similar story came from Helen who said,

I was born into an Irish Catholic family with a drunken
father. My Mom and Dad had to get married. She
was pregnant with me before the wedding and my
Dad always thought it would happen to me too. I was
determined it wouldn't. I wanted to do something really
special with my life. In the eighth grade I loved the
Sisters and decided then to go to the convent. It meant
I didn't do much with the boys because I knew I was
going to the convent.

June had an Irish father of another temperament. She describes her childhood relationship as having an "Oedipal thing" for her father,

> He was a wonderful father for me. He was handsome and very masculine. The kind of the quiet Irish man in the John Wayne sense. He was not overly demonstrative but he had ways of letting you know he approved of who I was. Ways of saying boy you look nice, ways of a smile, running around opening doors for me when I was a young, young child. That's why I say I can recognize at least from that a lot of the oedipal thing. I'm sure there are times when I would have gladly shoved Mom out and taken over. I think the most tragic thing for me was that he seemed to have changed when I got back from the convent. He seemed to have lost his sense of humor and his lust for life and I blamed myself. I think later in life as I talked with my Mom after we became friends I realized it was really between the two of them, but at the time I thought it was my fault that I'd killed Daddy when I left home, he wasn't very happy about it. If I see my Mom through my own eyes only and shut out my brothers and sisters, I see someone who I always tried to measure up to. Somebody who was always physically, so it seemed, more adept than I am. There were long, long times that I sought her approval in a lot of ways. I remember that after I was married and had quite a family, I had never been able to do anything for her of any value. My grandmother died and my mother called me and asked if I'd go over and help her clean up before my aunt came out for the

funeral. I cried and she said "what in heaven is the
matter?" I said that is the first time you ever asked me
to do anything. It was overwhelming that she actually
needed me for something. She was the dominant one.
Her mask was there, wasn't anything she couldn't do.
Yet she was full of fears with things that shook her to
her roots. She was so insecure that she would never
go outside her family circle. In general I had a good
home life; they took good care of us. We all felt loved,
but once we grew a little they kept us at arm's length
so a little more physical love would have been good.

June entered the convent at 16 years old after the family of the
young man she had been dating insisted upon their separation. She
entered more or less on the rebound from this unhappy experience,
although I understood that she had intended to enter prior to meeting the young man.

The common themes running through these stories are silence
around sexuality, alcoholism, lack of affection among the parents
and continuing this attitude in their interaction with their children.
There are common traits in the discipline they experienced and
a feeling that the convent was an escape from this dysfunction.
Another very frequent theme which evolved, was the neglect the
women experienced from their mothers. Some were emotionally
absent, some extremely abusive. There was a continuum of behav-
iors in between. Some of these themes are illustrated in this short
dialogue from Alison who said,

I don't think my parents had a good relationship.
When I look back on it now, my father drank a lot, and
I remember being very surprised when my mother was
pregnant. My mother and father slept in twin beds;
I don't ever remember seeing them in bed together.
In my teens I don't remember my father and mother
being especially affectionate, yet my mother was very

affectionate to me but my father was not. He didn't
show his affection, he was a man's man. I didn't know
my father very well. He had high expectations of
everyone but particularly of me. It set sister against
sister. Going to the convent was a way to escape what
my family was; it was always my refuge. We were
asked many a time and told the convent's not an escape hatch for you. If you're not happy someplace else
you're probably not going to be happy in the convent.
I would have denied that then but I think I've come
to the point where I'd acknowledge that now. But I
probably did enter religious life to escape, and I don't
know what I was trying to escape. I think I felt that I
couldn't make it in college or whatever. I was never
the brightest kid, maybe I thought I wouldn't be successful and I thought I would have some semblance of
success in my life by entering.

Parental control of sexuality was maintained in a variety of
ways. Sophia's story has similarities with others as she spoke of
the control over her sexuality by her father.

I'm the oldest of three I have two younger brothers.
Father was extremely strict; I guess I knew I dared not
be sexual. I went to Catholic girl's boarding school
and when I went to college I was very close to the
nuns. When I lived at home I had to be in at a certain time, and he always checked what I wore before I
went out. My mother was very passive, now she's still
very passive, he's a very old man but he still rules the
roost, and very, very, Catholic. When I left the convent
I wanted to do something completely off the wall, I
went to work on a cruise ship. My father was not a

happy camper, not with me living that kind of life. He
thought I was a harlot. I wasn't. I still wasn't. He was
afraid I was going to be sexually active and I wasn't.
When I finished University I dated, but I still wasn't
sexually active. My sexuality just went away. A
friend I'm dating now says, "you were hiding behind
things for years weren't you?" I have to say, my father
would become upset and angry and so we learned
not to get him upset. He's not a drinker, I know from
talking to his doctor now he says he's a classic alcoholic, but no, he never drank. He's a control freak, if
he didn't get his way he would yell and so we learned
to get around it. We got the message you'd better keep
yourself good. I went out on a date and my mother
bought me a dress and I had to go home and bend over
for him to see whether or not I was showing anything.
He thought it was too revealing so I had to go back
and have the lady at the store fix something so that
it would cover me up. It never occurred to me or my
Mom that there was something wrong with him, he
was really controlling.

Intuitively I felt Sophia had experienced physical as well as
emotional abuse at the hands of her father and I asked if she experienced physical violence at his hands? She responded,

Oh yes but he stopped when I wouldn't cry. I just decided I don't need to cry if you're going to hit me and I
didn't do it. He got frustrated and just left the room. He
said to my mother "What are we going to do with that
girl?" But he never did it again. When I entered the
convent he was very happy, I think he had a big problem with sex. Sexuality was not a reason for going in, it
was a blessed event.

Abuse on this level was quite common amongst the interviewees. The extreme was demonstrated in three interviews where I would assess the damage to have had lifelong traumatic effects on the women. Incest, psychological and sexual abuses are very common issues uncovered in therapy when dealing with a religious client pool (anecdotal accounts from therapists in California. and Washington State). Although this area was not initially anticipated in my research, sufficient cases surfaced during my interviews to warrant mention here. Anecdotal evidence from professionals dealing with these people together with the previously mentioned empirical research by Chibnal, Wolf & Duckro, and evidence given by Sipe, points to a high incidence rate of abuses both in priest's and nun's childhood. To quote one therapist from a major in-patient treatment center, "A fair proportion, if not everyone, in the program had been abused. Some women would go into religious life to avoid sexuality and they always tripped up, they ended up in therapy." Virginia said in her interview, "Nearly everyone I knew in the convent was in therapy." I asked for clarification, "everyone?" "Yes, I didn't have a friend who wasn't in therapy for years." When questioned on her thoughts as to the main reason these nuns sought therapy, she answered,

> Family of origin issues. I think a lot of people were doing repair work in therapy; that was at the heart of it. A lot of women used the therapist as an intimate relationship to have a place to go, to talk about what you're thinking and feeling and what's important to you, in place of a spiritual director. What's important about that is that people were very reflective, very aware and working on themselves all the time. Who is your therapist? was the question, not if you're doing it. They're [communities] spending hundreds of thousands of dollars on therapy.

Doehring in the publication of her dissertation entitled, *Internal Desecration: Traumatization and Representations of God,* indicates that the God representations of those women in her study who had alcoholic parents were different from those who did not have such experiences growing up. The child with the alcoholic parent had a decrease in experiencing God as loving and a clear increased experience of God as absent or wrathful. Doehring further found that women who had been severely traumatized in their childhood most often experienced the wrathful absent God. In the case of the severely traumatized childhoods such as Ursula, Kathleen and Marian, their God representations in adulthood are gentle and loving, suggesting they have made some recovery from their earlier experiences. Ursula however recalled a time at age 27 when she had her first lesbian sexual experience; at this time she felt alienated from God.

A.M Flaherty in her book *Woman Why Do You Weep?*, examines how women who were victimized as children relate to God. She asks, "Does God become a part of the problem? Is this God just another figure of male domination? How does one learn intimacy again when intimacy has been violated?" She writes,

> Fear also becomes an issue in our relating to God.
> Fear of judgment, fear of God's abandonment. Having
> internalized much of the responsibility for what hap-
> pened to us as children, we believe we are to blame.
> These feelings of responsibility spill over into our oth-
> er relationships, and so we project that God will judge
> us as well. As survivors of abuse our self-esteem has
> been affected, which also encourages our feelings of
> worthlessness and self-blame.

Ione feels growing up in strict, sexually repressive homes and in a wider sense in a church which does not deal with the topic of sexuality in a pastoral way, adds a great burden of fear that God will also abandon them. This was a feeling expressed by the following women in their heart wrenching stories.

Kathleen was born out of wedlock. She thinks in retrospect that her mother had been raped by her own father and this was the reason for the terrible abuse she suffered at the hands of her mother.

As far back as I can remember, I was my mother's black sheep. I don't know who my father is, I heard stories about it being my grandfather. To this day I don't know who he is. I was raised with a stepfather but he couldn't be close to me because I was not his child and my mother would always tell him to mind his own business if he tried to come to my defense. She would never call me by my name, she would always call me by a curse name; even outside when she would call all of us children in at night, she would call them all by name and then say "And you, you----get inside." Every day she looked at me, she had to recall some-thing bad that had happened to her. It's a hard thing as a child not knowing why you're not loved, what you did wrong. I had very, very low self-esteem, craving love. It's the biggest sin any parent can do to their kids, to deny them that. Craving love and looking for atten-tion, and not being able to get it, especially from your mother; you knew to keep away. I didn't like women too much, I had seven sisters. The one that was born after me was mother's favorite and she hated me, so in the beginning I didn't like women. I couldn't go to my stepfather for attention because I didn't want him to get in trouble. What my mother did was drink a lot. They both were alcoholics. They went out a lot and used to leave drunken men taking care of us. One was a merchant marine and he would start messing with me when I was nine years old. Someone who had just got out of jail for being a child molester came to babysit because [my mother] wanted to go out. He was getting ready to molest me but a cop that lived in our build-ing found out about this and stopped it, so I was nearly raped at nine. Well, finally her dream came true and I got raped at the age of 15, raped real bad, I couldn't walk for two weeks. He was drunk and my mother had been paid for him to do it. I found this out years later, so she had me raped and it was terrible, terrible. I hated men more than I hated women. I hated everybody. I was kind of saying I don't deserve this but I felt I must have done something terrible so I did deserve it. An older woman who had two daughters studying to be nurses saw me and was very kind to me. One day she asked me if I was feeling alright because I looked so ill. I told her I didn't feel well, I didn't even know I was pregnant, I didn't know what was wrong. She helped me and told me where to go and it was the Children's Aid Society, to go there and tell them I'm Catholic and they'll put me in a place and I'll get help. I did and they took care of me until I had the baby. My mother was still cruel even then, she came to the hospital, she was pregnant herself with her 10th child, and screamed and yelled at me and called me a little witch. The hardest thing I ever did was to sign the papers to give the baby up for adoption; but if I loved the child I had to die to myself, to give him up. I didn't want him to go through what I'd gone through. I wanted to keep him because I wanted something to love because I'd never known love, but I didn't want to be selfish, I didn't want to hate him later, which I was told was a possibility. Every time my mother looked at me she remembered what had happened to her. The nun who helped me was so loving and accepting, I knew she was holy, just to be near her I felt special. I guess it was the only time I got any kind of attention. They took me out of

> this Sister's group and moved me to another, they had
> different nuns in charge of each group, and I felt like I
> didn't want to live. I cried, I couldn't eat, I can hardly
> talk about it without crying now. I felt nobody can love
> me, I was so unlovable that they took me away and I
> couldn't figure it out. I was so confused, but then I said
> I will do anything, I will become a nun, anything that
> I can be near her, anything so that she would like me.
> So I joined up there.

Kathleen told me that there were two "levels" of nuns in the order she joined. One was for girls such as herself and was called "The Magdalene's."

A story of similar intensity to Kathleen's was Ursula's. The agonies suffered by these women at the hands of those who should have loved and protected them were very difficult for me to listen to. That they should be as emotionally strong and able to share their stories with me in such a trusting open fashion filled me with an even deeper respect.

Ursula was French. Some of the transcription may appear to be incorrect English. However, I have attempted to keep her own words as closely as possible for authenticity. At the time of the interview she was 75 years old. Before we began the interview she prayed before a small altar in her home, to be as honest and helpful to my study as she could be. The story of her childhood follows:

> I came from a broken dysfunctional childhood. There
> were four of us children, two brothers and a younger
> sister. There were daily wars of religion in our home
> because my father was a Protestant and my mother a
> Catholic. My father never forgave my mother for hav-
> ing changed her mind to bring up the children Protes-
> tant. She tore up the piece of paper when she had the
> first child, and she was in such agony the first son died
> after a few months. The second child died at birth.

> Then came me, then my sister and then twin boys. My
> mother was extremely religious but despotic, and I
> believe that my mother was either sexually abused in
> her childhood or was a true victim of a very narrow
> and despotic up bringing in an orphanage with nuns,
> medieval type nuns, this was some hundred years ago.

Sadly this kind of treatment was not just a historical specula-
tion. In my own story I spoke of the life my mother must have
experienced in her orphanage in early 20th Century Ireland. The
evidence of such severe monastic practices was the subject of a
documentary in Southern Ireland called "Dear Daughter" (Lown-
stein). The film was based on the true story of a young girl growing
up in an orphanage in Dublin in the 1950's. It details the atrocities
she and other girls faced at the hands of Sister Xavieria and her
"regime of nuns" the Sisters of Mercy. Some of the abuses that the
Sisters inflicted on the children included ritual beating with chair
legs and rosary beads. These revelations caused the reopening of
a 40-year-old case involving the death of an 11-month baby. The
result of this documentary was the subject of an article in the National Catholic Reporter. This reported an apology for the alleged
abuses from the Sisters of Mercy in Ireland, and the establishment
of a hotline to provide support for former orphans who still may
be traumatized by their experience. "By mid-March, the helpline
was said to have received calls from more than 600 people." Sister
Xavieria alternatively named "Sister Severia" was accused of beating children so severely that they needed medical attention. She al-
legedly threw boiling water over another child. The subjects in this
documentary talk of mental illness and stories of profound cruelty
defying reason. Forty years later these Irish women re-lived the
horror of their lives with the Sisters.

The true enormity of this case exploded over the past ten years
rocking the Church in Ireland to it's very foundations. Not only
were the nuns vilified in the case but by the end of the decade the
order of Christian Brothers were also held accountable for unspeak-
able abuses. Once again I want to take this opportunity to remem-

ber my mother and acknowledge her early years and the tragedy of life for these unfortunate children living in orphanages under such tyranny.

It may be a source of consolation to read that in contrast, the respondents in my study virtually all speak of their dealings with nuns in glowing terms. Thankfully, none have experienced any of the atrocities experienced by the former generation of children who grew up to perpetrate such damage on their own children and children in their care.

Ursula continued her story with further reflections from her childhood and information about her mother,

> My mother never talked about it, [her experiences in the convent] but she was a very bitter woman, her solace was strict religion. This was quite a bad atmosphere. Sex; we did not speak of sex. Priests, nuns, nobody dared say the word "sex." This was the period of my upbringing. Now I'm 75, when I was 60 I went through a biofeedback process and just to tell you how traumatized I was about sexuality, the counselor who was doing the biofeedback named a few words and suddenly she said "sex." The machine jumped including myself, and so I became aware of how painful sexuality was in my life, how twisted, what twisted thinking and feeling I had about it. Even at 60 years old I still believed that intercourse is dirty and even as I speak now I can still feel something dirty about intercourse.

> I shall go back to my childhood. I was raised in a very strict milieu, and on top of this my mother abused me emotionally. Because she was very unhappy and I was very willing and out of nature very tender and affectionate, and I always mean well. I may be very wrong sometimes but I always mean well. After the

second sexual abuse, which my mother witnessed at
13, every day she called me dirt of a pig or dirt of an
animal, every day until I was 20, practically every day.
This created a tremendous fear in myself and a kind
of self-hatred, a disgust with myself. When I was 30
I really thought that I stank, I couldn't see myself, i
was ashamed of my hands, my feet, my nose, because
I was constantly criticized by my mother. When I was
10 years old I was molested by my uncle, my mother's
brother. I was not aware that it would mark me and
my sexuality; I didn't know, I was too innocent. He
molested me for about three weeks, and because it was
my mother's brother I couldn't say anything to her or
to my father, I couldn't tell anyone; I was too ashamed.
I know I was so ashamed I wanted to die. At 13, a
similar thing happened in the school with a priest, and
the horrible thing that happened I really wanted to die
then. When I was in his arms being submitted to this
horrible happening, he was molesting me but I thought
it was horrible, I wanted to die on the spot. That man
kept me prisoner there for hours and so my mother
came to the school and found me there. My mother
had already had no affection for me; I was always the
black sheep. When she saw this she practically broke
the door, tore me away from the man, screamed at him
and going home screaming, pulling me by the hand and
kept telling me I was a pig, I was the worst pig in the
world and I should be ashamed of myself. Then she
imprisoned me in the kitchen, she told me I had to go
to confession and that I was going to hell and all that I
knew was I wanted to die. My mother called me daily,
dirt of a pig, or dirt of a beast. I suffered so much that

by the time I was twenty when she said it to me one
more time I screamed, and 55 years later I still can
feel in my whole being the scream which started from
the bottom of my inner, inner self, it welled up and I
screamed. Probably the whole neighborhood must have
heard. I said to her, that's it, I cannot kneel before you
and beg forgiveness every day, I had been doing it for
five or six years.

This background plus being brought up in a private Catholic
school Ursula claims was the reason for her always connecting sexuality with fear and guilt. "Sex, you just wouldn't speak of sex and
to my mother of course it was absolutely taboo." Ursula responded
to one of the questions regarding Catholic education affecting your
sexuality negatively or positively, she said,

I should circle this one with red blood. Ah boy! And
so many are still twisted because of that stinky education, I still feel the anger! When I got my period
I was 13. I was petrified of my mother, I was even
afraid to ask my mother anything. So I was bleeding,
I didn't know where the blood was coming from, I had
no idea of my anatomy. I told my mother that I was
bleeding, once more she found a good occasion to beat
me and scream at me to lock me in my room and say
"you hypocrite, you know damn well what this is," I'd
known nothing. At 13 I believed this was another mark
on me, instead of my mother explaining to me what
was happening she beat me and I was sobbing like a
fool, this was also after the second incident, the second molestation. She locked me in my bedroom with
the shutters locked, I hated that room. It marked me so
much that every time I had my period, (I stopped having them when I was 52), every time I went through a

74

crisis of despair. I was ashamed anyway; my mother
had a regimen of fear and of shame.

I asked Ursula why her father had not interceded for her against
her mother's abuses, she avoided telling me why she thought he did
not defend her in her young years and instead answered,

I had a very tender affection for my father, and when I was
15 or 16 I didn't pass the official exam in France and my father
rejected me and put me in the same boat as my sister who spent
her whole time flirting and got pregnant at 15. My mother had
always hated me, now my father rejected me. I wanted to go to
the monastery at 20, but my father said for a Protestant this was
not normal, so he made me go to the city. I know he meant me to
meet a man and get married. He told me if I still wanted to go to
the monastery after one year then I could. After one year he denied
saying that and would not give me a dowry, also the war was on
and the Carmelite monastery I wanted to join had its Mother House
in Italy and we couldn't cross the border, so I gave up the thought
of it for many years.

Ursula said her experience of God throughout her life was "like
a rope leading up to the hands of Jesus." She was "always loved
and lovable to God." When at the age of 26 she had her first sexual
relationship with a woman she felt she had lost God's love that she
was truly "dirt of a pig," as her mother had accused her. All through
her life she has never stopped attending mass and the Sacraments.

Ione's was also an Irish Catholic family, with several very specific differences.

It's kind of weird, because the only way religion
came into our home was that we had to go to Catholic schools. My Mom tried to get us to go to Mass
on Sundays but my parents didn't participate. I'm
the most religious of the bunch, I'm the only one still
connected to the Church. I was sexually abused by
my father. My Dad is mentally ill, he's now institu-
tionalized. As a child I was pretty close to my Dad

which was opposed to my mother. I never felt very
close to my mother, so I was very close to my Dad
and then when I was about in third grade he started
shutting down emotionally. He was pretty much
unavailable because of his depression and his diagnosis of schizophrenia. When I was in the convent, he
would call me up and make inappropriate comments
to me so I had to stop them, and I haven't seen him in
eight years. My mother was an alcoholic when I was
growing up, those years were very chaotic. I think
the abuse started pretty early and stopped when I was
about ten. I don't really know when it started but it
went on a long time, it was just sealed off. My mother
even asked me once when I was in college if my father
had ever touched me inappropriately and I said "no."
She had noticed that my father and I had a very close
relationship, that my father spent a lot of time with
me. Because of the abuse, my sexual life was pretty
shut down, the memories were really repressed and
I didn't remember about it until about two months in
the convent. I was on retreat and the memories started
to come up when I was praying. After the retreat I
just slammed the door, but about six months later they
started to come up again and it was awful. I thought
I was losing my mind; I had two years of intensive
therapy. I had a teacher who was a nun in the eighth
grade; she became very much the parental figure for
me all the way through college. I started to admire
the Sisters and found them strong women and having
a strong sense of self, doing more than housework that
was the experience of the women in my neighborhood. I think my interest in God and the spiritual

life probably started in the sixth or seventh grade. I found going to Mass really comforting because my home life certainly wasn't. I would help this Sister with class work and stuff and through her, I met other nuns. I don't think I was in love with her or anything; it was more an emotional attachment on a motherly basis. I would go to her with my problems and she would take the time to help me with them. An interest in the spiritual life developed as I went through high school, also because it was a community of women I think unconsciously I was attracted to having relationships with women. Therapists have asked me. I think it's complex. Maybe I went into the convent because of a fear of sex, I think it was also because it was a women's environment. They were different from any women I'd ever met and then also the interest in the spiritual life also attracted me. Some of the most amazing women I've ever met I met in the convent. Women of vision working for justice, who will go into Africa, into El Salvador, or Peru, with all the violence. The most courageous females I've ever met were nuns. I think if my only reason for going in was sexual I wouldn't continue a relationship with them now. I continue to be interested in the spiritual life. I'm a very liberal Catholic, but I would say my interest in the spiritual life continues.

Margaret's story was different from the others in that she was the victim of incest. The perpetrators in this case were her older brothers and friends of theirs. She said,

We had six kids in our family; the first four were only two years apart and then the last two were five years and five years so the last two weren't as close a part of the family as the first four. We were a middle class family, my Dad had a good job, my Mom stayed home but she was sick a lot, which is probably why the incest thing was allowed to go on. That was with my two older brothers. My oldest brother was eight years older than me, and then my next brother was only two years older than me. The older brother had a lot of power in that family because my Dad was gone to work and if my Mom didn't feel well it was "listen to your brother and do what he says." I never really figured why this started with him except it may have been the kid down the street who was a few years older than him who wanted to do this, and I was a good target. I was about four. Some therapists say they think I was younger than that, but I think it was around that time. So he started that and he showed my younger brother and he showed his friend up the street who told another friend.So at one time there could have been five different guys who wanted to do this at any one time, until I was about 12. This was intercourse, oral sex whatever they wanted - the whole thing. My older brother was mostly into intercourse, the boy around the corner liked oral sex a lot, but he also liked intercourse. Sex was wrong, it was dirty, we just didn't talk about sex. I think I was around seven before my older brother said "well don't you know that's where kids come from, that they [the parents] did that." I was angry that he should say my parents did that that they would do something bad, because to me it was just bad. So I never felt good about it. You know at school when the other kids would talk about it, I would just pretend I didn't know anything. I thought if I said anything they'd know I know too much. We moved house when I was 10 years old so that cut out all of those kids but my brothers still wanted to do it. Then my older brother moved on but my younger brother and I still continued. I'm not sure it wasn't because we were just so used to it, it didn't seem that awful any more. Then we just seemed to grow out of it. With my older brother it never felt like it ended, like if he came back at any time, even though I'd say no, it felt like I should still do it and he'd want it. I remember when I was 15 or 16 years old saying out loud, "I am never going to let any guy, ever, do that to me again, it's never going to happen again." I mean I just hated it, the whole idea of it was just disgusting. I liked boys, I wanted to be around them, we had a great time in high school, but I would never date anybody unless there were at least 10 of us, we were just having fun. I went to a convent high school and met my algebra teacher who was this wonderful person who made it all look like a wonderful place to be. So I went with the idea that now I could be a good person; plus I think at the back of my mind I went with the feeling, I don't even want to deal with the sexual thing. I can get away from it I don't have to think about it.As I continue Margaret's story in subsequent chapters, the childhood trauma she suffered will be re-visited.

Virginia shared the following story:

This seems quite important to me. I was molested by my uncle when I was very young. There were two or

three incidences of fondling, making me touch him. I
worked on it at various times, but I don't think it's had
an enormous impact on my life. I always knew I never
repressed it. I rarely said anything but if anyone ever
asked I could remember.

This experience was to impact her life in the future when she
had a meeting with a priest whom she described as extremely sexist. He was "a divide and conquer type of boss" whom she claims,

Evoked the penises, right up to the Pope. He said, "I'm
responsible to the Archbishop and the Archbishop's responsible to the Cardinal and the Cardinal's responsible
to the Pope." I had this image of all these penises wearing their various hats, up to the Pope with his miter.

This quote was amplified in the recent Meryl Streep movie
Doubt. In the role of Sr. Aloysius Beauvier she accused Fr. Bren-
dan Flynn (played by Philip Seymour Hoffman) of abusing one of
her students. Virtually the exact imagery above was evoked by
the accused priest when he was attempting to defend his right to
impunity.

It was evoking a prior sexual assault, it was clear then that this
was like a rape. That my beliefs about women and the sexism in
the Church was so challenged by the way he did this that I felt it
like that and it triggered a similar experience.

Chibnal, Wolf and Duckro estimate 9% of religious women
report sexual harassment in the work place, mostly by priests.

The concluding story in this chapter was in many ways a most
inspiring one. It was narrated by a courageous woman named Marian who spoke to me in the terminal stage of leukemia. Her story was
all the more profound for being told in the final chapter of her life.

I grew up in a family that's nominally Catholic, of a
Catholic culture. I'm first generation Italian and
Portuguese. I had a grandmother who was very
Catholic, but my parents were Christmas, Easter

80

churchgoers. My father was a night club owner and
my mother was really more his mistress than his wife.
There was 21 years difference in their age. He had
had an unsuccessful marriage because a child had died
of syphilis, and my father, being a traditional Italian
man, believed the problem was his and it was not. So
before my father was willing to marry again, it was
important for him to know that the woman would bear
him children; so my mother was pregnant before they
married and I think they had a marriage of convenience. She was from a poor family, very bright but
poor and he was a moneyed man with, I found out
after he died, some Mafia connections. I was 14 when
he died. I grew up in that milieu. The home I grew up
in was purchased when I was ten. It had a fully
stocked bar, it was like a nightclub with a lot of exit
doors. They had a lot of gambling there, as is not
untypical of this kind of a family. Part of why I paint
this picture is, I had an older sister, 16 months older
than myself and my mother really didn't like children.
She just wanted this ticket into being with this man.So
we, as really small children, maybe three or four years
old, spent a lot of time in nightclubs, a real inappropriate way to raise children. Naturally there was a lot of
drinking going on. When I look back, it was almost
like we were little prostitutes in that men gave us a lot
of money and there was inappropriate behavior. When
I look back I remember one particular overt experience when a man was actually molesting my sister and
I came in to kind of save her. I also remember a
sexual experience of my own when I was quite young.
My mother would have us go to the show [at the

nightclub] on Saturdays unchaperoned. I was sitting next to a man, then again I was young, maybe sixish; he exposed himself and ejaculated and put it all over me, over my hands and that sort of thing. It just wasn't a healthy environment. There was a large party where my father I believe, rented a resort. We were the only kids. There was a band and lots of drinking and partying and dancing. I remember the dress my mother had bought me, which had eyelets; it was just a see through top and a non-see through bottom. I was very developed at 12. One of our friends brought this man as a date. He was very old to me at that time, and I danced with him all night. I felt like kids do some-what, that I was coming on to him, but he had a hard-on most of the night when we were dancing. My sister and I were in a room together downstairs and didn't know where the adults were. This man came in at night and said if I didn't come with him he would hurt my sister, and the hurt I got was a real physical kind of hurting her. So I left with him. There was this beautiful beach and he rapes me in the garbage part where the garbage cans are. I blanked a lot of that for a long time but there is one sexual position I've not been really prone to and that is the puppy dog position. I realize that's part of what happened there. When I started uncovering it and when people would share with me any kind of sexual trauma or even profound physical trauma, I started hurting in the back of my legs. That memory would block out and come and go depending on where I was. I don't know quite how much went on sexually as I grew up, but way too much. That is a backdrop to my growing up. I am conscious of twice saving my sister at my own expense. When I was 13, I had my first consensual sexual experience. I was fairly wild, hanging around with motorcycle guys and that sort of thing. We had a situation where there was an adult movie on TV. Now we're talking about 1950-51, so I don't know what an adult movie would have meant in that period. Three couples were there and my sister was allowed to watch it because she was 16 months older than I. That left me as a fully developed young girl with a 14-year old and a 15-year old boy in a huge house to hide in, left to our own designs. We could outdo any adult movie, it was my first sexual experience and it ends up being a *menage-a-trois.* It involved everything except genital intercourse, I mean finger fucking the whole bit. At some point my father came back and found us, I know I came out of the room and I have a scar here [pointing to her face] where he actually hit me and his ring caught my face. We had done the horrible thing. So then news spread, you can get what you want from Marian, so that was very difficult. I was also very sexual, very aware of my sexuality. I'll tell you one thing that was very sexual being raised Catholic we get all those stories about the martyrs and whipping and all that. There was a little place in our house that we would climb up to that nobody would ever find us. My father had a whip and we wouldn't actually hurt each other but we would do all sorts of S-M kind of things and really enjoy it and getting all the permission psychologically from saying "well we're just playing saints." That was a little wild. So by 13 I was pretty well fully sexual; luckily I never got pregnant. I had a traumatic experience with my father's death; this plays in heavily. I really loved my Dad, we were really good buddies and he was incredibly generous, he was primarily a man of the earth. In many ways I was his son and we would cut trees and go fishing, and I knew he really loved me. He didn't like my mother or my sister, we'll leave love out of it, he didn't like them as people, and I picked that up, their values were so different. My mother was quite a hypochondriac, but at 14 I couldn't differentiate between what was real and what was not. She had had a surgery that she led me to believe was very serious; later I learned it wasn't serious at all. My mother and father fought horrendously, and she told me that if he wasn't good to her that she'd have to go away and be in a sanitarium. So I'm facing the abandonment of my mother and so at that time I decided I wouldn't show anger. I did all this repression as a child, around family, always. My Dad had just built a summer home. It was a way for him to get away. So this was our first time up there. He brought my mother a tray at breakfast and they fought which was typical. He came out of their room--I have this vision really clearly of him, wearing a white T-shirt and dark pants, and here is the person who is so significant to me--and I said, "I wish you were the one that was dying." And the next day he had a heart attack and I watched it and he died in two weeks. I know for a long time I believed I was guilty of causing it. But I think what I did believe was that if I loved someone, most particularly a man, I could kill them if I got angry. Before my Dad died he made my Mom promise to send us to Catholic school for the education, and I was pissed because all my gang was certainly not going to Catholic school. I had no way out of it. I remember in my freshman year I ran for student president as a lark and I won it. I turned my life around. I went out a lot. Five boys asked me to marry them my senior year. I knew that wasn't the route to go and I still had that lingering feeling of if I get too close I'm going to kill them. That was more of a pervasive thing and probably why I went out with so many guys. The choice of going in the convent was a really good one, in the whole spectrum of things, very wise. I was 18 when I entered and I stayed in for 13 years. I needed to get out of the house. I think my mother was very jealous of me which was an interesting phenomenon because I was always heavy which just drove her crazy. Her belief was that I couldn't be successful or happy and be heavy. I ended up the most successful in terms of personal satisfaction than anyone in my family. But she said if I ran for and got student body president she wouldn't pay for me to go to college, and there's tons of money. I spent a lot of my life saying I'll show you, so I ran and won, and she refused to pay for me to go. I didn't have the humility to say I have no money and apply for scholarships, so I know part of my reason for going to the convent was to get the education.

Ritter and O'Neill in their book *Righteous Religion. Unmasking the Illusions of Fundamentalism and Authoritarian Catholicism*, refer to family of origin of clergy. However, I feel for many of the women in this study a similarity will be immediately apparent. Ritter and O'Neill write,

Individuals who are drawn toward ministry in righteous authoritarian religions are most often those who are compensating for low self-esteem. As mentioned previously, many were reared in homes where they felt uncertain about their worth and lovability. Thus such individuals gravitated toward the clerical state wherein they could enjoy the prestige and importance that automatically come with the role of minister or priest, [or in this case the role of the nun].

In conclusion, the themes emerging from the narratives up to this point are, silence, fear, guilt and shame around sexual issues. A variety of parental sexual and physical abuses, perceived emotional neglect, particularly by the mother, were accompanied by the need for the women to "gloss over" these areas in some cases. Alcoholism, where present, was usually apparent in the father but occasionally in both parents.

Chapter Five
Spirituality and Sexuality

The goal of spirituality and the goal of sexuality are the same, It is the experience of intimacy and union.

— Elizabeth 1998

Young women choosing a life of celibacy and asceticism must necessarily substitute a love of God and religious life for the abandoned desire of physical attachment to another human being. The question examined in this chapter will be how the participants in this study viewed their sexuality during the transition into the convent and their time there. Their collective reasons for entering had little to do with a desire for asceticism. For the majority, celibacy was either a relief or appeared to be a "non-issue." Few of the women described themselves as tremendously religious prior to entering, although many said they were daily communicants. Did these women see their sexuality as being honored? What did they do to preserve that part of themselves that would have been labeled sexual? These are some of the questions I hope to answer.

Catholic children of both genders learn at an early age and in complex ways that they must deny and sublimate their sexuality in a variety of ways. In their recently published book *Righteous Religions,* K.Y. Ritter and C.W. O'Neill, compare fundamentalist patriarchal religions to our image of the nurturing family. The reality for many children growing up within the confines of these religions was far from nurturing. Often the children are exposed with impunity to "authoritarian misuse" from angry, repressive parents in a Church which teaches that parents are God's representatives on earth and must be obeyed and honored in all things. According to Ritter and O'Neill this belief applies to members of the Catholic and funda-mentalists religions in particular and children of these families.

> They are continually threatened with exclusion and
> eternal punishment at the hands of a parental angry
> God unless they abide by the dictates of righteous law
> and authority. Members encounter a belief-system that
> assumes that they are flawed and evil children and that
> only out of fear will they stay in line. In this regard,
> believers are terrified into obedience by frequent
> references to Satan, hell, and a final judgment presided
> over by a jealous and wrathful God.

An example of this was apparent when Caroline described an incident that happened to her in high school.

> We'd had teenage missions where you'd go off for a
> week and the priests would holler at you. I remember
> sitting there one night and literally they would holler
> at us for five nights in a row. This night he was talk-
> ing about French kissing saying how evil it is and how
> can you do this, and I'm sitting there thinking what
> is it? I didn't even know what he was talking about.
> I was more embarrassed not knowing what it was.
> I couldn't look in either direction. I just pretended I
> knew what it was. I thought it must be a terrible thing.

As illustrated in Chapter Four, many of the participants en-dured paternalistic, dysfunctional and often abusive homes. Au-thoritarian religions give parents, priests and teachers absolute power. Only one of the women in this study had attended a Catho-lic co-educational elementary school. In addition, 100% of them attended single-sexed high school, further re-enforcing the model of a "good Catholic girl." By the time they were 16 or 17 all of the women had made their pledge to enter. Two entered when they were 16, one when she was 39, the remainder entered at 18 years. This figure was consistent with the data from the larger study, which found the majority of women to have entered between the ages of 16 and 19 years old with 49% entering at 18 years.

Caroline's story held an insight that was repeated by other women when they recognized that during their time in the convent they were able to play and be children for the first time in their lives.

> I know I went into the convent for a number of reasons. I went because in the convent I got to be a kid. I wasn't the oldest. I didn't have to do everything right. I got to be a kid in the convent. It was like joining this big family. I broke all the rules. I did everything wrong, all the things I didn't do when I was the oldest of six and the Student Body President. If there was a rule to break I'd figure out how to break it, and have a great time doing it.

Miriam had a similar experience upon entering her convent,

> I would have been in the Peace Corps, had it been another time; except I went to a Catholic school and was taught by nuns and I was attracted to their altruism. I think the religious life continued my adolescence. I thought it was a real challenge to beat the system. I remember stealing ice cream from the locker and being found out by the novice mistress with chocolate ice-cream running all down the front of me. I was a novice then. When I look back at all the things I did, I know I went from one family to another. I took authority very seriously. My mother is a very dominating, angry woman and to me she was replaced by the mistress of novices, so I was scared shitless of that. When it came to sexuality, I used to

laugh. But I entered in the 60s, and I have to say the
novices all laughed at what the vows were. We had
this crony Dominican priest telling us about them,
and what made us really laugh was "particular friendships." Now the point was we all probably had one.
The holy cards in our missals. I still remember that
and it makes me laugh. I did not have any sexual feeling about women but I liked being close to them and
having girlfriends.

Although Caroline would break any rule she could, the rules
relating to chastity and personal friendships were never challenged.
More or less the only gift sanctioned by the novice mistress was a
holy card with saints' pictures, prayers or spiritual sayings. These
were kept in the nuns missals for reflection at meditation or to look
at before sleep and were precious. Miriam poked direct fun at the
personal friendship rule and was conscious of breaking it, by passing a holy picture to a fellow novice to carry in her missal. However, she never attempted to form any sexual liaisons. Caroline
continued her story,

In the convent when I look back, people have asked me
if there were a lot of lesbians. I wasn't aware of any
sexual fooling around when I was there. Now when
I look back on it I'm aware that so and so was having
an affair with so and so, but with people I really didn't
know. My friends and I really weren't doing it. What is
interesting is that when I got to the convent I was 17. It
seemed like somehow we all paired up; like we all had
a crush on this other novice, you know we were postu-
lants with the older novices. It wasn't sexual but now
I look back on it and it definitely feels like a crush. So
there were no sexual feelings for me in the convent.

Looking back she recognized the feelings she had as a "crush."

However, she differentiated "crush" from sexual feelings without explaining how she understood the difference. I therefore asked her where she thought her sexuality went while she was in the convent?

> I just think I felt, I'm not going to feel this. I'm not
> going to deal with this. It's too scary. It's just too
> scary. I don't want to feel this. Another reason for
> entering was there was a very strong spiritual yearn-
> ing at a young age. I could have joined the Salvation
> Army or something, but I entered the convent. The
> other reason was a great fear of the world, fear of men
> and sex, fear of life really. I was thinking of God,
> and fearing what I would do when I was out of high
> school. So there were many reasons for entering--all
> the fears, the need to belong to a big family. There
> was a spiritual need and there was a need to do some-
> thing big for the world and I think the convent filled
> all those needs for me.

Margaret was vociferous with praise for her convent years. Following her experience of being the victim of incest at the hands of her brothers and their friends she proclaimed at 15 years "No-body will ever do that to me again."

> I went to the convent with the idea that now I can be a
> good person. Going to this order seemed like a won-
> derful place to be, and it turned out to be a wonderful
> place to be. I loved those people. There were 125 of us
> who entered the year that I went in. Those poor people
> who were in charge of us; I look back now and think
> how in the world did you put up with 125 adolescent
> kids? There were a few college kids but "yes that was
> it." So we had a great time; we had a lot of fun. I was
> lonesome I wanted to go home. I had this idealistic

picture that we had this wonderful family; that we all
cared about each other, that my parents were wonderful. It took me a long time to realize there's some
big problems. I loved the structure, knowing nobody
is going to break this structure. Nobody came from
behind and said now we're going to do this. It all
worked with the rules. I liked this stuff. The biggest
thing the convent did for me was say you're a woman,
and you have power as a woman. You have talent and
we're going to find it and use it. I got through school.
I got to be a teacher. It was something I respected
and felt good about. I feel they helped me become
a very strong person compared to what I was. Not
strong, maybe because I hadn't begun to deal with the
incest yet. So there was a lot to be done before I got
to a point where I really felt good about who I was. I
wound up with a lot of good people to live with; not
everyone. There were some that I didn't like, but
they would never have known. I was a "yes" person.
But the rest, I loved them. So the convent was a real
growth place for me. They gave me the opportunity to
be away from the sex when I didn't want it and didn't
even want to think about it or deal with it, but also
gave me a time where I could grow back into the idea
that it's not a terrible thing. I went from being a kid to
being an adult; and being able to look at it in a whole
new light. To say, "wow, you have choice out there."
Sex is something that people enjoy and it's something
that people don't look at and say this is bad and it's
terrible and you shouldn't do it. By the time I left,
after seven years, it was something I looked forward to
again. I thought by then I'd like to have a boyfriend,

I'd like to have a husband and children. I think it was like growing in a safe place. In the few times we had sexual instruction in the convent it was always treated as something that was fine. It was good, and being a woman was a good thing to be and you should be the best woman that you could be. I was proud of that. There were lesbians in the convent, just a few of them. I never quite understood that a whole lot. I never ran into that as an adolescent growing up. It was way out some place and nobody ever talked about that you know. Not then back in the 50s and 60s. Today my 6th graders know about it. I never encountered any sexuality when I was in the novitiate; maybe other people did, but not me.

Alison told me she was aware of sexuality in the convent, but saw it in a "negative way."

We were very much prohibited from being alone in the same room with another nun, for heaven's sake. If you were caught talking to someone in the closet, God! They had the Holy Water out, exorcising the evil spirits that evening. What did they think we were going to do? Did they think the convent was a breeding ground for homosexuality? We never talked about it, but I suppose that was the undercurrent. They were afraid that you would become sexual with one another. But they never said that. They just said, "Don't talk, don't meet." We had grown up and gone to Catholic all-girls high schools, and all we had were girlfriends. Your girlfriends were important to you and just because you had a girlfriend didn't mean you were going to start experimenting. I just felt that was weird to me

and that was the negative message that we got. I don't
ever remember any actual sexuality between anyone,
not in the 11 years I was there. Maybe I was just naive, it never happened to me. I was never approached.
I'm sure it probably happened, but I didn't know about
it. I didn't even know that some of the sisters got
alcohol and drank or went in and got the altar wine.
Oh God that totally blew my mind. Did I have tunnel
vision or what? I just didn't think of it. I didn't know
about any of this until after I left. Did I have such an
exalted perception of religious life that I really felt that
I didn't expect people to act on their sexual impulses?
I think on some level I still have that expectation of
people who make vows of celibacy and chastity. Sure
we're all sexual people but those of us who have taken
a vow of chastity and a promise of celibacy don't
get to act it and I think that's probably very narrow
minded but I still have that expectation.

Lisa entered because she felt her family had spent her whole
life preparing her for religious life. She was extremely introspective having spent many years examining her sexuality in particular
and societal expectations in general. One of the conclusions she
came to in the interview was that it was rare for our society to explore sexuality. She said,

I think I understood even from very young, that one
can be close to people spiritually, intellectually, emotionally, but when it came to physically, suddenly that
piece of us was not to be allowed. We're told, "Oops!
That wasn't good." Where no limits were placed on us
around the other emotions, physical touch and closeness was banned.

On reflection she holds no bitterness or regrets about the decision to enter, and said,

> I treasure the decision to enter, and what it has brought me to. In retrospect, I think I made that decision for a lot of the reasons a young woman gets married right away. I was not ready to be out on my own, to go to a public college, to interface with men, to do the adult thing. I felt so--so, not handicapped, so young. I felt so inexperienced. I think I felt the convent sublimially as another womb; as another home, as another place to protect me from making decisions on my own and challenging my relationships with men, which I was just really fearful of. The convent was actually my birthplace in a sense. That again, in a protected place, I was gradually being readied to be an adult in the world alone.

Lisa's insightful memories have no reference to her feelings toward God. In transcribing the tapes I was struck by this omission. Her childhood was so devoutly religious; all her memories of childhood play were spiritual in nature, yet when she reflects on her religious life, there was no reference to God. She does say that she did not enjoy all the religious practices in her home but participated because her parents expected it. Also the prayerful nature of convent life, she did not enjoy yet she still felt "called" to religious life.

The process of separating the young women from human love and devotion begins early. Many had already begun the process before entering. Their parents, school and Church prepared them in advance for the sacrifice. The name given to the introductory period in the convent was "formation," aptly titled since it was a time of change and of forming the character and personalities of a group of *individuals* into a *collective,* forever after recognized as a member of a *community* and undergoing the process of "dying to the self." Individuality was a flaw, to be disciplined and prayed out

of the young women. This was the process in the early 60s and 70s.
I realize this is not the case today. Reasons for the bold changes
which have taken place over the past two or three decades will be
explained in a following chapter.

During formation, life was so ordered and controlled only one
of the women addressed the subject of sexuality as being an issue
during that time and this was Ione whose incest issues were re-
remembered in the first months of convent life. For young women
entering the convent every waking moment from the first bell at
around 5 a.m. to the last bell announcing the Grand Silence at perhaps 9:30 p.m. was completely full of activity and closely controlled. The desired result of this isolation and indoctrination was
the sublimation of the body and the mind. Of course each order
was different depending on the particular rule followed. However,
what was systematic throughout the experience of all but two of the
women was the reality of control that followed them through each
day. According to McNamara, the very strength of character which
had enabled the women to choose religious life was "ruthlessly
disciplined" in order to "create a harmonious community devoted
to self-sacrifice and worship. The proud and adventurous brides of
Christ had to learn humility." There were two exceptions to this,
only one of whom gave permission for her story to be included; Sara
who entered after Vatican II. Sara did her novitiate time in Nigeria
with a missionary order. She returned to her Motherhouse after her
time in Africa, where she did experience many similar restrictions
as the majority. The other women in the study had all entered before
or during the transition stages. In the pre-Vatican II days there was
no individual private conversation allowed, particularly during Formation. Two people speaking alone would be considered breaking
the rule denying particular friendships or P.F. The definition of P.F.
according to R. Curb and C. Manahan was that it "refers to friendships between two sisters which exclude others, considered harmful
to community living and prelude to Lesbian relationship." There
was plenty of manual labor to tire the body and lots of theology and
scripture to tire the mind and their work used most of their energy.
Forty of the women received their entire adult education and pro-

fessional training whilst in their convents. The larger sample data shows went to Catholic colleges and more than attended Catholic graduate school.

The entire group spoke in glowing terms and with great respect for the individual nuns who had influenced them in their early years and the lifestyle they represented. They saw a place where women were exalted, with none of the drudgery of home. As Grace said,

> I saw nothing but female role models. Who made the decisions? Who cooked the meals? Who ran the hospitals? Who had power in a group and who didn't? But it was all women. There was nothing a woman couldn't do, because in my experience, women did everything.

Often in the interviews I heard stories of kindness offered, motherly love and gentleness shown, guidance and strength from older nuns lovingly showered on the children in their care. This was experienced often at a time of great personal need and tremendous vulnerability to many of these young girls.

This story described by Ione, was quite common. Even though Ione's family situation was more extreme than many, in that she suffered incest at the hands of her father. She spoke about her early experiences with nuns.

> I had a Sister when I was in eighth grade. She became very much the parental figure for me all the way through college, and I started to admire the Sisters and found them strong women and having a strong sense of self, doing more than housework. That was the experience of the women in my neighborhood. I don't think I was in love with her or anything; it was more an emotional attachment on a motherly basis. I would go to her with my problems and she would take the time. That was in 6th and 7th grade. I found going to Mass really comforting because my home life certainly wasn't. My story is interesting in the interrelation-

ship between my spirituality and my sexuality because my sexual life became part of my prayer life. I had experiences of dealing with and coming to terms with the sexual abuse and understanding myself as a lesbian. My prayer life was very much involved in that. You know the Church doesn't have very good teachings on homosexuality so there was a certain amount of feeling guilty or wondering if it's bad. My prayer life was very much integrated in my coming to a sense of my being lesbian. I realized it was how I was created, not some aberration or that it was some consequence of the sexual abuse, because I don't think it was. I know some Sisters have relationships and remain in the order, but I pretty much feel it's a question of integrity. You're saying that you're going to be celibate but not doing it. Some people are having relationships with lay people or whatever. I feel it's not fair to the person you're having the affair with because your primary focus is not on the community. A lot of people think going to the convent is running away from the world. But when I went, the opposite was true. In the novitiate they gave you lots of time to go to therapy, to go to spiritual direction, to think [each woman would have had a personal spiritual director, usually a priest, who would help with issues of a spiritual nature; similar to a counselor]. I had to interact with all these people, so all my personal issues were bubbling up all over the place. You were always being challenged because a lot of the Sisters are therapists and lawyers and doctors. When I went to dinner I was challenged intellectually, I was challenged emotionally; I knew people were going to challenge me on everything. I was in the convent

for five years and have been out for 10. I was more
challenged in the convent than I am now.

The reasons given for entering religious life were varied.
Some said they wanted more choices of career than their mothers
and other women in their lives had had. Further, some said they
needed to escape an abusive home environment with the added in-
centive of receiving a good education. The love and adoration of
God was rarely verbalized as a reason for entering or for staying.
Many spoke with love and fondness for their communities. Yet, it
was rare to hear words of adulation toward God. Ione was one of
the exceptions and she addressed the issue directly when she said,

> When I was a young nun I used to struggle with the
> idea of being celibate. There was a place in me that
> was only for Jesus and that place was the most inti-
> mate thing in my life. I took it very seriously, but now
> it seems to have passed.

It was also rare to hear feelings of devotion, intimacy, and
utter renunciation of their sexuality in favor of spirituality. Kate
and Hazel were exceptions; their stories follow. Where conscious
awareness of the spiritual transubstantiation was lacking, there was
an understanding in most cases of suppressing sexuality and trans-
posing it with a life dedicated to good works and humanity as a
whole. Most of them made the commitment to enter religious life
in grade school or during high school. For the remainder of their
adolescent and teenage years, they remained loyal to this decision.
In the years after they entered religious life many of them matured
in the nurture and the safety of the convent.

For those who entered to escape dysfunctional homes, the
peace and security and therapy provided by the convents allowed
them to recognize their full potential as human beings and also
recognize their sexual needs. Many of the women in this study
became teachers, their commitment to their designated field often
kept them in the convent long after their subconscious had told
them to leave.

Kate stayed in her convent for 28 years even though she said she knew three years before she actually left that it was over.

> I felt to leave would be totally disloyal. I'd given my word and I couldn't go back on it. That comes from being the child of an alcoholic. I'd been disappointed so many times in my childhood that I thought I'm not going to disappoint anybody. It's like, if I say it, I'll do it.

Kate spoke about the intensity of her feelings toward God in response to my question if she was aware of the sexuality of others in her convent? She gave an emphatic,

> No, never, never. I was attracted to some of the women mainly because they were assertive and smart; they were the leaders of our community. I was attracted to those qualities but not in a sexual way. I think I just shut it down, totally, because since then I found some of my friends that did have sexual relations with other women in our order. I was even living with one of them while she was in a sexual relationship with another woman in a different house. I didn't have a clue. I'm pretty alert, I think I would have picked up on it if it had been blatant, but people were careful and discreet. Since I left I heard more about peoples' experiences than when I was in the order. This is very important, and I guess it was a way of sublimation of all these sexual feelings; I was totally in love with God. I had this fantastically intense emotional, and well, not physical really, except that physical in the sense that it would make me smile. I would feel so happy and proud of how close I felt to God and how really connected we were. So I know I took a lot of

my sexual feelings and sublimated them into this love
affair with God. I think it was really valuable.

Hazel did not speak directly of transplanting her sexuality with
spirituality until close to the end of our interview. However, she
told me very early in our session about a fellow student nurse who
suggested the reason she was going to enter was because she was
unhappy in love. Her response spoke for many when she answered,

Oh no, it's all about love. To put my love, the capabili-
ty of my heart, at the service of others. I really did not
see myself giving up, as much as I was gaining something, going into the religious life. I just didn't see
myself as denying anything. Sexuality was not a part
of my life. I think if I was really honest with myself,
I wonder if I just plain didn't think about it, in light of
my style that I had learned early on. I learned "well
you just blow that off and you don't think about it."

As Hazel said, with her wry laugh and courageous insight,
there was a heavy price to pay for that kind of thinking and she began to pay for it in the convent. Hazel initially denied understanding what exactly went wrong after she entered. She speculated
perhaps if under hypnosis she might be able to unravel the mystery
but said she doesn't try and analyze this anymore. By the end of
our two-hour interview the mystery unraveled somewhat and she
reached some conclusions. She didn't pay particular attention to
her feelings toward God as she described her time waiting to go
into the convent. On entering very little was said about her emotions regarding a life dedicated to God, and in sexual sublimation.
At almost every juncture of her story, she focused on her parents,
particularly her father. Three months after she entered she began to
have what she now suspects were hyperventilating attacks.

This was in '57-58, the year of the Asian flu epidemic.
When I started to demonstrate these symptoms, lack
of balance, I'd almost pass out. I don't think I ever ac-

tually lost consciousness, but the fainting feeling was awful. They attributed it to an inner ear problem.

She saw many doctors. The nuns were exceptionally diligent in her care, taking her to different specialists. However, her condition continued to deteriorate. The nuns would ask her if she were happy.

They would say, "We don't know what's going on." I didn't know what was going on and they would ask me, "Are you happy?" I would say [cheerful laugh] "I am so happy." Even the dumb little chores or charges we had to do, I would do with great joy. Cleaning a classroom, can you believe it? I look upon that as an indication of how happy I was. I did not see that as demeaning. I remember the fun things that would happen in chapel and we would sit there with our shoulders heaving, we were laughing so hard. We weren't supposed to. I was always in line report-ing that I was in two's. We weren't supposed to be in two's. I just couldn't get to grips with that; other people were so important to me. Particular friend-ships, I'd have to report that and do my penance, that didn't seem such a big deal but I thought, "Oh well." We were following the rule of St. Benedict and we were taught early on, you keep the rule and the rule will keep you. A Christian burial is the only thing you have a right to in religious life. I didn't see it as some-thing dreadful, I thought, "Isn't it freeing?" Prepar-ing for the vows particularly the vow of poverty, to be free of material goods, I didn't see that as a problem at all. Chastity, I didn't think about it. I just didn't see that as something I needed to deal with. I mean of course-- sure-- and Obedience--well-- I'll deal with

102

that as I go along. But I did continue to be sick and they thought it was part of the Asian flu. The diagnosis and the treatment were miles apart because they didn't know how to treat it, there wasn't any treatment. After five months they sent me home. As soon as I got home I was fine. I was home for two weeks and I was well again. But I persuaded them to let me go back. I wrote to the powers that be and said I'm fine, please let me come back, I really do believe that I have a vocation. They didn't realize, and I didn't realize that it was quite significant. They thought I'd just recovered from whatever the problem had been. I went back. I picked up where I left off. My group gave me a great welcome back. I received the habit and I took my mother and father's names as my religious name and began the canonical year. I entered into my novitiate year with great delight, but soon the symptoms came back. I'd be sitting in a classroom and then I'd become so nauseous from this lack of oxygen, I expect that's what it was. It went on for months. I was spending more time in the infirmary than with my group. It got to the point where I was losing the feeling on one side of my face. I could hardly talk. We went through Lent but Easter Sunday morning I was in the infirmary again. My Novice Mistress came to me and said, "I think it's over" and I said "Yes I think it is too." I knew I couldn't go on. I was home a week and I was fine again! Well you can imagine how I felt at that point, "Dear Lord, I want to give you my life, and you don't want it!"

Without further analysis, Hazel went on to describe how her career path had continued. I interrupted her to ask whether her superior in the convent ever suggested she see a psychologist for her problems. She answered,

> No, they sent me to more doctors. I was paying an
> enormous price for not being in contact with, God
> knows what. My sister saw me before I left and she
> told me later, "You were on the verge of a nervous
> breakdown." I don't know what was going on but I
> sure wasn't able to cope with what was happening.
> But you're right, I don't remember them ever saying if
> there's something other than physical going on here.
> Yet they sent me to the best doctors, and they kept
> saying "Are you happy?"--"Oh yes, I'm very happy."--
> "Then what in the name of Heaven is wrong here?" I
> was broken-hearted when I had to go home, and I truly
> went through a time when I wondered, "Now what?"

Hazel proceeded at this point to discuss her father's failing health and once more addressed her family's propensity for denial. She left the convent in April of '59 and she continued,

> Daddy's health was in bad shape at that point, and
> you know I almost hate to tell you this, my sister and
> I were talking about this very thing just a couple of
> months ago. He died in September of '59. There were
> two practicing nurses in that household and we didn't
> talk about how close to death he was. I said to my
> sister, "What on earth were we doing?" We were not
> acknowledging it. He was dying before our eyes. His
> heart was just failing by steps and he finally died of a
> myocardial infarction. But I think this is just incred-
> ible, the denial. We were two professional nurses

and we weren't even talking together about what was
happening to our Dad. Ah, mercy! It's fascinating, the
power of the human spirit to be a force for good, or not
so. I saw instances of both in my life.

This was the end of Hazel's self-analysis of her time in the
convent. She came to no conclusions beyond recognizing she was
in denial of something. That *something* remained nameless to her,
even as she reflected deeply on that period of time. She thought
that it would take hypnotherapy to uncover the reason for her illness. As her life story progresses she gave "The Good Lord" credit
for bringing her the man she eventually married. Her total devotion
to her God was intact and she exclaimed "But I just loved my order
and to this day I'm grateful for that time. It developed a spirituality in me that I'm not sure I would have had if it hadn't been for
that. God is my friend, my companion, my lover, my soul mate."
I asked how she conceptualized God as a lover and she answered,

It's not a person that's for sure, it's a presence. My
husband is obviously my lover but God is my lover
in the sense that he knows my comings and goings,
anticipating where I'm going to need help. There's a
relationship we often talk. It's due in large part to that
time in my convent. Yet there were some dimensions
that they did not complete that had to be completed or
opened up over the years. I have a Masters in Theology, the hunger to learn more was opened up in the
convent, for instance my love of scripture. I'm so
grateful for the experience.

I asked how she saw her spirituality and sexuality being
merged.

It's so deep, I'm not even sure I knew what that meant
when I was in the convent. I didn't masturbate or do
anything sexual. I had very little knowledge of my

body, even as a professional nurse. Even my language now when I see God as lover, it's not physical. It's lover in the sense of being cherished, being special which is true of all of us. I don't mean in any way to imply that I would see myself as any more chosen than anyone else. I just think that all of us in some incredible way are chosen. I don't think it's any less perfect for not being physical because I feel it's been completed by my love for and with my husband. I don't think I've ever thought of this before, it's like I intuitively know that, but haven't intellectualized it, put words on it. I don't think I've ever done that before, this is a great opportunity. I feel these are treasures I'm bringing up from a long way down and saying look at this, and polishing them. These are treasures of my past, and it's wonderful to look at them again at this stage of my life.

When Hazel spoke of the treasures that constituted the memories of the past, which she took out now at our interview and "polished," she said,

The clarity of the memories is accompanied by, hopefully I can say truthfully for me, an affection. An affection for that young girl, for that young woman, who was idealistic, not sure of what she was seeking. It was denied to her, and yet it has still been given to her, over the years.

Hazel and I discussed the value of looking back over one's life from the vantage point of age. At this point I introduced again the issue of her illness in the convent by asking whether on some level she was aware of wanting a sexual life or a family of her own and if that may have contributed or accounted for her fainting?

I think you're absolutely right and nobody would say that. And you know what happened early on in our marriage? I said "Oh Peter, let's have a family." Those babies came along boom, boom, boom, six in seven years. Fortunately he was as pleased as I was. We lived in those days when we didn't have much choice [All forms of contraception were still banned in the Catholic Church]. A significant time in my life came after the last child was born. I suffered a prolapsed uterus. I can see why. My obstetrician said he needed to take the uterus out. Oh he was so rough, that was a terrible experience for me. I was a terrible patient, going to the hospital at the last moment, being hostile. It was just very difficult to accept the fact that it was the end of childbearing. I'd come to value that experience. Thank God, I didn't have any more. I've come to see, okay I had to go through that, but that doctor gave me no choice. He told me what I had to do. Having children was such a value in my life. But putting it in the context of what you're saying, that I was paying such a price at the convent for not being in touch with my sexuality, for what I was giving up as far as love, marriage and childbearing in that order. Nobody asked me that question, least of all me [the doctor did not ask for her opinion before removing her uterus which she experienced as a great offense]. Why didn't someone else ask that question? Were the people responsible for formation back then so out of touch with the psychological well-being or lack thereof, of their candidates?

Finally, Hazel verbalizes what she had always known, that having babies as part of a loving family relationship was what she wanted. Earlier in her story she said how she negotiated at the beginning of her marriage by refusing to argue with her husband. She recognized that it didn't work, seeing the practice as another form of denial. Hazel was in the convent for 18 months. It may appear a short duration to have such a powerful effect on one's life. Suffice it to say the disciplines of convent life are 24 hours a day, seven days a week, 365 days per year...every single waking moment. Most of the women were well prepared by their family of origin to be docile and obedient. The experience stays with you, as do many of the tactics to protect oneself from the truth. A willingness to explore and comprehend their reasons for leaving was a very common trait.

Sara entered her community after having travelled extensively with volunteer groups around America and having completed part of her college career. She was sent to Africa to complete her novitiate due to lack of entrants into her order. Sara said her "experience in Africa was a paradigm shift" which forever changed her understanding and appreciation of everything she previously believed about her religion. She anticipated major opportunities for women in the Church and wanted to be in the vanguard of those changes. The reality was quite a surprise to her.

I was the only novice for the whole of my novitiate.
We had consortiums with other convents for classes
where they only had one or two novices also. That was
nice, lots of friends. But when I got the opportunity
to go to Africa, I really wanted to go. It was a very
tumultuous time in Nigeria. The Muslims had just
overthrown the Christians and were basically slaugh-
tering everybody that didn't agree with them, and
were trying to undercut the influence of the Christian
groups. I wasn't prepared. They said to me, "So you
want to go to the novitiate in Nigeria?" And in two

weeks I was there. There was no preparation, I was 24
and had been in the convent for a year. It was horrible.
We lived in mud houses on the edge of the desert. I
was the only white thing; well there were two novice
mistresses. One Irish the other American, but they
were a little darker so I was treated like I was weird by
the Africans--well not weird, mystical, because I was
so white. I was taken aback by these people looking at me as if they'd seen a ghost. It was shocking,
absolutely shocking to come from America to absolute
basic life, it scared the hell out of me. It was a lot of
culture shock.

On Sara's first day at the convent station she was witness to
the execution of hundreds of political prisoners caught in the coup.
The convent was the only place with a television and the message
she said had come up on the drums that if people wanted to see
what happened to the prisoners to go to the place with the television at a certain time. The relatives of these people came to the
convent and Sara watched with the natives as the men on view
were tortured and executed slowly by being shot from the ankles
up. Sara went on to describe how her spirituality and view on religious life had altered in view of her experiences.

It was totally transforming. It just shattered all my
understanding, any worldview that I had. It just put
me back to square one, scared out of my mind. My
symbols, everything I had were gone and you really
had to look at life in a very basic way and re-think
things from bottom up. The Church that I was a part
of for the first time said you had to cover your head
and wear a veil and all that, we didn't wear a habit and
it was never anything I'd wanted. It was also very oppressive of the native cultures. I was so alienated from

the structure I was a part of. I didn't want to be a part
of an organization that was more and more conservative, and I felt the Church at that time was becoming
just that. Spirituality for me was very different. It
was still very comforting but after you've seen and
gone through that kind of an experience it changes
you. To me it had more meat on it and it was a lot
more real and I felt comfortable enough to walk out of
the structure. I was just about to make vows, not that
I was a sexual person but chastity was a real--Obedi-
ence was a big one, I can't just go along with a structure that I feel is so foreign and destructive. I don't
know if that was just youthful rebellion or a real life
system but it was something that I was trying to figure
out. The community was trying to deal with chastity,
and sexuality and religious life, at a time in the Church
when I really feel women were being relegated to very
subservient levels, and not credited for brains or being
capable of ministry or that kind of thing. I didn't want
to be in a structure that was defining me that way and
I was conflicted enough I didn't like the symbols and
I didn't like the superficial level you had to work with
people as a religious. I didn't hear enough people
within the community struggle with the issue of sexuality. We had a number of workshops about sexuality,
but the people who were responsible for you in training to the point of vows; it just wasn't an issue for
them. It was "just pray more, pray more," and the more
you quote/unquote, "pray more," and thought about
it, the clearer the questions became. I just didn't find
room for those questions. It wasn't as if I was hanging
out horny for anybody, it was just an area that I ducked

from and didn't want to shut myself off from for my whole life. I knew they wouldn't let me go back to the missions because they wanted me to work in administration. That's not where I wanted to go. A lot of them had built their lives the way they wanted them to go. A lot of them had very close relationships with priests that didn't stop at spiritual direction. I think it went further, and there were a number of people who were having ongoing relationships with other people, men or other priests. I wasn't aware of lesbianism within the community. I knew of homosexual priests, I didn't care to find it but I knew of many priests having relationships with other men. I don't know. I was 30 then, and I'm thinking, I don't want to live a divided life. I don't want to sit there and say celibacy and find someone to keep me warm on a cold night. I want something to be whole for me and I couldn't see it being whole for me in the community. It wasn't clear that they were willing to put me through law school, so I put it all together and moved out.

Ill health is not uncommon among those women who repress feelings and continue to force the body and attempt to control the mind in a lifestyle wholly unsuited to their true needs. Of the participants in this study, one woman developed breast cancer, five had nervous breakdowns, one left in a severely emaciated condition, one was diagnosed as being deathly allergic to what she finally decided was the religious life rather than to the physical environment. Clinical depression appears to have been fairly common amongst the women. Unfortunately this was an area that I did not address in my questionnaire and needs further study.

Marian was one of the women who became dangerously ill while in the convent. She prefixes her statement with,

The choice to go in the convent was a good one,
very wise looking at the whole spectrum of things. I
entered at 18 and stayed in for 13 years, so I came out
at 31. While I was in the convent I really repressed
things. After a while I was very sick, I had a hysterectomy in my 20s, and a surgery that was much more
dramatic and serious than that.

Marian thought her condition was congenital, owing to the fact
that she thought her mother attempted to abort her. I am inclined to
believe that a lot of internal damage may have been done by all the
sexual activity she experienced as a very young child. This would
seem to be a much more plausible reason for internal organ damage
than would an attempted abortion by her mother.

As previously stated the length of time spent in the convents
does not appear to be as important as having made the decision
to enter and been exposed to the rigors of the life. Ursula was in
religious life for only six months after having waited until the age
of 39 to enter. She told me "My search for God is so ferocious; it
is far stronger than my sexuality." Ursula has spent her life locked
in the torment of trying to make peace with herself and her sexuality. Her attempts at denial of the existence of a sexual nature have
caused her to spend a great deal of her life castigating herself. The
result was that, at over 60 years of age she finally began to examine
the roots, the genesis of her sexual aversion. She discovered the
roots lay in the sexual assaults perpetrated in her childhood, compounded by the "despotic" behavior of her mother. Doehring, in
her book *Internal Desecration* said that subjects who have suffered
an extreme level of trauma in childhood and adolescence suffer
inflexibility in adulthood in all cognitive domains. "As adults they
may have fixed religious systems as their only means of coping
with the representations associated with traumatization, which lie
at the deepest level of their personalities." Ursula illustrates many
of the characteristics described by Doering and parts of her story
will be included in most chapters. Ursula's representation of God
at this stage in her life has moved on from seeing God as angry

and now sees Him as her savior. However, after her first lesbian encounter she felt God had deserted her. At this point in her life she believes her love of God to be the only thing that saved her from committing suicide on several occasions when her life became intolerable. Most of those times were when she allowed herself to experience physical sex.

After being denied the opportunity of entering the convent when she was 20, Ursula once again attempted to enter a community in her native France, when she was 35 years. The Superiors in that order suggested she may be happier in America since she had lived in this country for five years. She returned to America and eventually entered a strict, monastic, cloistered order of Carmelites. This was how she reviewed that period of her life..

> My sexuality had never interfered with my desire for
> the monastery. I forbade myself to think about the mon-
> astery when I came to America. I wanted to be open for
> maybe marriage because I did not realize exactly, my
> nature. At 39 I thought I could go into the monastery
> and live perfectly normally and have no sexual desire
> because I would pray, that's what I thought. There was
> no sexual attraction when I was in, although there were
> some very beautiful women. I was attracted to them
> again like a mother because I know that there is some-
> thing very important about that lack of mother love. But
> I fear, fear, so much fear, I was ashamed because this is
> something very strong with me, that I am fearful when
> facing a beautiful woman. I feel they will judge me,
> that I am a lesbian. So in the monastery I never had an
> attraction, but I had a fantastic fear. So much so that
> every day when we had to have recreation together for
> two hours, facing all of them, and some of them were
> very beautiful, I wanted to hide. I was so ashamed of
> myself I got diarrhea. Something had to give in my

body, and it was the worst diarrhea in my life. In the
end, I was so afraid to go to recreation I would get
diarrhea before we went in and as soon as I sat down it
would begin again.

Ursula was finally asked to leave after six exhausting months.
Nobody at the convent or at any time in her life suggested therapy
or psychological counseling. She was simply asked to leave and
went away feeling even more defeated by her own body.

Virginia discussed a romantic relationship with God.

When I entered in 1969 there were some talks given
on what celibacy was all about. I thought a lot of them
were pretty ridiculous except for the one where you
have a romantic relationship with God or Jesus. It made
to sense to me to be celibate to be more available to
work; that was the most stupid thing I'd ever heard of. I
disregarded that as a possible motivation and the retreat
experience was so powerful and personal it wasn't at all
romantic or spousal in its experience. What it evolved
into quickly was spousal in that God became the object
of my life desires. I felt like the Bride of Christ image in
as much as that image was being discarded at the time.
That didn't fit with most of the people in my group, but
it fit my motivation. I think a lot of my sexual energy
got pulled into the psychological experience that I was
having and so that's what I did with most of it, I knew
right where it was. I couldn't really imagine any other
way that it would work.

Lua Xochitl [self named] was one of those women who entered
essentially to escape. She shows great insight as she examines her
reasons for entering and staying 12 years in the order. In two areas
of her story she refers to how she handled her sexuality before and
on entering the convent and where she thought the energy went.

114

She said,

In high school in terms of sexuality, goodness no,
none of that. Every Friday we were asked, "What
are you doing this weekend? Who are you going out
with? Remember, French kissing is a sin." They didn't
even know what French kissing was, isn't that a trip?
God! Women have been so violated intellectually. My
senior year I decided to go to the convent, never having shared with a man and done that French kissing. I
thought if I did it, I was going to hell or get pregnant.
With all that, as I look back now on my childhood, I'm
wired to be a person of joy but there was this hiding
of the deep pain that was going on. Then I entered the
convent, and took on all that meant. What that meant
to me personally was, being a member of a family.
I fell in love with it. On the surface, up in my head
I entered with a thread of spirituality. I was doing
God's work. But deeper down where it really mat-
tered, in my core, I was running away. I was going,
following my higher self. It was only in my early 50s
that I realized that it was integrity that I maintained
during those years. It was then, in my fifties that I
was able to say, the convent saved my life. I became
one of those activist nuns and I really promised myself
that I deserved to bomb a Church before I left this
planet. Now it's not important that I do that, it's dying
by itself. Thank you, Goddess. Also, I've come to a
place where I know it saved my life. In terms of my
sexuality, I was dead, and where does your sexual
energy go? It goes to cleaning up the house, waxing
floors, and cleaning schools; that's what sexual energy

was for in the convent.

I wasn't aware of sexuality in the convent. I wasn't
awake to it. I remember talking to one wonderful nun
about this subject. We went out on a walk and I asked
if any of our nuns made it with each other or at all? I
was so naive I didn't know. She said "Well you know
Sister Mary, it's like women in prison. Living in a
convent in close quarters, the more women become
affectionate, develop friendships." Now we had been
taught not to have particular friendships. She went on
"Let me tell you, I've never seen anyone in our community doing anything inappropriate; what would
be inappropriate for you Sister Mary?" I said, "Two
Sisters kissing," and she answered; "Well I've never
seen that." Then I said "It would be inappropriate
but it would be fine wouldn't it?" She just smiled. I
understand now that she was accepting and it was a
young woman with no judgment. One time she said
she saw two nuns in the trunk room with their arms
around each other, but that was it. She said she did
know of one nun who was making it with a priest and
by that time had left the community. I knew this nun
to be the model of the perfect Sister. What that did for
me was a shock at the total hypocrisy of it all. A voice
inside of me said "What a sham."

The trunk room is the special storage room for the girls' lug-
gage upon entering. A point of interest about the part of the story of
the two women in the trunk room was that both the nuns discussing
it overlooked the fact that this may have been the innocent farewell
scene between two friends, one of whom could have been departing
the convent. There are many such stories of snatched moments of

privacy in the trunk room from other former nuns' memoirs since this was the only private place to speak freely prior to the silent exodus the following day.

Although these words read with an element of bitterness, there was none in Lua Xochitl's demeanor. She spoke dispassionately of her dormant sexuality in those years. Her earlier anger so well expressed was replaced in these years with a certainty, a knowing, a "crone's" knowing as she would have described herself. She has an understanding that she was saved by her years in the convent, and became the strong loving woman she is today because of it, not in spite of the experience.

Elizabeth knew as a first grader that she was going to be a nun. As previously mentioned in Chapter Four, she believed in past lives and felt as if she had followed religious monasticism in many of them. Her awareness of a personal spirituality was evident from the moment I met this quiet spoken, peaceful woman. She told me,

> I think because I had my heart set on going to the convent, the sexual part of me was probably split. And when I did enter, I remember thinking, it's having babies that I'll miss rather than the sex. I grew up around babies and I wanted babies. It was very hard for me to give up, but I didn't have a sense of the intimacy, I didn't have that at all. I think I got that more through prayer, later. But I didn't have it then. I did violence to myself, I really stifled the joyful, fun part of me to do this right; I thought, I'll show them. Sexuality, I think it was put into a desire for celibacy, a desire for more spiritual application so I think that was what happened at that time, unconsciously. I think I was repressing it and putting it into spirituality, because that was my focus. I was studying theology for my Master's. I ran prayer groups and taught religion wherever I went but I think it was spirituality. So I think I put

all my sexual energy into spiritual energy. I always
felt that a lot of the energy that would have gone into
being a mother went into being a teacher; I was really
present for my students. That held a lot of satisfaction
for me personally, on one level. I wasn't aware that my
needs weren't being satisfied because they were, as far
as I was concerned. I wasn't sexually involved with
any of the Sisters. I don't think there was a lot of that
going on when we were in formation. There was later,
I know of two novices who were involved with each
other. I also know of women younger than I am who
were seduced by other people. I was oblivious to it at
the time.

Elizabeth suffered many years of very serious illness but remained in the community for 29 years working in high office. The
Chibnall et al., data states:

We found also a notable frequency of sexual trauma
perpetrated by women, often on other Sisters. At least
13% of the respondents reported some form of sexual
trauma as an adult at the hands of a Sister. Among
those who reported sexual exploitation, 25% reported
that a woman was the perpetrator. These percentages
are conservative. If some of the unclassified sexual
traumas occurred in religious community, they would
be increased. The respondents reported details only
on the most painful trauma in each category.

Maria, who entered at 16 years old and left almost 20 years
later, felt as if she grew up in the convent. As stated she also entered to escape from home. Maria expressed clearly how her students satisfied many of her maternal and sexual needs. She rarely
mentioned any religious or spiritual experiences of her years in the
convent and when she discussed her observations of nuns and their

possible sexuality with each other or with clerics she clearly was aware of close friendships but denied intimate knowledge of physical contact.

I think a lot of my interactions with the high school kids that I taught had some growing up for me. I don't remember any stirring or sexual feeling but a lot of the boys would hang around and we would talk and listen to "Peter, Paul and Mary" records and hang out together. So I think I got some satisfaction that way. Knowing that the boys were pretty attentive to me and liked being around me. Still to this day, some of them come to see me. Just a couple of weeks ago one of the men I had in my class over years ago came by to see me when he came to town. Some of the connections have lasted. So I think a lot of the attention they gave me was somewhat subliminal sexual, nothing was ever acted out. It was very interesting; if the nuns needed anything, they would tell me, call your kids. Whenever they could be used it was an okay thing, but if it was just hanging out then it was looked upon askance. Somehow, I weathered all that. I wasn't aware of anything physical between the nuns. There were always pairs of them that we called "Uncle John and Aunt Ellen." Those were the names as nuns, we gave to those people who were always together; they spent the summers together, things like that. They weren't usually on mission together but at other times such as holidays. I never had it in my head that they did anything physical, so I have no idea what acting out could have been, in that sense. There was one nun when I was about 20 who showed movies on Friday night. We were watching the movie one night and she leaned over and held my hand, it shocked me, it just shocked me. It sent shivers through me and I was very concerned but we never spoke about it. I never said "don't do that" I just didn't have my hands free from that point on. I think that was an interesting beginning of seeing how there could be sexuality in the convent, yet I was pretty strong against that, it was not what I would choose.

This comment from Maria was quite interesting in the light of the transitions she made during the final years of her year stay in the convent. The story of how she met and fell in love with a young priest will follow.

Where women lay emphasis in their own stories was significant. For all participants the period when they were in the convent held many poignant, moving memories. This was where major discoveries happened for some, where others grew safely and securely in a loving environment. For some it was the place they learned how to be rebels and branch out completely away from the Church they had dedicated themselves to. Ursula's memories of convent life added to her concern regarding her gender preference, in that to be confronted by "beautiful women" on a daily basis was difficult for her. For others, the time spent in the convent was not the most significant area of interest as they scanned the years of their lives. As the chapters in this work unfold stories from other women will be introduced as their own histories apply best to the points being made.

CHAPTER SIX
SEXUAL TRANSITIONS

But surely infantilism is destined to
be surmounted. Men cannot remain
children forever; they must in the end
go out into "hostile life." We may call
this "education to reality."

— Sigmund Freud, *The Future of an Illusion*

The decades of the 1960s and 70s saw a revolution of sorts in the Western world. Major incidents such as the assassination of President Kennedy, the Vietnam War and the Cuban missile crisis were an assault on the American bedrock of faith, and created a very uncertain world. There was a movement away from authority, away from conventional sexual and traditional lifestyles. Feminism was gaining momentum. In all areas of life it seemed dramatic change was taking place; music, space travel, air travel and finally the sexual revolution culminating in the spectacle of Woodstock. Crisis was also brewing in the Catholic Church. The Second Vatican Council or Vatican II opened in Rome on October 11, 1962. The impact of this meeting of all the prelates of the Roman Catholic Church was to have a profound effect on women in their convents all over the world. Vatican II was probably one of the most decisive influences on male and female religious in the past century. The First Vatican Council was convoked by Pope Pius IX on 29 June 1868, after a period of planning and preparation that began on 6 December 1864. Its best-known decision is its definition of papal infallibility. As stated, the message of this revolutionary Council was "change," forcing personal responsibility on religious men and women and changing monastic practices centuries out of date. Some of the women in this study reported entering the convent because they felt called to do something "bigger" with their lives than being wives and mothers. They wished the Peace Corp had been available for them. Incidentally, if it had been available, the commitment involved would have been only two or three years. These women were prepared to make a lifetime commitment to religious life.

My data show 76% of respondents felt sexuality played a role in their decision to enter, with the same number feeling it was an escape from sexuality. Ten percent saw it as a way to live in an all female environment. Further information from my data shows the average age of women entering the convent to be 19 years; the average age for leaving was 32 years. Seventy-five percent of these women had professed vows, which means they had been in the convent for more than three years. The average age of all respondents was 54 years. Thus the majority entered and left within the time frame of the greatest unrest in the Church. The effects of Pope John XXIII's call to modernize, plus the establishment of the Peace Corps, were integral to the great exodus of women from their convents and the dearth of others to replace them. Hedrick, in her autobiographical musings, *Whatever Happened to Sister Jane?* addressed the issues in a similar fashion to that I heard in my interviews. She said that there were others like herself "swept along on the idealism of the 50's into the realities of the 60's." She goes on to say that many women like herself had entered because the Peace Corps was not available. They did not want to go into the armed forces or get married and so religious life was the only option open to them. Hedrick's statistics show by 1977 there were 130,804 women in religious orders or institutes. This number was down 50,000 from the all-time high, which peaked in the 1960s. By 1990 the number was 102,504. The 1993 Catholic Almanac reports 97,751 women religious in the United States. The Tri-Conference Retirement Office for Women Religious in 1993 lists the membership at 92,857. This is a drop of 88,564 in 27 years, a 44% drop in population.

Sipe, says, "Before the 60s, celibates were presumed to have no sexuality." Sipe was referring to priests; however, the same could be said about nuns. Vatican II was pivotal in re-directing the entire approach to religious life. Pope John XXIII is often quoted as saying he wanted to "throw open the doors and windows and let a little light in." Many of the women in this study felt he was speaking directly to them. For not only did he throw open the doors and windows, but threw them open so far that thousands upon thousands of religious, both male and female, marched right on out. Vatican II forced religious men and women to think as adults instead of being forced to believe that the way to Heaven was to think with the mind of a child. Translated, that meant, "Do as you are told." As Hazel said previously, "Keep the rule and the rule will keep you." What the rule really developed was a child-like devotion, but now they were told it's time to wake up and begin to take personal responsibility.

This relaxing of the rules and establishing of more personal accountability resulted in many changes. For women such as Lua Xochitl who had suffered from body image issues all their lives, this was a traumatic ordeal. She expressed her feeling in this way:

> When we were told we were going to get out of the
> habit, I cried for three days. I hadn't looked in the
> mirror after I put on the coif because I had been taught
> I was ugly and I believed it. So now I had to put on
> street clothes and the thought was terrifying to me. So
> I had to unlearn all that. The process of unlearning is
> more painful than the learning. What was happening
> also was a sexual, spiritual awakening.

Lua Xochitl was insightful enough to recognize the bigger picture. Once the nun is taken out of her protective ancient garb, she is perceived by those around her and even more importantly by herself, as a woman. The relaxing of the stern old ways had other ramifications, notably the formation of open close friendships, which would have been terminated in the past. San Giovanni says it is a basic sociological truth that sex roles are never static. Data from the wider group show a move away from strictly heterosexual throughout the transitions:

SEXUAL IDENTITY	N = 45	N = 47	N = 49
	BEFORE %	DURING %	AFTER %
Heterosexual	89%	79%	67%
Bisexual	9%	11%	21%
Homosexual	2%	11%	12%

For some of the women, experimenting with sex roles was part of their progress which culminated in their leaving community. Eight women had varying degrees of sexual relations with priests or brothers whilst still in their communities. One met a layman and began a relationship. From the data I found that 54% were aware of sexuality between the clergy and nuns, and 36% knew of nuns and a lay person being sexually involved. Three out of this group were sexual with women during their time within the convent. Two had same sex relationships once they had left. The remainder did not admit any same sex experience. However, 44% admitted to knowing of its occurrence within the convent. Further information from the questionnaire shows, 26% had lived openly with a same sex partner for an average of six years. The minimum was one year and maximum 25 years.

Virginia had an observation on this subject. She said, "I think living in a primary female world all those years moves people to a more bisexual place. I think it can't not for most people. Even if you're as heterosexual as they come when you move into that experience, there's no way it doesn't influence you--psychologically, spiritually, and sexually. There's just no way you can avoid it." I asked, "but very few have acted out on it, did you?" She answered,

No, I could fall in love with a woman; I haven't but
I could. Now, I wouldn't let it happen because I'm

committed. But if a woman came along before my husband, I would have struggled with it because of the edges of homophobia that are still there; but I think I would have let myself have the experience. There have been a few people I can remember who I have been briefly infatuated with. At the front end it just felt like infatuation it didn't feel sexual at all. I just felt like a good friend. That's the full extent of 30 years living with women and I never fell in love with one of them.

I will continue later with the theme of same sex partners. First, I will complete Virginia's story, which describes how she began on her road out of the community after more than 18 years. Up to that point she had one relationship which began several years after she entered. After being assigned to work in a community center she met a young priest,

We became good friends and by the end of the first year I fell in love with him. It was a very powerful friendship and we talked about how we were beginning to feel. He wasn't feeling similar so we cooled the friendship but by a year from then we were both very much in love. I feel that my intention always to get beyond this, not that I didn't enjoy it, but I was clear that I didn't want to act on it and move it into a sexual friendship and that didn't happen. I would take breaks from the relationship then we would have contact and have it be okay, it was 99% in love emotional reaction. At some period of time we would go on romantic dates holding hands, a couple of times we would kiss but it was very limited, very controlled in the way we acted. I didn't see him after that, and I didn't think it was right to need him like that. I knew during that time that I was playing with fire in terms of the stress I was feeling in the form my relationship with God took, and I now had this real live person that I was in love with. That relationship ended very badly as we both slowly just abandoned it and as he made a choice to go forward with his ordination. My take on it was that this relationship does need to change but we can't just abandon it, but he had nothing to say. Then within two years he identified himself as gay and was acting out. He caught AIDS and died. All that happened within two years. A lot of the way he managed the relationship was around his being gay. For me it was around the fact that I had vows and I wasn't going to act as if I didn't. He wanted to pursue the sexual relationship more than me, I think he was in such denial about his sexuality which he later said he knew about in high school but had been put underground. He said I'll either leave and we'll marry or I'll be ordained. To him there were two options, since you're saying no to me, I'm just going to move forward. I think if I had been willing to be sexual we would have left and married. When I think of it now; imagine what it would have been like? Two kids later to find out he's gay, oh that would have been bad. When our relationship ended I felt cut off, abandoned.

I think the sexuality question in that is, the first decade I was held and I had this channel for how I understood my sexuality. Then I had that period of time when I kind of fell apart because the relationship shifted the way I dealt with my energies. I had the attempt at recovery that never happened, if it had I would have weathered a lot of the other issues. I think the sexuality question is central to the whole story. It's central to getting me in and it's central to why I ended up leaving and I never thought I would have the relationship I have today.

After leaving the convent she met a man and they moved in together. The relationship became sexual very quickly. She said,

We had sex every night for two or three months. I think he thought he'd found an Amazonian. I said I've been waiting 50 years for this; lay down and shut up! I was very aggressive and very ready to do this; I knew exactly what was happening. I'd walk into work and shout I love oral sex. They just looked at me, I was talking about it all the time. Here is this very modest man and I would run around naked all the time, it was like this all the time. I have this modest little man with this wild woman who's telling everyone everything. I was still processing it.

I asked if she felt this euphoria was due to the fact that she had denied herself sexual pleasure for so long and now delighted in the free expression of it? She answered,

Yes maybe in a different way than when you're 18. It's so many things all at once. It's the first time so there's all the newness, but you're 50 when you're doing it for the first time, that's a really different meaning to it. It's been contained for so long. I'm more sexual than he is. The focus of it is what makes it as good as it is. The relation between having it all and it being as good as it is, is sort of how it came together with my spiritual experience of it too.

Nuns by virtue of their avowed celibacy are denied the role of wife and mother; they are expected to subordinate their sex roles to the demands of religious life. San Giovanni, says "Paradoxically, while a nun was discouraged through convent law, ideology, vows, and routines, from defining herself and acting in terms of her role as a woman, the very same structure of convent life, grounded in Catholic theology, reinforced traditional feminine values and behavior." The data shows 65% of respondents wanted children and that long-term marriages, i.e. 12 years, is average.

This period of change and turbulence prompted by Vatican II catapulted members of communities out of medieval centuries into the 19th Century. Thus, once the rigor and ritual was removed and more feminine dress was added to daily life, those who had stayed in the fixed mode of thinking were now forced to re-evaluate their lives. It would take much more pain, therapy and education before they would enter the 20th Century as fully contributing members of society and in control of their womanhood. For those women who would eventually relinquish the celibate life, one major key was in recognizing, challenging and eventually owning, their sexuality. This is a remarkable transition from turning over their minds, their aspirations and their virginity to Christ as His Bride. San Giovanni describes "two primary themes" which she sees as motivating forces for women leaving their convents. Those who were "pushed" out, as a consequence of change and convent politics being too slow and restrictive for them; and those who were "pulled" out by options and alternatives unavailable to them as long as they remained nuns. Maria is an example of one who may have considered herself to have been pushed out because Rome was too slow in allowing priests to marry. On the other hand she was pulled out because she knew outside the convent she could have sexual relationships with impunity. Three of the interviewees fit into the first category. Those were the political radicals who became frustrated and could not conform to convent life any longer. The remainder was enticed back into the world because of their desire to make their own decisions amongst other things.

Several of the participants had intimate relationships during their time in community. Lisa had an intimate relationship with a fellow nun during her 15 years in the convent. In remembering this part of her life it triggered an emotional response which surprised her. As her story progressed she wept and told me,

> On and off in my religious life I had thoughts, should I leave or should I stay? And I always recommitted myself to staying. During most of my religious life I lived in small communities, a big part of that time I lived with a woman who I became very close to. We were very warm with each other physically, we never got into genital sex. You know maybe some of the things we did with each other could be construed as sexual. I remember thinking of her, if I could marry anyone I would want to have married her. I loved her and I continue to love her, I don't have the same feelings toward her now but I look back and I see a lot of that sexual energy I had in those young years in my twenties, definitely directed towards her. Throughout the course of years we shared a room in some houses and had separate rooms in others. We were parted for a year, and I wrote a love letter to her every single night for a year. It would be the last thing I did every night. There was nothing inconsequential; it was almost like a diary of that year, I wish I'd kept those letters, because I'd just tell her everything. She also wrote to me almost every day and I remember rushing to the mail box. There was another nun I lived with who had a close relationship with someone but they didn't write letters and she would say "Oh, I envy you, I envy you." We were having an affair in a sense, it was long distance, and sometimes she would come up

to where I lived on business and we would be together for the weekend and it would be, it was like heterosexual couples would be like, and I never felt guilty because I loved her and if I could have married her I would have [married her] and she me. We are still very close. If I were to say who my dearest friend is, she is that person. Even when we were in the convent and were having some difficulty with our friendship she said "no matter what you decide to do, I will always love you." I remember experiencing that love is a matter of choice, not a matter of emotions. When my emotions that I had with her for so many years were beginning to wane, I made a choice to continue to love her. That experience taught me that love is beyond feeling, there is choice to love, and when you are in a relationship with someone, sometimes the feeling isn't there but you can choose to love. It was kind of a love beyond feeling which so much of our love is in our world today; I don't feel love so I'm just going to go. It taught me you can continue to love without all the emotion. I actually saw that modeled in my parents in their marriage, they were together for 50 some years, and they made a choice to be with one another for the rest of their lives even when the emotion wasn't there. After 15 years of re-commitments my dearest friend left. She had been with the community for 25 years; she had her own reason for leaving. She entered the convent because she wanted to make sure that her father went to Heaven and she sacrificed her life for that. She found out that's not the way it works so she left and got married. I stayed on another year. I didn't want to leave because she had, even though I'd been thinking about it, so I took my time. I finally decided to take a leave of absence for a year. I went home and told my mom and dad and mom just smiled, a lot of priests and nuns were leaving at that time so she just accepted it, it wasn't a surprise to her. My father's eyes welled with tears again and he said, "Do you remember what I told you when you entered? Well God is just giving you back to me again." I was overwhelmed with that. A couple of years later I took a weekend workshop on co-dependency and this story came out. The leader of the workshop told me "you know your father had no right to determine your destiny. That was your choice." When she said that, it made sense to me. Not that I love my parents less for that, they did their best from where they were coming from. It became so clear to me that my time in the convent was just part of my journey; it was not going to be my whole journey. It was like a second womb. I had this home that protected me and loved me and taught me some wonderful things about life and relationships. Then I needed to in a sense die out of that life, be born into another, learn something's there, die to that, be born into another and so on. I believe there are lessons to learn and then you move on, that's what happened in the convent. I've been out now for 18 years and I'm learning things in this third lifetime. Yes three very different lifestyles. I don't think my real death will be very different for me. I do believe that I will go on. At the time when I left I had a lot of fantasies about what it would be like to be with a man, and my fantasies were a lot grander than the reality it really is. I mean sex can be really wonderful, but it's not all that it's cracked up to be. I wanted to discover that. I think my first penis-vagina sex was when I was 33 years old; I was a virgin up till that time. It was a homely guy I'd met at work. He dated me and I wasn't all that attracted to him, he was very attracted to me. He was always very nice and I thought, "Oh Lisa, let's just get it over with, let's just do this thing!" I remember feeling "Oh finally I'm a woman." I remember going to work the next day, I finally did the woman thing, and now I can get on with my life. I don't know why I waited until I was 33, but I just wasn't ready, and it wasn't as if I was waiting. I've talked with other people who say they wanted to do it with someone very special, but by the time I was 33, I didn't want to wait around for someone special, but he was very nice, and he was very inexperienced. If the man I'm with now had come into my life when I first left the convent, no way would I have been ready for him because he has had a lot of experience sexually, and I think his relationship with me was the first time he'd been monogamous. So I guess I began to go out and experience men. At first I was resistant to telling people I'd been a nun because if I did it was like they had certain expectations; like, I guess you don't like sex, or have you ever had sex? Here I was 33 years old. It was kind of hard and there was this 15-year vacuum. One man had the gall to say well you mustn't like men, if you're this age and not married well then obviously you must be gay. I can still count my sexual liaisons, about 12 to 15.

Although we did not discuss this at length, it is surprising to me that Lisa said so little about her bisexuality once out of the convent. She did in fact speak about attending workshops which were

132

"very sexual" but did not give details about her participation. She did however admit to many same sex relationships although her primary lover is male and she appeared totally comfortable with her sexuality.

When Lisa spoke about knowing people who wait until just the right man comes along before becoming sexual, I thought of Mary. I was troubled on a number of levels after speaking with this woman. Her voice was flat and emotionless throughout the entire hour we were together. Even though the topic of our conversation and the content of her story was emotive, her voice showed no reflected emotion. She is a therapist herself, so the time allotted was exactly the time allowed. Although she made me feel very comfortable, and I believe she made a true and considered attempt to be frank in our interview; I did, however, feel a sense of sadness upon leaving -- that here was a woman desperate for something she didn't have the dialogue to ask for. Mary was one of only a few women who left the convent primarily because of the vow of chastity (the majority of the others left because of obedience) with the express wish to be sexual and after ten years out of religious life, still remained a virgin. This was another woman who as a nun had a life-threatening disease, this time in the form of breast cancer.

> I think having been so close to death and age wise, I
> was thirty when I got cancer, I just wanted to be more
> free basically. During the process of all the treatment
> and things that happened to me, it became evident
> to me that I was a very different person. One of the
> things that I wanted was very much connected to early
> religious life, which was to be open to all kinds of
> relationships. I was aware even before my first profes-
> sion at the age of 21 that I was crying because I knew
> it was connected to not getting married; I stayed for
> 21 more years. I do remember each time I took vows
> contemplating leaving around the marriage factor.
> There were other people leaving to go with people

they'd met in college and things. That didn't happen
to me, I do remember being attracted as a sister in
those young years. I dated tremendously the year after
I left but I wasn't ready to form a relationship, I was
still in transition.

She went on to explain how a series of events overtook her life: her
father's diagnosis of cancer, her studies for a Ph.D., and a very busy
work schedule cumulatively making a social life impossible for her.
Even having just moved into a new condominium housing many
single men who could be potential partners, she said she was just
too tired and was busy with her own activities. I asked if she had
ever considered just having anonymous sex, to get it over with?

Yes, I thought about going out and being a prostitute
or something. I think for me it's so caught up in love
and the whole package. But there have been times
when I've considered just finding someone and just
doing it. But I've never known how to go about doing
that in a safe way to tell you the truth, and I always
go back to the fact that it will be so different if you
really love the person than if you're just doing it. If I
was afraid of it, the pain and all the rest of it I feel all
that would be okay if I really loved the person, so it
just doesn't make sense to me. As I said I feel like my
family was very affectionate but I also feel my mother
had a lot of problems with sexuality, just listening to
her talk now. My mother will talk about the fact that
they didn't have sex after a certain age, quite young.
I get the feeling that she was pretty frigid; she's a
person who holds herself pretty tight. There's never
been a soft side of her. I don't feel like that at all, I
feel very soft most of the time. The men I'm attracted
to are spiritual, growthful and I don't meet many of

134

them. I have to say one of the men I met nine months after I left community, I had to chase him out of my apartment because he wanted to go to bed immediately. We had only gone out a couple of times. I don't feel I have to be married or anything to do it, but I do see myself as needing to love the person and wanting to embrace them in my whole being. I feel the only piece of me that isn't fulfilled is sexually and so in the last year I feel very open to it. I feel like if it happens, if I moved into an intimate relationship that my life would be very different and I would not be working like I'm working now. I would be spending a lot of time with that person. When I left community, I wanted it to happen, I was pushing it and it didn't happen. Now I'm at the point where I would like it but it's not necessary. I feel like if it happens that would be great and I feel open to it but I also feel like I am who I am. I have men as well as women friends, I feel very complete that way. I feel it's just the sex act, if I was with the right person I think it would be very fulfilling; it's just that I've never met the right person. In the nine years since I came out I've never been that close to anyone. When I was in community there was that automatic protection there and when I was in high school, there were guys I kissed but it was just not something that happened.

I asked Mary if she was aware of sexuality in the convent.

Yes, that's another thing I felt extremely naive about because that was happening all over the place in the convent, and I was really not aware of that at all initially. That was even happening amongst our group;

there were 19 of us, and things would happen at night-
time. I thought I pretty much enjoyed people and had
a good time, I felt like a very young adolescent college
kid who was acting out. We did a lot of acting out the
first two years. We did things that kids do, that teenagers do. I never was attracted to another woman but
it became evident to me later as people were leaving
that it was because they had become sexually involved
with someone in the community who wanted to stay
or that they just needed to get out because it had become too intense for them to stay.

I asked, of all the vows, which was most responsible for your
leaving?

The celibacy, yes definitely. I think it was probably
the obedience, a combination of them. In my letter I
think I mainly talked about celibacy, but I think for
me I just needed to do my own thing.

As the interview progressed Mary began to delve into why she
seems unable to "do the act" and comes to the conclusion,

I looked at the possibility with the help of my therapist
that I may have been sexually abused as a child. This
just doesn't make any sense to me, I can't even picture it or imagine it. I've thought about it and tried to
imagine it. This is when I start to wonder about other
lifetimes, I don't know, it just interests me. There was
no sexual abuse at all. If anything I'd say my mother
was physically abusive. I have vivid incidences that I
remember that the boys were more treasured than the
girls. Father was definitely loving, but anything else, I
don't know.

In a closing statement she refers to the question previously discussed regarding the possibility of child abuse and said that if something is going to come up for her regarding the sexual abuse question, she feels it will come up when she has sex for the first time. That's why she protects herself and wants to make sure it's the "perfect man." It occurred to me on reading this transcription that Mary did not speak about psychological or medical counseling regarding her sexuality following her mastectomy. I ask myself what effect a disfiguring surgery such as breast removal would have had on a 30-year-old virgin. This woman who has never attempted to be sexual when her body was intact has to enter a world of extraordinarily body conscious individuals and establish a sexual relationship. I anticipate this to be one of the underlying problems. Mary denied any experience of self -pleasuring, and again I suspected her body image may have been part of the issue.

Grace entered the convent not so much because of her dedication to religious life or for the love of God, but more because she wanted to devote her life to a higher calling than marriage and family. She would have gone to the Peace Corps had it been available. When referring to her time in the convent Grace said,

> We were in transition time where they used to know how to form nuns but were moving to a time where they didn't, so we were right in the middle. We were the experimental children. It is changing a profession. I did have one close friend in the novitiate; we could be naked together in the shower and there would be nothing, but there was another woman, however, that I had kind of a relationship with. I don't know if she ever realized that it was an expression of my homosexuality, and it was all very invisible to the nun in charge. You were not supposed to have particular friendships, and we were doing exactly what you weren't supposed to do. She eventually left, nothing stopped for her because we were still friends, what

stopped for me was having it be some sort of sexual expression. We only did back rubs, nothing else.

Lois' political and life intentions were similar in some ways to Grace's. She saw religious life as a means to fulfilling a political as well as a professional spiritual life. She was totally unaware of sexuality in the convent and said she wishes she could be a fly on the wall now to see what goes on because she was just oblivious to it when she was in community. She said she was really good at keeping custody of the eyes and therefore was unaware if things were going on around her. She was asked to leave because of her political opinions and up to that point, when she was 21 years old, had no sexual experience whatsoever. Her first real experience came after she had left the convent, when she met a young man on the Vietnam protest lines. She was 24 years old by this time and he was 22 and as in Lisa's story, Lois decided "it was time" and virtually planned the seduction of her date. She described it like this:

We had sex for the first time on Valentine's Day; I planned it that way. I started sleeping with him in October and I was like sleeping with him with my clothes on. He was my first kiss, my first necking, it was perfect in terms of as I got more comfortable with the contact it got more intimate. I love having Valentine's Day, I love that I chose, that I made the decision. You see I made the decision to come out of my family's house and decided I want to explore sexuality now and how am I going to do it, so I chose him. I invited him over to my apartment. My roommates were out. I fixed him a big dinner, and then we went over to his apartment. Trying to perform intercourse was too painful, I was too tiny so we stopped and we started again in the morning and that's when it happened. Lois' sexual development was rapid after this and very convoluted. She went on to have numerous partners,

69 men and then she came out as a lesbian. This is an unusual story, which continues in later chapters.

For eight of the women, molestation, rape, and incest were the means of their sexual initiation. Kathleen was raped at 15 by a drunken man who paid her mother for access to the child. She was impregnated by the incident, gave birth to a son and put the child up for adoption. Ursula was doubly traumatized in her childhood, first at 10 years old by her uncle then at 13 by a "de-frocked priest" at her school. Ione endured years of incest at the hands of her father, and Marian, self described, was like a "little prostitute" from her earliest years and was also raped at the age of 13 by a friend of her father. This is a tragic way to become sexually aware. Marian was consensually sexually active from an early age.

Ione began work on her incest issues early in religious life through therapy. It was during her early years in the convent that her sexual orientation began to be clear to her. She said,

> After three years in the convent I fell in love with my novitiate mate. We started a sexual relationship that probably went on for about a year, but we were kind of tortured by guilt over it because we were sisters and made promises to be celibate and we weren't. So then we decided to put an end to the sexual relationship, and we did pretty good. At the time we were living together and then she got transferred and that made it easier. We kept the friendship and emotional attachment but we weren't sexual after that. The year after that I met a woman at a party and was really sexually attracted to her, and kind of the same thing started again. I felt I had a responsibility to be celibate so I decided to leave the community. I left pretty quickly. The woman I left the convent for broke up after six months; that was pretty devastating for me. When I was in the community I went to graduate school, I

met a young man who I was interested in and he was with me, but I was still a sister. We went out a bit. I was very confused. All my sexual abuse issues were swimming and my sexual feelings were swimming. We went out a couple of times but I said this is ridiculous. I can't get involved with you. So I said, forget it. I still had feelings for men. After I left the convent I started to date men again. I met a lot of men at parties and bands but I realized the only reason I was dating men was because that's what people expected me to, I wasn't having too much fun. I remember something switched inside me. The man I was dating started to get sexual and I felt really uncomfortable. I knew it wasn't that I didn't like him or anything. I was seeing another man at the same time but I never had the same deep emotional feelings I'd had for the woman. I really didn't know what to do then. I thought I'd just fall in love, and I didn't try and put a label on who I was going to fall in love with. I fell in love with a woman I was working with. We had a relationship for about six years. We never lived together. I wanted to, but this was her first relationship, and she was really uncomfortable with it. She was very afraid that someone might find out. Up until about four years into the relationship I didn't see myself as a lesbian. I was seeing a woman therapist at the time, and I said well maybe I'm a lesbian since I'm falling in love with women. Then one day I looked in the mirror and said I'm a lesbian and that seemed really true for me. Up until the time I identified as lesbian I still would have fantasies about men, I wouldn't find women on the street attractive or anything. Once I said to myself I

140

was a lesbian my feelings towards men began to adjust to seeing them more as brothers. Then I began to be more attracted to women or other lesbians. It's been an interesting little journey. Now that I look back I think that I have always felt different from my girl-friends when I was growing up. I always thought it was because I was a tomboy, and didn't really do girlie things. They started to wear make-up and do things, some girls would just go along with that but I decided I just wasn't going to do it. When young men started to come into the picture I remember feeling jealous and thinking the guys were disrupting our little group. I think I was brought up in a very heterosexual environment, like the thought of being with a woman never even occurred to me until I went to college, girls on campus were identifying as lesbian. The way I grew up in a Catholic family, went to Catholic schools, I never met a gay person.

The fact that she never knowingly met a gay person is not surprising. Catholic theology and politics of the day would have denounced homosexuality. A study commissioned by the Catholic Theological Society of America entitled *Human Sexuality New Directions in American Catholic Thought* reports from a 1970's study that 86% of the general American population disapproved of homosexuality and that three-quarters of the general population that attended church weekly still disapprove of it. The same study reminds us of Catholic tradition over the past centuries, when evaluating moral behavior. "Masturbation, any premarital sexual pleasure, adultery, fornication, homosexuality, sodomy, and bestiality were considered intrinsically evil acts, seriously immoral, and under no circumstances justifiable." The way Catholic families in those days dealt with issues such as these, which would be destined to bring "the wrath of God" upon them, was to ignore them.

Silence and ignorance was the order of the day. My own mother quite frequently told us "where ignorance is bliss, it's a folly to be wise." Which was her quote for "don't ask?"

Whereas Ione's sexual abuse did not lead to precocious, promiscuous behavior, Marian began consensual sexual activity at a fairly young age. Marian jokingly quips that her "first real sexual experience, at age 13, ends up being a *menage-a-trois*, and it involved everything except intercourse. There was oral sex, finger fucking everything." Although Marian was in her own words "very sexual" she remained a technical virgin until she married, in that she had never had vaginal penetrative sex after the rape. We had a little fun at this point during the interview since she compared herself to an inside joke with Catholics, "the girl who says I'm a virgin but I do blow jobs, I like oral sex, anal sex anything but vaginal sex because I want to be a virgin when I marry." She thought she typified this picture. She met the man she was eventually to marry when she was in high school and they dated. He was the only date with whom she was never sexual. This man entered a religious order independently of Marian; they had already ended their relationship. As previously explained in Chapter 5, Marian had a radical hysterectomy when she was 25. She said,

> I think there was some knowing in me about that. I wanted to go to the doctor about it when I was young and my mother told me to save my money and I could go. I did that but she telephoned before my appointment so that when I went to see him, without even examining me, he told me I'd be fine once I got married. Had I gotten married right away it would have been horrible because of all the expense and stuff. I definitely wanted a family; I knew I wanted a support system. I wasn't ready for it when I went in the convent, though it did deal heavily in my wanting to leave. By the time I wanted to leave, I had dealt with a lot of the issues. I repressed some. I masturbated. I

felt my feelings. But there was enough aversion, not
to sex per se but to the context of marriage and family and closeness to a man that it detoured me. As I
say, it gradually came back in, maybe in the last five
years and then it became quite apparent that it was a
part of my life that I wasn't willing to live without,
among other things. Of course Vatican II was the great
hope for us. It opened up a lot, and along with many
other nuns I was a political social activist. I could pull
a lot of stuff off in some places. Of course we were
assigned to wherever they want you to go and that
was crushing for me because I would become very
attached to people. In fact when I left the convent I
didn't leave the area.

Kathleen was similarly abused and gave birth to a child when
she was 15 years old. Her time in the convent as stated was three
years and mainly in response to the adoration of Mother Magdalene
who had shown exceptional kindness to this young girl. Once she
left the order, Kathleen continued to work with the nuns in their
orphanage. She had not, up to this time, experienced a consensual
sexual experience.

I loved children. Not being loved as a child, I loved
children. I knew how important it was. I had a hard
time thinking I was lovable and thinking someone
could love me. I had a few boyfriends and I thought
the only way was if I did something I didn't want to
do, I hated sex--I hated it. I was afraid of it, I was
afraid of men; but I knew if I wanted to be loved,
that's what they wanted. It's all the wrong ways; even
as a child it was all the wrong ways of learning about
sex and about love. I have one man that I've loved
since I was a little girl. He's the one who found me on

143

the street, beat up by my mother. He knew that she
was abusing me, knew that I was getting hurt by men,
and I have loved him since I was about eight. He was
a reporter and he found me and brought me home. I
never told him my mother beat me but he must have
known. He checked up to see if I was okay and was
always checking up on me. I felt this was a fantasy
love of the heart. I loved him so much. When I was
13, he sent for me and told me that he was getting married, it broke my heart. Those were the two people I
totally loved Sister Magdalene and this man. I loved
him so much. He got married and he used to call me
his little girl. He's the only person that ever gave me
attention, he's an outsider of the family, but he was
caring and I was googoo-eyed over him. When he
told me he was getting married I said please can't you
wait till I'm 18? I'll be a good girl, please wait for me.
I begged him to wait for me. He said "Oh foolish little
girl, you're going to grow up and you're going to laugh
at all this." But he died a year ago, and I'm not laughing. He knew that I loved him a lot.

Kathleen spoke about the time after she left the convent when
she met a man who lived next door to her. They began to date and
to go to church together. She said,

I finally thought I had someone of my own and that he
was going to marry me. I found out he was dating me
and another girl at the same time. He told me about it
and then I thought I didn't want to live no more, I tried
to commit suicide. I thought I'm not worthy to marry,
I'm not even worthy to live. I wound up in a mental
hospital for about a month and it was just this desper-

ate thing to be loved. It's a terrible thing for anybody
to experience, because I didn't learn to love myself. It
took me 50 years to learn I was lovable [she pounds
her chest as she cries]. But now nobody can mess me
up. I wound up marrying my husband because the
woman he was supposed to marry found out he was
divorced, and because she was a very strict Catholic
she couldn't go through with it. I felt so sorry for him.
I said, ah I'm not doing anything I'll marry you. I
loved his children. But before I married him I went to
see my friend Laird. He hadn't seen me since I was 13
and now I was 22. I told him I have to see you, I have
to tell you I've loved you all my life but I'm going to
marry this man, he needs a mother for his children.
That was really the reason, the wrong reason to marry
someone. I was terrified, terrified of sex, terrified of
everything. I let Laird know that; I settled it with him
and then I married my husband. He had to be very
gentle with me and teach me, because I didn't trust
men. After a while I trusted him so much I hadn't
known anything except that it hurt and that it was
painful and bad. He taught me to enjoy sex and all
that stuff. The sad thing is we married for the wrong
reasons. It's 35 years later; I won't end it unless he
wanted it. I didn't love him the way I was supposed
to. I loved him enough to stay to raise his children.
Even when he cheated on me, I left and came back,
twice. I trusted him like God; I thought if anyone
would hurt me it wouldn't be Peter because he idolized
me. He idolized me for taking care of his children,
but you can't think that anybody is that perfect. That
was my problem; everyone was better than me. I don't

think that any more. It happened in my own house
when I was pregnant. One night I got up to go to the
bathroom and heard the TV, I went in and saw my husband and on his lap kissing him was the woman from
upstairs whose children I'd been looking after. It was
like I'd been stabbed. I thought again what's wrong
with me, it must be my fault? The priest told me I had
to forgive. I thought perhaps I'd loved the other man
too much, so I did everything to restructure myself
to give him the attention, only to find out when he
came out here to find us a place he was cheating on me
again. The woman told me herself that she was a call
girl and that while I was waiting to move here, she had
been taking care of him for me. So then again you can
imagine how sick I was; I almost went crazy with it
all. And the saddest thing is he would give anything
if I could have my youthful belief in him, but I can't.
I don't love him, I pity him. I'd never let myself love
again. Just my children, I love my children, I lived for
my children. I feel all my life I've been a Cinderella.
I've suffered, I always worked very hard and now I
have my children; named after the two people I loved,
and I do the things I want. I live my life the way I
want to live now. As far as sexuality now, we have a
good sex life as far as it goes. He had heart surgery
a couple of years ago and he's afraid. I never deny
him but it's not the way it should be, the way I think
it should be. I might fantasize about the man who I
never even touched who never touched me. If I did
ever dream, it was with him and now he's gone and
he's with Mother Magdalene.

Kathleen told me that she and her husband have had separate bed-rooms for many years and he "visits her" occasionally. Her story returned to Laird,

I went to see him three years ago because his wife said
he had the disease where his mind eventually goes,
and he kept calling for me. In the end he loved me. He
realized how much I loved him. His wife even said
you would have been a wonderful wife to him; but I
said, I was just a little girl he didn't love me that way,
but in the end he did. When I said goodbye I knew,
he told me. He said I loved you, I just didn't know
you were always around and now it's too late. He was
17 years older than me, but my husband is 11 years
older; today it wouldn't matter. I adored him; to me
he looked like Tyrone Power. I found out why I loved
him, I told his wife and wrote a poem to him, because
he used to call me foolish little girl and I told him,

Foolish little girl that's what you always called me
for loving you
Foolish little girl who lives in a dream world.
A dream that can never come true.
I know it can never be.
Foolish little thing you're going to grow up and
laugh at all this.
Foolish, foolish man, my love for you still exist.
Although we live apart because God has made it
our fate in life
Today I have a husband, you have your lovely wife.
But this foolish little girl, she'll love you till the day
she dies.
She keeps asking herself, but why, but why?
And as through the reflections of my mind I do try,
I found the answer there.

It was so easy. Because of you my foolish man,
I saw God.
He was the only light in my childhood.

He could have taken advantage of me, he could have
done anything. He never did. Sister Magdalene was
the second, two finer people they never made again.
She used to say don't think of me as a Saint, don't
think like that, she brought me closer to God. I used
to go to Church, I'd made my communion and everything but I didn't know God, she was the one who
brought me closer to God.

One area of Kathleen's story illustrates the strength of her ability to fantasize the life she would have chosen. It again revolves
around Laird and this time also illustrates a spiritual connection.

I had a dream, it was 15 years ago. All I ever wanted
to be was Mrs. Laird...

If I could have been that I would have been the happiest girl in the world. You know, fantasies; and then
it [the dream] comes with Mother Magdalene and the
priest and God and says you can commit spiritual
bigamy. You can be Mrs. Laird you have to go to
St. Patrick's Cathedral in New York and find me and
you can commit spiritual bigamy; you can marry him
spiritually and treat your husband as you would treat
him. That helped me become a better wife. On this
certain day, October 17th, I went to the Church. I had
a white veil my mother-in-law gave me, I bought a
white dress, and I went and I prayed and I had to look
for Jesus. There were many altars of Mary and all the
Saints and finally there was the altar of the veil of Jesus
and I knew that's where I had to be. In my dream I

was told to bring a little Yarmulke and a yellow rose and leave them at the altar, so that's what I did. And I said in my heart Oh God I hope he knows how much I've loved him all my life, and I want to be his wife spiritually. Months before this I'd written to him and told him of my dream, that on October 17th I could be his wife spiritually, and I forgot all about it, I didn't talk to him again. Then I went and did it and as I was leaving on this beautiful day I was happy. I was leaving and opened the heavy door and got such a surprise because I didn't know anybody, and who's there but my Laird. I said what are you doing here? He said, "I'm not having my little girl come all the way to New York and marry me and not be here." He made it special, he came; he took me to the Rockefeller Center for a glass of wine and a piece of cheesecake. He said, "I must be crazy, I don't know why I'm here." He made it so much fun, I said, "Okay where's the honeymoon going to be," he said, "On the Subway" it was a day I'll never forget in all my life. I guess that made him feel safer too, we became closer after that, he was always there for me. And Mother Magdalene was the same.

Kathleen shared the deep sorrows of her life story. However, I came away from her with a sense of her strength and acceptance of the sexuality of others. When she told me her daughter had come out as a lesbian it was without a trace of judgment. She told me how happy she was to talk to me because her story deserved to be told. I am honored to tell it and wish I could include more.

Ursula, at the age of 75 still struggles to identify her true sexual identity. Her experiences as a young girl in pre-war France were traumatic enough to leave their mark for a lifetime. When looking at sexual awakening, it is somewhat curious that in the case of this woman all but one of her sexual encounters happened prior

149

to entering and in her life she had a total of four voluntary sexual experiences, all with women. She was introduced to sexuality at a young age by a pedophilic uncle and a priest. She did not speak at all about regular friendships of same age boys and girls during her childhood, although in follow-up conversations she said as she grew up she was always friendly and had no problem making friends of both genders. She spoke of being aware from the age of 16 that she was attracted to women but does not explain what that meant to her at the time. She had no consensual sexual experiences until she was 25. However, when she was 22 she left home and went to Paris for the enforced year before her father would allow her to enter the monastery. At this time she fell in love with a married woman with whom she worked, who was 15 years her senior. Ursula wanted to go to bed with her "to feel her body." The woman did not reciprocate the feelings but was gentle and kind and called herself "mummy." To compound the confusion Ursula said she was molested by the husband of this woman. Specifically this man attempted to seduce her and did succeed in digital penetration. This was the third such experience for Ursula. In the course of her life Ursula had two more relationships with men where she felt she was violated. The female friendships, which became genitally sexual, were traumatic to her and she said after three or four months they always reverted to spiritual, platonic friendships because she couldn't handle the sexuality. This is the only woman in the group to enter in her later life, for although she expressed a wish to enter at 20 years old she did not accomplish this until age 39. When she left the convent, breast cancer changed her life. She described herself as a life-long celibate and continued her struggles against a need for self-pleasure. She also remained in a dilemma regarding her sexual identity.

Maria had been in the convent for 16 years and had up to that time had no physical sexual interaction. Her only emotional experience had been a fondness she held for her students. This was until she met a young priest who lived across the road from her convent. The religious couple worked together and were friends for a long time. She asked him to give her a ride to their work but he refused because he said the rule was that he was not allowed to give anyone a ride in his car except for women as old as his mother and even they must sit in the back seat. Maria said she would always absolve herself from rules for which she saw no reason. This was one such rule. She denied any sexual interaction whatsoever before this period.

> In the last two years, especially after Vatican II, things changed dramatically, inside of the convent and inside of us individually. Throughout my career in the convent there were always priests who were very attentive and we would chat and be together and so forth, but only on a professional basis. But I could tell some of them preferred to be with me than with some of the other nuns. So not only did my students give me attention, the priests did too. By the time I was in the Convent for 16 years I was sent to the place where Michael was originally placed as an assistant priest. He was very young and I kind of liked working around him, I used to think he was wet behind the ears but I loved the way he celebrated the Eucharist. The attraction I had for him originally was the way he celebrated the Mass and then we started working together teaching the kids. He was going on to get his degree in counseling and he wanted to get some experience working with the kids in our school. We had to go back and forth from where I lived to the school. I thought it was stupid to drive two cars. So Michael and I started working, and spending more time with each other and eventually we began to read Eugene Kennedy's book, *The Third Way*. In the book he talked about people who are dedicated. Like the first way would be married. The second way would be

single and chaste or celibate. The third way would be these single and celibate people working together in such a unique way that you could have a relationship. It was very supportive of the work you were doing and allowed you to be compatible sexually. This was a whole new idea for me but it seemed like it could work. It was a step beyond platonic because you could get into being genitally sexual but it wasn't like you had to leave this major work to go and be together just the two of you. So we tried this for three years. We were still in the whole habit. By that time I was living with a nun who was pretty open-minded. I went to a store and bought myself some shorts and T-shirts. When we went out with another couple, who were also a priest and nun; we would take these clothes and go to a gas station. We'd get undressed from the habit, put on these clothes and go out and have a picnic or go to someone's home that was given to this priest; not knowing it was going to be used for this double date thing. We would neck, and they would go into the bedroom and rub against each other and pet and stuff. I was still saying we can kiss and we can be with each other and hold each other close but there was still no petting and then finally one night when he did drive me somewhere, we drove back into the rectory garage. I started to get out of the car and he was all hot and he said to me "Lick this" and I said "What?" He pulled down his zipper and took out his penis and said, "Lick it?" I said, "Why ever would I do that?" He said "Well because it feels good." I said "Oh." So I gave him a blow-job. That became one of the things that would happen frequently when we got together, but he

never would do anything for me. It's very interesting.
I read the journal from our honeymoon recently and
I realize it's the same, it's exactly the same, and I feel
resentful at times. That I would give him pleasure but
there was never any reciprocation. I'm sure as I speak
to you that he could have read it that I was pretty
resistant to someone touching my breasts or whatever
and so I can read it like that. But then I think no way;
because over a period of time I got to a place where
I could say to him, if you turn me on you'd get more
turned on. So it's like you don't even have to think
about what's happening to you. It was pretty interesting when I read that last week, what does change? The
zebra keeps his stripes. We've learned a lot going to
workshops and he does try to please me, but it's still
not enough.

I asked Maria when had she become aware of her needs for
more sexual attention. She told me,

I think there was a point at which I loved him so much
in our early connection that I think that I made some
statements in my head, that it was such a privilege to
be connected with him that like it didn't matter. There
was some wiring going on that read, if I can keep
him happy, if I can do what he wants then he won't
be sorry he left the priesthood. I'm sure I realized
it between 1969 and 1972. I left in 69 and he stayed
in the priesthood until '72. We were waiting for the
bishops to allow a married clergy, and so I said originally I'll wait a hundred years, and then I said I'll wait
fifty years and then it was three years and finally when
I left I was shortening the time. But it was during that

time '69 to '72 that I realized I wanted to be pleasured
and pleased and so forth, but I was still walking in
a very tenuous line because he was still a priest so
it was a lot of that being the primary thing for me to
look at that if he did leave for me he might go bonkers,
so I didn't want to be real demanding. I decided to be
very independent; it was a time of growing for me. I
decided I wasn't going to *need* him so that bolstered
him because it kept me spinning with I serve him but
he didn't have to serve me. But between '69 and '72,
I still wasn't sure Michael would leave the priesthood,
and we continued to be with each other. He would
come to my apartment; it was easier to make contact.
He was always wanting to make love, and so was I,
so that was a very powerful connection for us. When
we first began to get connected, I still had my vow of
chastity and he had his celibate role. I think we just
created this third way, that we were still doing this
great work and so this particular vow wasn't as important as it was before that. I knew we were rational-
izing. Even today when I get down about how much
more he wants, I realize if he could rationalize way
back then why would it be any different today. I was
very involved with all the changes going on in our
order, with the habit and everything. I knew I wanted
to be out as soon as I could but I was in "Chapter" [as-
sembly of delegated members of a religious community for elections and decisions on other governance
issues] that summer and so I couldn't leave then. I
waited until Chapter was over and in August I decided
I'm going to leave. I went over to see Mother General and told her I wanted to leave, and I don't need to

go through a year of probation. I want out as soon as possible. I think I told her I'm in love with a priest. Within about a month I had my papers. A little later they started to make people wait, but I was in that rush of years of the huge exodus of priests and nuns. I was in the earlier phases of it within our community, so I just said I want out and it happened pretty quickly. When I was in the convent The Third Way was sufficient but once I left it wasn't anymore. The two of us were trying to hide it but others can see the juice. My family had met him when we were both still working together, eventually his brother convinced him to "shit or get off the pot." It was probably two months later that he left. He lived in my apartment; until we got married. My mother came to visit for Mother's Day, and we had moved all his things over to the apartment where that other couple lived [former nun and priest] we used to double date with. My mother gets up on Mother's Day when I was going to be entertaining his mother as well because we were going to be getting married in a couple of months. My mother says, you know Mrs. Brown isn't going to like to see Michael's shoes in your closet. I wondered what she would be doing looking in the closet. I always had that quick retort, she never said anymore, but I was probably the only one of the six of us who lived with someone before marriage, who probably screwed before marriage.

Maria's story and Helen's which follows, are representative of two women who truly felt they were blazing a new trail. The atmosphere of change within the Catholic Church was so pervasive; they thought it was just a matter of time before priests would be allowed to marry. They did well not to wait in their convents and presbyteries for the Vatican to make up its mind.

Helen married a priest the same year as Maria. Their stories parallel each other's in that their love affair began before they left their respective communities. However in their case, both partners decided to leave at the same time and moved to an apartment together. Helen was vague in her details and description of her early relationship and religious life. The interesting part of this woman's story is how much she neglected to tell me about her own coming of age sexually. She is guarded around the early years of her sexuality. What she said is that there was no shame or guilt in her relationship and how she was "able to hold on to the warmth even though it was on hold for all those years." She was in the convent for 15 years. Beyond referring to her comfort in having the relationship before she left her community her story picks up when she tells me her husband became an alcoholic and they divorced. She was very disillusioned, because she felt they had the perfect love, one they had both given up religious life for. During the break up of her marriage she said she felt "I'm not enough, I'm not skinny, I'm not earning enough money. That was just a stage. I was in therapy at the time and I knew it wasn't my fault." Her most memorable sexual encounter came when she met and made love with a former monk; this experience she describes as "the full expression of my womaness." Although she only made love with this man once she said it was enough. They remained very good friends, but she never felt they needed to repeat the act. Helen's story will continue.

Pamela refers to having sexual dreams and fantasies and considering whether or not to declare these at "Chapter of Faults." This practice is described by Chittister et al., as "Weekly Culpa Chapters [in English called a Chapter of Faults] the sisters confessed those personal mannerisms or minor accidents which had become part of a regular community script. Each day, time was set aside in the schedule for the examination of conscience, or particular *examen*, a practice designed to uproot faults by counting daily transgressions and comparing the results to previous counts." Pamela said,

I used to love sexual feelings, and then I thought, "Oh now I've got to say those in the 'Chapter of Faults' but I didn't, because I thought they were very normal. I guess when I was in my early 20s, and I got out and went to summer school, there'd be all these cute guys. That was really hard. I remember telling our Superior for the summer and she said "poor dear." I thought, "I'm not a poor dear at all." A couple of times when I did want to leave, I'd shave my hair to stop me going. Looking back I loved teaching, so all of these feelings were going on inside me but I kept on thinking, no I must continue to be this nun because that's what I said I would do. I became good at it, I was a good teacher and my family thought this was great. My sister and brother had eight children between them and I was very close to them, and when things opened up a bit I could go stay with her five children when my sister went on vacation. I was a real close aunt. That helped compensate my maternal instincts. As we got more open and we could talk more openly with people, I was able to get closer to other priests and people generally. Not thinking about leaving or having any kind of sexual relationship. Then one of the priests who came to say Mass for the kids (I'd known him for about three years), asked me to the park with him. I told him I really didn't want to go, and then after a while he asked me again and said he wanted to marry me. I burst out laughing, poor man. I told him it made me feel really uncomfortable, and there was no way I was going to be anything more than friends and certainly not leave the convent and marry him. Meanwhile I was meeting all these different people, men and that. I guess I was getting ready to leave. I don't know, but, they were very interesting to me but none that touched me so emotionally that I would want to leave. Then I met a brother who taught religious programs with me. I fell madly in love with him, and that's my husband. The whole time we became really good friends and I didn't really have sexual feelings because we were really good friends, and then all of a sudden it happened, really, really fast. Does that make sense?

He's seven years younger than I am. Oh God, this is a story! He seemed so much older than me at the time. But he was 22 when he met me and I was 29. I thought he was 32 and he thought I was 21. We never talked about age; we had talked about getting married. It was my 30th birthday, and I said to my parents Charles and I are going to get married. There was a horrible upset, but I said for my birthday why don't you have Charles over for dinner. When they found out he was 22, well! He bought me a beautiful pantsuit to wear to dinner but I said I had to wear my habit, wasn't that weird?

I asked Pamela, "So you decided to marry before you left the convent?" She replied,

Oh yes. I don't know if I would have left if not. He said "I want to spend my life with you" and I said "I want to spend my life with you, too." That's how it happened. So here we were at this birthday party and he was shocked to hear it was my 30th. But he left the brothers.

I asked what the transition was like for her, from a life of repressed sexuality to this.

> It was incredible. I felt two things; first it was really
> good to feel somebody love me, I'll never forget that
> feeling. I was loved by my mother and father, sister,
> brother and friends. But to have someone who just
> loves you and wants to spend their whole life with
> you, is such an incredible feeling. With that other
> priest who wanted to marry me, I had no feelings, but
> with Charles it was so freeing it made me so happy
> and alive. It was wonderful. I guess it happened little
> by little. We became friends, he got to know all the
> other nuns; because they all worked with me and had
> gone to high school with me and were all the same
> age. There's a lot of painful things. My mother was
> very bitter, that was real hard. She did not want me
> to leave, and that I was leaving to get married. I guess
> it was like a scandal. My Dad was really good, very
> accepting and whether he agreed or not was just a very
> loving father.

Pamela talked about how naive she was at 30. She said she
was totally naive sexually and that Charles gave her sex books and
manuals before they got married. I asked her if that was how she
saw herself being initiated into her sexuality.

> I don't think we even kissed. We may have held hands
> and hugged or something because I still had vows. I
> felt it was a phony thing, but I thought it wasn't that
> long to wait. I don't know if it was a legalistic thing,
> but I said "Let's not do anything until this is final."
> We didn't have sex until---we were going to get mar-
> ried in December and then at one point he said, "You
> know I think I might want to go back into my order."

This was because of the change of life style he had
to endure once he left the brotherhood. From being
a scholar about to begin a Ph.D. to working anything
he could get. Then when we were getting married he
started teaching, but he felt lost and so broke down. It
was so painful. Then three weeks later he came to see
me and said "I just miss you so much and I want to be
with you forever." So that night he said, "I want to get
married" and I said, "Fine." We had sex that night. I
conceived my daughter that night, the very first time
we ever had intercourse. I think we had been brought
up so strictly I felt so bad about having sex, so Charles
said "Fine we won't have sex again before we get
married." But I was already pregnant...[she laughs an
amused laugh]...we didn't even do it all the way, we
did withdrawal! Three weeks later when my period
didn't come, I went to a doctor and the test was positive. I told Charles and he said "We're not waiting till
December we're getting married right away." Well
my father had big plans and I had to tell them that the
big wedding was off. We told them after dinner one
night and my father stood up and said, "Let's go have
a drink and celebrate." He was always so stern, but he
was a real good dad. Of course the Catholic Church
refused to marry us. I threw away the stuff I got
from the Pope, my dispensation papers and stuff. We
had been in the Parish for 30 years; our Parish priest
had known us all those years. My family was very
prominent my father had been on the parish council
for many years. They didn't refuse me because I was
pregnant, they refused me because I had just left the
convent, and I didn't have the dispensation papers. I'd

thrown them out. Anyway, we had a lovely ceremony
in another church and it was wonderful. My mother
was cruel. She said, "You got pregnant so that you
could keep Charles." Oh my God, I think she felt so
hurt to say that. She never said it again, and before
she died, she and Charles were best friends. But I
think it was a very different society at that time. I
don't think society cares now, but it did then. I felt so
nervous during that pregnancy, and I'm very angry
that I was put through that. A lot I might have put
on myself. My brother and sister were wonderful but
once in a while my sister would say "Well we had to
wait, you didn't." I guess that made me angry because
I thought this should be a wonderful time of my life
but I was upset all the time because people looked
down on me, and I really didn't care, but it still hurts.

Pamela's children were grown at this time and yet she still
remembered the hurt of her mother's cruel words and her sister's
thoughtless conversations.

Whereas some joined the order with the express mission
in mind to become a radical Catholic, Lua Xochitl on the other
hand grew to this place, in part, as a result of the changes in
her order brought about by Vatican II. This woman became a
revolutionary after twelve years in traditional religious life and it
began with a chance meeting and comment from a fellow nun:

When Vatican II told the women religious either
modernize or close your doors, my convent wrote a
new Rule. It took them two years but with regard to
sexuality it said each sister was responsible for her
own sexuality. What did that do? Well, it gave the
sisters permission to experiment. It opened the doors
to allow women to get married and still remain the

sisters of this order, they could do that. It was the
first Rule not based on Francis, Benedict, Augustus,
Dominic or Aquinas. These were the five men who
wrote the Rules for women, and we were the first
group of women religious to write a Rule not based
on any of those cats. It was great to be part of the
Church at that time. The new Rule said sisters could
not teach in the classroom without their B.A. I for
example, started teaching twenty years ago without
any preparation. The grace of God was to help me to
teach and I was to teach 50 children in a classroom
with no preparation whatsoever. So I went back to get
my B.A., after 11 years of teaching. In 1968, the week
before I was to attend a weekend workshop, one of the
women who entered at the same time as me came back
from Chicago and was living the new Rule. The other
nuns were outraged and wouldn't talk to her. We were
allowed to drink alcohol and smoke in the confines of
the convent in our own rooms and outside if we were
not wearing the habit, at that time we wore modified
habits or lay clothes. I was the last one to catch on to
things like this, I was so naive. One day this woman
stopped me in the corridor and asked me to get some
7-Up and come up to her room. This was the woman
who no one spoke to. I was always the supporter of
the underdog and I was so naive I didn't know what
the 7-Up was for. I bought it and went up to her room.
She served me a drink of bourbon and 7 and then another. She asked me "'Why aren't you involved in the
Chicano walkouts?" And I said, "Well I came back
to study." She said, "Why aren't you involved with
Caesar Chavez?" I answered, "When I graduate I'm

going to go back to work in my school." She looked at me and she said "You know you are no longer Al.....'s daughter." [Lua Xochitl was Latino and the daughter of a very prominent activist in the Latino community]. When she said that to me, I know it was the drink, but my response was; "No white bitch is going to tell me who I am" [click of her fingers] it was just like that. She said, "Good it's still there."

What followed for Lua Xochitl was months of affirmation of her Latina heritage and a slow and steady change in her attitudes. A fundamental catalyst for this change began when she experienced the weekend workshop discussed in Chapter Seven. This to her "was the beginning of the unlearning of the lies." She began her journey out of the convent that weekend, yet before she left, she began to fight for the rights of the oppressed. She said she heard people say "What's happened to Sister Mary she used to be so sweet, now she's talking about racism?"

I stayed in the convent because my community was in transition and I was waiting to see if they were going to live out the new Rule. The first sentence in the new Rule was "We as sisters of ...will give witness to the political, social, and economical needs of mankind." You know that was mid 60's, that was the edge. When I saw that they weren't going to do it, I said I'm leaving, my integrity would not allow me to stay. It was nothing to do with sex, it was political. When I saw it was a lie, and it was not going to change, I couldn't stay. I stayed a year hoping it would change. I loved my community, even as I was becoming ostracized.

Lua Xochitl had gone to her superior on two occasions requesting the community "as women of the 20th Century" take a stand and issue a statement on behalf of political issues congruent to their new Rule and the request was refused both times. Up to this point she had not become sexually active except in the emancipation of her personal pleasuring because she said her self esteem was still so damaged from her childhood as to make her feel unlovable. By the end of her final year, as she said, she was,

> ...pretty much what you would call a political activist nun, I was marching and boycotting and leafleting and masturbating and loving it all. Still not sexual, the men around were EuroAmerican, and I just didn't turn on to them. They weren't juicy to me. I've grown since then, and I stopped relating to men by their race anymore, but when I would see Latinos or brothers who were political I would wonder, yes, yes, definitely, but I was in the convent and I was in my warrior self. My inferiority complex would get in the way if I felt anything. I was going to be thirty-three and I began to know my body and be comfortable with my body when I was 30. January 1st of 1970 I woke up in a park in LA with $3.00 in my pocket. I told my family I was leaving and no one said "come home" so I left and spent my first night in the park.

I asked for clarification here, wondering if her community actually let her leave with nowhere to go and no money? She answered,

> Yes, yes, but let me explain. I didn't want to be beholden to my community. I had entered from a very poor family, so I had no dowry. My older sister had already left and my political self could not accept anything. So for me I was totally free. I stayed with different friends until I went to Cuba to cut cane. What it is to be young, to be warrior and to be woman totally

unto herself, and feeling okay with it. Six weeks later
I was en route to Cuba where I had my first sexual
sharing with a man. The inferiority complex was
still there but I was riding high on my political self.
I was older than everybody else. This was the time
of the progressive youth of America and I was 32, so
that kind of put out of my mind any possible encounter with any man that fit the old conditioning. The
political part of me was very affirming and my trip to
Cuba was all for that, the sexual part of me I just put
away until my last week there. I just thought I'm too
old now, my time has passed and besides I know how
to take care of myself. I remember a Cuban brother
coming on to me and my response to him was, I didn't
come to Cuba to fuck, I came to learn the revolution. So there I was, that sentence said it all. My first
experience sexually was fairy tale like, very romantic. Not orgasmically as it would be today or what it
was like when I masturbated by myself, but the whole
experience of being with a man who wanted to be with
me who didn't know any of my history. I remember
saying to myself, he doesn't know you feel inferior, he
is just seeing you right now. It was just really wonderful. I remember Fidel was there that night and he had
spoken and we were dancing, and the man that I had
attracted was this beautiful man from Haiti. He was a
political escapee and had come to Cuba as I had to cut
cane. This was the first time that I ever allowed myself to feel a man come on to me and he had to tell me
very clearly, he had to ask me, because I didn't get it.
I think a couple of things were going on, one I think
my warrior self was so vibrant that it didn't let the

other part of me come out, up front like. We cut cane
and this Cuban had wanted to bed me all night long
and I had resisted because I wasn't turned on to the
guy. So now in the morning, I'm tired and I'm paired
with this beautiful Haitian to cut cane. He asked me
why I was so tired, and when I told him about the
Cuban wanting to make love to me and keeping me
up late he threw back his head and laughed. He asked
me "Why didn't you make love, because you were a
teacher?" And I said "No, not because I was a teacher." Finally he kept asking questions until I told him
I'd never made love to a man because I had been in a
convent for 12 years. And all of a sudden he turned
and he said "What, you in a convent, why?" I was too
tired to talk. So we walked back together for lunch and
we worked together in the afternoon and we talked
about our lives and he asked me what I'd learned. I
told him, "I learned the most subtle nuances of racism,
so I know when I'm being bullshitted by anyone, and I
learned about sisterhood and nothing on this planet is
more important except the revolution and sisterhood."
He said, "I'm glad you said the revolution first!"

On the way back to the camp this "beautiful" man proposed
sex to Lua Xochitl. He asked her three times how she felt and each
time she gives him a brush off answer saying "Fine, really fine."
The fourth time he asks her "How do you feel about you and me?"
She answers almost coyly "I said, oh this is so wonderful, this is an
opportunity of a lifetime, and he stopped me and he said, 'Querida,
I am asking you as a man would ask a woman, how do you feel?'"

I was blown away. I looked at him and I said, "I feel
wonderful, easy;" and he said "Do you feel excited"
and I said, "Yes;" so he said, "Good, we will go to din-

ner tonight." Of course going to dinner meant going to dinner with a thousand other people, but from that moment on was when Lua Xochitl opened up to being looked at as a woman, as a sexual woman to another person. It was wonderful, all the tapes were put away for that time because he was a beautiful looking man and there were all these beautiful African sisters on the brigade. I always have and had this bad body image and here he was choosing me. Everyone around was aware of it and was happy about it. That night at dinner he wore black pants and a red cummerbund; the brother looked fine. In the middle of the dance he said "Let's go walking" and so we went and I was just open to whatever would come. I was so aware that we would make love, but I didn't know what to do. He was so careful and caring. He cut off these two palms and lay them down, took off his sash which covered the whole thing. I said to him, "I don't know what to do" and he said to me "Querida, what I know is that you know how to play. We are going to play, and you're going to tell me what you like and I'm going to tell you what I like" and I said "Oh, okay," and I got undressed. I remember that this was like a fairy tale, it was a full moon, just fairy tale. I had never had anyone touch me, he combed my body. He asked me if I had ever made love and I said "No," and he asked me what I knew about my body and I said, "I know I can make it vibrate," and he said "I think I can do that too." We played and he asked me "What do you like?" and I asked him "What do you like?" and I did it. I remember he asked me "How was it?" and I said you're pretty good, you're pretty good, this is okay, and he said "Just okay?" and I said, "Well I've been doing this for two years and I understand you just don't know my body." I was just totally fresh. Orgasmically it wasn't what it would be like with other men later, but at that time I didn't have it in my head yet that a man could make me feel great. I already had the experience of me making me feel great. I think it saved me a lot from putting it on men. I remember people talking about sex being bad and dirty, but we had oral sex, I didn't even know that existed, isn't that amazing? I led a very sheltered life but once I learned that this is my body and I can do whatever I want with it, there was never any guilt anymore.

Caroline had a problem remembering when she first recognized having sexual feelings. She identified a time after she took her vows:

There was this older nun, much older than me, she was about my Mom's age who really took a liking to me. When I look back on it now and it was really mothering. She was someone who would listen to me, someone who was physically loving to me, not sexual, all the things my mother wasn't. Stirred up in all that I began to have sexual feelings. But again it was very interesting; I couldn't have named those feelings. They frightened me, and I swear to you, if someone would have said, "Are those sexual feelings?" I would have said "No, I don't know what they are." There must have been a part of me that recognized what they were because then I began to worry that I was homo-sexual. Oh, this is interesting. I remember writing in my journal about it, and I was really worried and I

stayed away from this nun. I went to talk to a psychologist in our community about this and she asked
me who I was talking about and said, "Oh no she's not
homosexual." But she didn't give me any information,
I was just told don't worry about it.

In many different areas of Caroline's story she complains
about a lack of knowledge and a perpetuation of ignorance which
seemed to restrict her quest for sexual information. She began to
suffer from bouts of depression. When she became aware that by
staying in the convent she was hiding from her deep fear of men
and her fear of sex, she decided she did not want to do it anymore.

That was the beginning of the decision that I wanted
to leave the convent. I did base my decision on that.
After the decision to leave the convent, while the process was taking place, I called up another psychologist
that was on the faculty of my college. She had been a
nun but had left. When I went to see her, I wanted to
talk to her about the fact that I'm leaving the convent
and I'm scared to death, and what I'm really scared to
death about is men and my relationship with them. I
remember going in to see her and it was terrible. She
was sitting at her desk and I was standing in my trench
coat. She never asked me to sit down and just said,
"Well, what are you here for?" and I said, "Well, I've
made the decision to leave the convent and there are
things that are scary to me and I want to start dealing with them." She said, "What's scary to you?" I
said, "One thing I know is sex and men," and she said,
"What are you afraid of?" I said, "I don't know where
to start." So she started this exercise where she said a
word and I had to answer with the first thing that came
into my head. She got to the word, I think it was "pe-

nis," but what I heard was "pubic hair," and I said, "Oh
I'm scared," and she said, "Okay, if you don't want to
do the work you come back when you want to work."
So I left and I thought wow, how am I going do this?
I look back on it and I hated her for that. I felt really alone. I was in years, so I was 22 when I left. I
remember, going out on dates and felt like I was out
with a Martian. I was very stiff and I always thought
what is the fun of this? I'd try to neck and I put myself
through it but it never felt fun. I don't know how to
describe it. I wanted it but couldn't do it.

Caroline talked about one date where the man put his tongue
in her mouth and she said,

Again I was so naive and inexperienced, and here I am
at 22 years old thinking I've done something wrong.
Rather than let my body feel what it was feeling, it
was this sense of always being on guard. I did feel
a lot of sexual feelings toward him but he was not
very strong in pursuing me. We eventually went our
separate ways and a few years later after I had had a
couple of relationships with men, I ran into him again
and we were talking. I asked him, "Are you gay?" and
he said "Yes I am" and I was dealing with that at the
time. So it was this wonderful piece of information,
to put the pieces together. I decided to get into therapy
to seriously explore my sexual issues. Just at the point
in my life where I was about to get myself on track my
young brother committed suicide and that catapulted
me into space. I didn't know which end was up. Just
at this time a woman, a lesbian came into my life. The
funny thing is, I wasn't attracted to her, physically;

170

she wasn't beautiful. Fundamentally I think, again I
needed someone to mother me.

Again in these narratives I was aware of hearing a common
theme, one of a woman who was flattered that someone was interested in her. But also one who needed to be mothered, listened
to, touched, and loved. It took Caroline a long time to break this
relationship and she ended it when she was 30. Up to that time, she
had not yet had sexual relations with men or women except for petting. She met a woman who was a lesbian, and she said there was
an awareness of wanting to get to know her own body with another
woman who really appreciated a woman's body. In regards to establishing the relationship she said,

> It was from my place of integrity. I did not want to
> make love with this woman because I didn't want to
> make a life with this woman and again it was like
> wrenching myself from a motherly relationship.
> When I look back on the way I was with men, if one
> should like me I didn't get it, I really didn't get it. I'd
> say later "God, he really liked me!" What I learned
> really well was to put up a lot of protection. It is go-
> ing back to my relationship with my father; you're not
> going to appreciate me as a woman. Therefore, I'm not
> going to put myself in a place so that you can make
> me look stupid. I realize that's what I've always done
> with men, I won't relate on that level, I'll relate as your
> good buddy.

After years of profound depression and treatment she finally
found some resolution on medication. She was 38. This was the age
when she had her first truly sexual experience. He was her "Zorba."

> We just had the best time together, we had so much
> fun. One night we had been out together and when
> we got back it was obvious he was coming on to me. I

couldn't do anything but a few nights later I told him
I'm scared to death, I've never been with a man. He
was wonderful; it was the most wonderful experience.
All he wanted to do was give me pleasure. In fact we
did not have intercourse for a long time. First of all
there was a fear of AIDS and secondly there was the
fear of pregnancy, I was clear I didn't want a child
at my age. We started smoking dope together and I
didn't realize our relationship became more and more
dependent on the dope. He began to experience bouts
of depression due to issues in his family. The more
depressed he became the less present he was in our
lovemaking, he was no longer really there, I didn't like
it. I felt more and more like an object. I can look back
on it now and know the truth, at the time I thought
there was something wrong with me. I think I was
falling in love with him but he was not loving me. He
didn't know how to do relationships, I see that now.

Since her Zorba she had one more relationship which ended
in disappointment; he wanted a family and she didn't. She told
me that she still had problems being freely sexual and needs to be
under the influence of dope before she can relax enough to orgasm,
which was a concern for her.

Hilary was sent for therapy after being in the convent for 10
years. She left her order after 14 years. The primary reason she
was sent into therapy was because her Superiors thought she was
"too quiet," and that she was also possibly anorectic. She had her
first intimate experience with the priest who had taken over for her
lay therapist. After he left the group she said,

I wrote letters to the people in my group, one of
them to the priest I'd had a relationship with and he
responded to the letter, which triggered me off. My

172

relationship was sexual but not sexual, for a couple of years. I was just nuts, crazy about this guy, and I had never been this way before over anybody. He was kind of stand-offish. He would come close and then I wouldn't see him for a long time. I'd call him on the phone or write him letters. He went away to another country and when he'd come back he'd come to visit me and I'd be all googly-eyed over him again. We never had overt sex but just petting, hugging, and kissing. I was 32 when I first met him, just when I was on the verge of coming out. I didn't leave because of him but he just was around at the time. Most of these things happened in the last four years that I was in the convent and I was in for 14 years. I left when I was 32 and stayed in my therapy group for a year with the priests and nuns even though I'd left. I was attracted to almost all of the priests in the group. At that time there were three young priests and a gay priest. Over a period of time I had feelings for all of the straight guys so I guess I was becoming more outgoing and healthy. There was one situation with a therapist I was seeing, sometimes there is a thing that happens called "transference," where clients like their therapist. Well this guy took advantage. You know? I was so naive, I'd one experience basically with the one priest and this therapist kissed me one time and I was really put off by that. It was a couple of years before I left the convent and he introduced me to oral sex. That shouldn't have happened, I realized it later, at the time I didn't really know it. I developed a feeling because of my relation-ship with him and my ignorance, that it was an okay thing to do and intercourse isn't because that would

break the vow. After I'd become more sexually experienced, having oral sex to me meant not going all the
way. When I was involved with other people I never
quite felt I was going all the way if that happened.

Later in the interview Hilary clarifies that the therapist had her
perform oral sex on him, it was not reciprocated. He led her into it,
she knew nothing about oral sex at that time, and in her own words
was completely naive. He encouraged her to pose nude on other
occasions. It took a year for her to appreciate that this was not
mutual and she ended it.

When I was out of the convent and was dating, I had
to deal with the guilt. I remember talking to myself
and saying "I don't think God would give us all these
feelings and then care if I went all the way; because
what's the point?" It wasn't as if it was should I be
married or should I not be married, it was should I do
it? It seemed to go as far as this oral sex thing but not
the whole way unless there was some more of a commitment involved. Although I did eventually but at
that point I realized guilt is something that's not con-
trollable, it's something you have or haven't because
of your past like being brought up Catholic. When I
decided to have sex, I planned it and even talked about
it in the therapy session. It was the right time I really liked him and had feelings for him. The actual
sex was not that great. He was uncomfortable with a
virgin or something.

Later in the interview she talked again about her priest friend
who she said she loved very much. She would see him occasionally when he would come to town. They would have extended
dinners and would pet on the sofa but she knew nothing would happen because he was a priest. It was a relationship that couldn't go

anywhere because he was a committed priest. Then several years later she had oral sex with him and that destroyed the relationship.

> It just wasn't that great and it shouldn't have happened.
> I guess it lowered him in my eyes to have let it happen.
> He was also talking about other relationships that
> he had. I presumed they were just friendships but then I
> started getting the feeling that he was really, really close
> to other people. I picked up on two other nuns that he
> worked with, and I started feeling that he was as close
> to them as he was to me and it started to feel not so
> special. This was seven years into the relationship.

Her relationship with the man she is now living with was unsettled for some time; they have now been together for a number of years and remain unmarried.

Another woman who was exploited by a therapist priest was Miriam. She had been held back in her novitiate because of childish behavior and breaking the rules. Her superiors gave her the option of having six visits to a particular priest therapist in order to take final vows with her group. She agreed. On each of her visits to this man he encouraged her to become progressively more intimate. Although he pressured her to do more, sitting closely with his head on her breast was the furthest this situation went before she complained to her superiors. Although her visits to the therapist were halted, her superiors made it clear to her that they doubted the validity of the complaint. Later, Miriam told me, the priest was found to have fathered a child.

Chibnall et al., looked at the incidence of sexual exploitation and found approximately two in seven nuns reporting some type of sexual trauma after entering religious life. They found the most common perpetrators of this exploitation to be the clergy, most often a spiritual director. Other common roles were retreat directors, pastors and counselors. "Most of the sisters reported only one experience of exploitation, but that single relationship may have lasted for months or even years. Almost 16% of those reporting sexual exploitation said that it occurred during formation." Of particular interest to the previous story is the finding that the aftereffects of sexual exploitation at the hands of a therapist are "guilt, shame, anger, depression, confusion, distrust of therapeutic relationships, sexual maladjustment, feelings of abandonment, suicidal ideation, and exacerbation of the problem for which therapy was originally sought." And finally that the victim may for many years protect the exploiter and even see the relationship in positive terms. Only after it ends does the victim truly experience the full impact and see it for what it was, not a mutual relationship but one-sided.

The final story from the group who never married is that of Kate. She entered at age 18 and had been in the convent for 30 years. She left community in order to live her own life, to have her own money. When she was in the convent she fell in love with a priest. She told me,

> I had a sexual relationship on a regular basis with him
> for about three years then off and on for maybe four
> or five more. For the three years I was a nun. It was
> at that time I really changed, emotionally I left when I
> started that relationship because it was so far outside
> of what I had promised to do; but I didn't physically
> leave until three years later. He left the area and went
> in a different order of priests. We just didn't have that
> much time together after that, he intended to go deeper
> into the priesthood. When I was about 35, I knew I
> wanted a relationship. I was about 39 when I met
> him; I didn't pursue him. I've had two huge love af-
> fairs and in both cases the other person pursued me, it
> doesn't enter my mind to go look for somebody. I sort
> of waited to be discovered, which is not very produc-
> tive sometimes. When I was in the convent I admired
> some of the nuns I lived and worked with but never
> had an attraction toward anyone. So then I left, I think

I'm still afraid to try and meet people. I went to some
places like dances, and I joined a type of dating service, but I didn't like any of them. So I wish I knew
an easier way of meeting people; other people do.

Kate had mentioned having "two huge relationships" in her
life. She described the first as being with the priest and then went
on to discuss her life once she had left the convent. No further
mention was made of the second "huge" relationship. I therefore
pursued the topic. Three times in our interview I asked if there was
anything else that had happened of a sexual nature since she left;
on the third questioning there was a little pause and an excitement
in her voice. But this time instead of moving onto another tangent
she told me,

About a year and a half ago where I work we had a
new director who's a lesbian and she totally fell in
love with me; which is really bad when you're working
together and she's the boss. She was always raving
about me so everybody knows she's nuts about me,
I don't think they know we're involved. Everybody
knows we're really close; we've been in a relationship now for about a year and a half. We just started
talking about it one day and she was freaked out that
I knew she was pursuing me, it was like, am I deaf,
dumb and blind? Unfortunately she's moving to
another job, again she's a person I don't think I could
have a permanent relationship with because she's so
impulsive, she's eighteen years younger than I am.
She's tons of fun and that's why I fell in love with her,
because she's very funny, very smart, very extroverted
and way out there and I'm way reserved and that's
where I think I was pulled to her as an opposite. When
I'm with her and she does weird things, I think its fun,

177

but I'd never do those things on my own. But she's
loving, incredibly romantic. But she has her problems.
She always gets involved with straight women so that
stops her having a permanent relationship. So now I
consider myself bisexual. I can't imagine being attracted to another woman. I'm totally head-over-heels
with this woman. It's made me more open to being
in love with other women, but I feel rather than think
that my basic orientation is to men, but now I had an
experience with both which were really wonderful,
very fulfilling, the woman more than the priest because she's way more available. I see her every day,
we spend a lot of time together and spend nights over
at each other's house. We go to the opera or the ballet;
she loves the same sort of things. It was a huge risk
for me, but I let my feelings take over. I told her that
when we started seeing each other and I said, I'm not
going to act on it. Famous last words. She seduced
me, she really did.

There are those in the group who left the convent and tried to
establish themselves as quickly as possible in the "normal" world.
Most of these women, June, Ruth, Stephanie, Sophia and Hazel, all
maintained their virginity until their wedding night.

Hazel has had a long-term marriage and has five children. She
had no sexual contact before her wedding night. She had known
the man before she went into the convent and on leaving the friendship was re-kindled. This time, however, she was aware that there
was "more." They married within the year. I asked Hazel how
important was sexuality to her once she became sexually aware?
She told me she would tell me with a story.

Our first sexual encounter of course was our wedding
night. It wasn't terribly satisfying to me. I didn't fear

it, I really wasn't quite sure what to expect. That's what it was. Some of the problem was the absolute fatigue of the wedding, and the stress newly married people had to go through. I'm not sure I can come out and say I'm in favor of premarital sex but there is something to be said for it. At least not having to go through all that as well as saying good-bye to family and everything, and stepping off into the unknown, as well as this experience of sex. It wasn't until the second or third night, [laughs] WOW! I had my first orgasm. Then it became a very important part of our lives. Nobody was there to tell me, but I think I made a smooth transition into owning my own sexuality. Which is really kind of neat, when I think about all the obstacles in my way prior to that. I choose to and want to give J credit for that. Making love and sexuality was very important to him but he was very patient and attentive.

While Alison was still in the convent she was sent on a mission to Alaska and there met a young man, she described as:

A handsome hunk of a guy, and I immediately fell in love with him. That's when the seeds really began to be sown that maybe religious life was not working. I always said that if I ever was to leave I wanted to do it in time to have a family and have a life.

Alison and her future husband met at the wedding of a friend while she was still in the convent. No relationship developed at that time. It was a year after her departure from religious life that they met again; they married within 18 months of this. The couple did not have sexual intercourse before the wedding because of fear of pregnancy and because they were both devout Catholics. She became pregnant very soon after the wedding. Alison stayed in the

179

convent for 10 years and left because she said,

> I could not stand to have someone tell me what to do
> every time I turned around. I could get around the
> chastity thing; I guess I didn't think of it as something
> unnatural. Having sex with someone is natural but
> that's what you give up. But is that all you give up
> when you take a vow of chastity?

Alison had more to say on the vow of chastity and spoke about masturbation in this context. Her comments are included in Chapter Seven.

I do not intend to minimize the importance of the stories not included in this chapter. I have attempted to give a representative view of enough stories to illustrate the diversity of this group. It has been a difficult task to choose, because the personal moment of transition from elective celibacy to being sexually active is of course such a profound moment in everyone's life. Each of the 28 contributors deserves her moment on the page. However, unfortunately, this is not possible due to space constraints and the request of some of the respondents.

Chapter Seven
Self-Pleasure or Sin

*A*ccording to Szasz, the word "masturbation" was not in use in the English language until the middle of the 18th century. The Oxford Dictionary recorded the word in 1766. The etymology of the word is significant; according to Szasz, it is a corruption of the Latin word manustupration or manual stupration, meaning to defile by hand. Haeberle says the genesis of the word is "manus; hand + either stuprare; to defile, or turbare, to disturb."

The Catholic Church in the 6th through 10th centuries developed a series of Penitential Books. These, among other things, explored the subject of sex in all its details. Every misdeed or sin was described and elaborated at length, and "penalties penances or acts of amends for sins were prescribed for each." According to Kinsey et al., early theologians declared masturbation to be a greater sin than fornication. The church, combined with parental fears of infantile masturbation, attempted to maintain its system of repression by nurturing the willingness of parents to condemn this behavior. By this system a child learns before fully understanding, that self pleasure is bad and fear of pleasure becomes inscribed in his or her unconscious mind, to the point when it can become generalized to include fear of pleasure in all its forms. The Church therefore concentrated a great deal of attention on this matter, seeking Biblical justifications for its views.

Although the Bible does not specifically refer to masturbation, Genesis XXXVIII refers to Onan's seed falling upon the ground. Significantly, Onanism became synonymous for masturbation as described by: Haeberle, Masters, Michael, Gangnon, Laumann & Kolata. This practice actually refers to coitus interruptus and relates to a story in the Bible where Onan was put to death because he failed to carry out the Judaic law, by which a man had to provide his deceased brother's wife with a child. Kinsey et al., claim "Few other people in history have condemned masturbation as severely as the Jews have." This view was adopted virtually unaltered by the Christian Church and then by the medical profession after that. The result is "the proscriptions of the Talmud are nearly identical with those of our present day legal code concerning sexual behavior."

Science displaced religion with regard to fear of masturbation. The credit for inventing masturbation as a grave medical hazard goes to a man identified by Haeberle as "Bekker." In 1710, Bekker, who had been a clergyman and went on to become a physician, published a treatise entitled *"Onania, or The Heinous Sin of Self Pollution, and all its frightful consequences in both sexes, considered, with spiritual and physical advice, etc..* In this work Bekker is concerned more with the sin than with the harm of masturbation. The Swiss physician Tissot spread the theory throughout Europe in 1741, with a publication entitled, *Onanism, Or, A Treatise on the Disorders of Masturbation* (Michael, et al.). This misguided philosophy initiated a century and a half of fear and medical warnings about the dire consequences of masturbation.

These works set the stage for many prominent physicians from around the world to follow. Acton and Maudsley in Britain, Pouillet in France, Rush in America (Michael et al., Szasz). Masturbation was blamed for a plethora of illnesses including, but not limited to: weakness, impotence, dysury, tabes dorsalis, pulmonary consumption, dyspepsia, dimness of sight, vertigo, epilepsy, hypochondriasis, loss of memory, analgia, fatuity, and death." Masturbatory madness was an invention of this time and many men and women were interred in mental institutions with this diagnosis.

Around 1858 a prominent London surgeon, Dr. Isaac Baker Brown, advocated the operation of clitoridectomy to treat masturbation in girls and women. To cure this "disease" he removed the "organ," because he believed that masturbation caused "vexing mental disorders of women." Klein, further attests to the fact that in America, removal of the ovaries was added to the clitoridectomy

182

and also infibulation, to prevent masturbation.

Infibulation is the the stitching together of the vulva, often after a clitoridectomy, leaving a small opening for the passage of urine and menstural blood. Today the Western world is outraged that this practice continues mainly in strict Muslim sects and most common in Sudan and sub Saharan Africa where millions of young girls suffer this fate at the hands of their mothers and grandmothers. Perhaps some pause for thought is necessary when one looks at our own history of sexual repression.

There are no records of exact numbers of these surgeries in Baker Brown's time; however it is estimated by Klein to have been in the thousands. According to Michael, et al., protecting people from themselves became a virtual obsession of American and British doctors and thus the God fearing populations of those countries by the middle of the 19th century. It was thought that certain food products could help quell the urge to masturbate. J.H. Kellogg produced corn flakes for that reason. Sylvester Graham created the Graham cracker with a similar purpose in mind. Both these men became popular sexual advisers. Graham prescribed that males eat grains and wheat rather than meat. Further, he advised sleeping on hard wooden beds and taking strenuous exercise to ward off the dire results of masturbation (Michael). Even though sexual reformers of the 20th century, such as Freud and Havelock Ellis, endeavored to stop the extreme cruelty prescribed by those people mentioned above, they too believed masturbation was capable of causing sexual dysfunction (Michael).

Further influence on the generation directly impacted in this study was the 1940 publication of the American textbook of pediatrics, Holt's *Disease of Infancy and Childhood* which condemned masturbation as harmful. Between 1897 and 1940, eleven revised editions were published. In the early editions the treatments recommended were mechanical restraints, corporal punishment in the very young, circumcision in boys "even if phimosa does not exist, because of the moral effects of the operation." [Phimosis: constriction of the opening of the prepuce, preventing the foreskin from being drawn back. This stricture is the primary reason for circumcision in older children under current medical standards of practice. Historically it was used as a deterrent to masturbation.] In girls the treatment was separation of the preputial hood from the clitoris, blistering the inside of the thighs, the vulva or the prepuce [the fold of skin covering the clitoris, similar to that which covers the head of the penis]. This therapy was recommended up to and including the 1936 edition. As time went by the tone became more uncertain. Szasz further states that as late as 1937 *Sex Hygiene Manual* of the U.S. public health services and the *Boy Scouts Handbook* for 1945 extort youth to avoid "wasting the vital fluids." Pediatricians armed with this misinformation would have influenced the parents of the women in this study. Further, general mores of the day supported this thinking.

The majority of current scientific and medical evidence points to the fact that at every stage of life masturbation is not harmful and in fact can be said to be a sign of healthy development: DeMartino, Hite, Kelly, Kinsey et al., Haeberle, Marcus, Masters & Johnson and Nevid et al.

A 1998 article in *Men's Journal* entitled *Masturbation's Midlife Revival, Hand Solo*, shows the topic of masturbation to be a current and lively source of discourse among baby boomers. With headings such as "A History of Hairy Palms," "Love Me, I'm a Masturbator" and "A Generational Legacy" this article cleverly leads us from the "eternal damnation…guilty of the Old Testament sin of Onan" to "taking cheer from modern sociology and sexology." Quotes from such respected names in sexological research as Ted McIlvenna and research findings from the University of Chicago help lend a clinical perspective to this lighthearted treatment of the subject. Significant numbers of respondents in this article report some level of guilt around their masturbation habit.

Sipe discusses a pamphlet commonly distributed in the 1950s to teenage boys during retreats. This was entitled "The Greatest Sin" and he further comments,

> One might think that such a title would be reserved for
> a booklet on genocide, or perhaps rape, or some other

184

injustice against women. Racial injustice or any number of sins against humanity might also come to mind. But no, this was a treatise on masturbation. Generations of young boys became alternately terrified and disappointed that at 13 years of age they had already committed their greatest sin.

Sipe says his education as a Catholic boy of 13 years taught him the connection between sex and sin rather "than the bond between sex and love, service and spiritual integration." Further in this quote Sipe says that the official teachings of the Church remain unchanged.

Every sexual thought, word, desire and action outside of marriage is mortally sinful. Every sexual act within marriage not open to conception is mortally sinful. And in the area of sexuality there is no parvity of matter - meaning there can be no venial sins when it comes to sex. Sex, not greed or cruelty...was the fast track to hell.

This tradition of crowning masturbation as the King of Sins is not recent. It is connected with the attempt to establish power by the use of guilt and began six centuries ago.

Statistics from the questionnaire data point to the late development in masturbatory practices for the study population. These data came from my own study.

AGE	N = 43	PERCENT
< 5	2	5%
6 – 10	9	21%
11 – 15	12	28%
16 – 20	7	16%
21 – 25	5	11%
26 – 30	2	5%
31 – 39	3	7%
Never	3	7%

Range = 2 – 39 Mean = 16

I compared these findings against Kinsey et al. The focus in this table is on female Catholic's masturbatory habits. The key comment is "in some of the most devout groups, as few as 41% had ultimately masturbated; in some of the least religious groups as many as 67% had such an experience."

Question 29 in my study shows that 22% or less of the females never masturbated during the time they were nuns. That is, 78% or more of them did masturbate during their time as nuns. This is a significantly higher percentage than the 41% - 67% in Kinsey's stats.

It is not possible to make a statistically accurate comparison between the two, because,

(1) The sample is different. In Kinsey et al., the sample is focused on a devout Catholic, Protestant and Jewish population at large, whereas this study focuses solely on Catholic nuns, and only on Catholic nuns who eventually left the convent. Additionally, the sample size was radically different.

(2) The time difference between publication of the Kinsey et al. Report and this ex-nun study may be a major factor, given the dramatic change in sexual attitudes over the interceding 45 years. Nonetheless, the 78% figure is surprising, given the fact that the nuns were very devout Catholics.

A later study was *The Hite Report*, which found 82% of respondents masturbated while only 15% did not; 3% did not answer. This was a study of the general population of women with no breakdown for religious influence and shows the nun group to compare quite closely with that of the general population. This is surprising because masturbation was such a taboo that one would have expected the numbers to be significantly lower and this was not the case.

The most recent sexual survey *Sex in America*, found that about 40% of women in the general population between the ages of 18 to 59 had masturbated within the past year. Further information from this survey shows that about one in ten women reported that they masturbate at least one time a week. My study showed the following frequency, comparing the shift in rates during their transitions:

FREQUENCY	N = 36	N = 38	N = 37
	BEFORE %	DURING %	AFTER %
> once/day	5%	3%	8%
>10 times/month	11%	10%	30%
>once/month	31%	32%	43%
>once/year	14%	13%	16%
<once/year	39%	42%	3%

The Michael et al. survey is the first to address why if masturbation is so common, does it still trouble people so much to talk about it. The authors of the survey conclude that the practice is still burdened by the severe consequences of it from recent history; both religious and medical consequences are described.

Of those participants in the interview group, none of the 28 women recounted totally carefree self-pleasuring. Only one denied that she ever felt guilt. However, even in this case a high school student friend told her how to do it. Before this time she had no knowledge of masturbation, which is in itself suspect. All participants experienced some sense that it was wrong. Of those who admitted to early onset masturbation, their stories recount feelings of guilt, yet continuing the practice. Four women from the group expressed few difficulties in their experiences. However the remaining 25 had varying degrees of fear, guilt, shame and refusal to even try it. This one issue of personal sexuality remained a current concern for a substantial number. It was the one question most reported having difficulty dealing with on the questionnaire.

These are complex stories. I have chosen to devote one short chapter to this subject in order to illustrate these feelings in the women's own words. The difficulty women have with self-pleasuring remained as a stark reminder that even as we come to the close of the 20th century many remain conflicted when it comes to being in control of their own sexuality.

In Grace's case she remembers a time when she did not think masturbation was wrong and recalls where the restrictions originated.

> I don't ever remember a time when I didn't masturbate. But I also know that I was unusual in the family. I remember my older sister discovering me. That was the first time I realized that if you're discovered then you must be doing something private, so private that you wouldn't want anyone to know. In my early days there was nothing I associated with being wrong. It felt good, it didn't hurt anybody, but I do remember learning from my mother and my sister that you don't touch yourself. It didn't stop me doing it, what it did was probably what my mother had intended which was to keep it private, it's not something you do out in public. She said more than that, I think the message she wanted to convey was that it wasn't right. I think a modern mother would probably realize that what she really didn't want was the acting out, that there was an appropriate place for that. I knew I was supposed to feel guilty but it didn't stick. I also knew somewhere else that that was baloney. I don't think anybody tried to sell me that God thought it was wrong. I probably felt ashamed when I realized you weren't supposed to do it in public but I never felt guilty. I confessed it once when I was in the convent. By then I had learned enough and talked enough

and I knew it was a perfectly natural part of who you
were, and if God made me that way then it was fine.
I remember going to confession, even though it was
something I didn't do very often. I remember being
very frank and the priest said God would forgive me if I
promised never to do it again. Well I thought, oh come
on, the promise never to do it again, you're supposed
to be so sorry for it that you'll never do it again, like
lying or something that's a bad thing. He said it with
the same conviction. I thought I don't share this view,
so it was something I didn't confess again. It never
occurred to me to confess it when I was little; maybe it
was something so private that it wasn't something you
brought to the confessional.

Grace illustrates clearly the conflict between childhood play
and the enforcement of religious and social dogma and restraints.
She came to the conclusion that it made no sense and therefore she
ignored that particular aspect of Catholic teaching. She continued
the practice of self-pleasuring during her stay in the convent without it jeopardizing her vow of chastity. This was true for many of
the women but by no means all.

When the question of masturbation was put to Elizabeth she
quite confidently said how comfortable she always was with it.
However, it became apparent that this wasn't always the case. She
was in high school before learning about it from a friend, suggesting some prior repression. Additionally saying "I didn't do it a
lot" was indicative of some feelings of knowing she shouldn't have
been doing it. Had she been thoroughly comfortable, the amount
she engaged in would not have been of import. She also implied
there was purpose for doing it other than pleasure. Elizabeth said,

Yes, I always masturbated. I never saw anything
wrong with it. I didn't do it a lot, it was more of a
relief, or just when I wanted to, I did it. There was a

psychiatrist who came to the novitiate before we took
vows. He was supposed to educate us about sexuality and what our vows of chastity would involve. He
told us it was wrong to masturbate but I didn't agree
with him, if it didn't make sense I just didn't do it. I
learned about it from my best friend in high school,
apart from her nobody spoke about it. She said it felt
good so give it a try.

Kinsey et al., points out that women talk less about sexuality
than males, and that boys often demonstrate to each other how to
masturbate. Women in this study often talk about their experiences
of sharing their information. However, only two women mentioned having learned how to masturbate through demonstration.
Sara was shown how to masturbate by her sister. Rachel learned
about it when a fellow nun came back from university having had
a human sexuality class. Sara told me,

My older sister was just a very conscious sexual
person and we used to share a room and she never
hesitated to pleasure herself. She basically said you
ought to try it sometime and showed me how and that
was it. I think it offered me great satisfaction when I
was lonely or just to know the peak of emotion or the
level of feeling you could get. But you always ran it
through that good girl, bad girl sense that you got, and
so I was never 100% comfortable with it. I did it anyway just to satisfy the urges or needs. I think the more
I found the lack of response from men the more I realized, I thought you've got to find some alternatives.

The second woman to be shown how to masturbate was Rachel. A fellow nun gave an impromptu sexuality lesson. Rachel
said she knew nothing about sexuality prior to entering religious

life and had never masturbated. Her development, she told me, was about that of an elementary school child today. She entered at 18 and said,

> When I really found out more about sex was just before I took final vows, at around 20 years old. Another woman who went to a Catholic university came back and was telling us about this Human Sexuality class she had been in. Apparently it was taught by this stupid priest. He drew a picture of a woman's body and was talking about erogenous zones. Well we didn't want to be taught about that, we wanted to be told about men. She went on to talk about sensitive areas of the body and masturbation. We all went out and tried it and came back and talked about it in class next day. I said well if this could happen in a Catholic university, it must be okay. So we all practiced again that night. That was my first experience. We were sort of given permission to do it but really I'd never thought about it before. In terms of sex and family and religious life, I had decided on religious life. The thing with religious life is you don't have a spouse, you don't have a family and that's it. That was out of the picture, a black and white issue. So we tried the masturbation thing and talked about it several times. It was interesting and pleasurable, but no big deal.

(34 years later Rachel does masturbate but not very often and with no pattern.)

Virginia knew masturbation was "wrong" but defiantly continued to do it. So even though she is among those who found pleasure in the act she also experienced a lot of conflict. She told me,

Oh yes, I did a lot of masturbation. I think I was
pretty young compared to a lot of my friends, between
fourth and fifth grades I just discovered it. Probably
I did it several nights a week most of my life. I knew
it was wrong, I don't believe that now but at the time
I felt really guilty about it and there were periods
of time when I tried not to do it. I remember early
years in the community worrying about it and thinking I shouldn't do it. My memories are of my early
20s talking about it to a very wonderful priest, sort
of friend confessor. He was very compassionate. I
remember eventually talking to other friends in the
community about it and that broke a lot of the guilt
around it because I found others who didn't carry
such an attitude about it so that softened my feelings. That was my main sexual outlet in the convent.
I have always suffered from insomnia and it's how I
put myself to sleep. I remember when I was younger
when I was trying to stop; what was hard about it was
that I couldn't fall asleep, not that I desperately missed
having orgasms.

Of all the women who admitted masturbating, the one who
had the most profound disturbance with it was Ursula. Having any
sexual identity at all was problematic for this woman. Yet at the
age of 75 she struggled to come to terms with her Catholic childhood and traumas suffered. Most troubling to her at the time of
our interview was the inability to completely control her urge to
self-pleasure. She said,

Masturbation created a great fear with me. I felt I
was damned. I had no understanding of sexuality. I
thought sexuality was abominable, it was taboo, it

was dirty. I have tried to live asexually, my life as a complete celibate. I was 19 when I started having orgasms in my sleep and I knew how it could happen, it happened about six times a year before I went in the convent. During my time in the convent it happened once and I thought I was going to die of shame. Now it happens about eight times a year. It happens when there is a build up of pressure in my life and I feel very stressed, then it happens. At one time I went six months without it happening and I thought, that's it, I'm free. Now I believe I have to deal with my sexuality and if I have a desire, if something happens I should not feel damn guilty because it's happened because it's my body, I don't want to hurt myself or anyone. The pattern of masturbation when it happens to me is when I get so busy running around for friends doing this and doing that, for maybe a whole week. It doesn't happen all the time but it's one pattern, it's one instance where the desire will come, then it's like an arousal. Suddenly after two or three weeks of horrendous pressure of being busy, I find myself home and I rest. I know now this time is for me, I get a movie, I have a drink and I rest and suddenly there is like a physical explosion. I've asked friends about arousal and so have discovered lately how it affects me. Another thing that happens is I go to bed, I've absolutely no desire or anything, I never, ever, go to bed with the thought of masturbating, because basically masturbating for me is still wrong, but I don't want to indulge in it, I don't want to make it a habit. I go to bed, I have no desire, but I cannot sleep, I toss to the right and

left. I have an agitation which is absolutely unbearable,
but no sexual desire, nothing. But then finally after
tossing around for about an hour and jumping around
I think the only way to get rid of it is by masturbating.
Masturbation brings quietness and I go to sleep. Then
those wicked priests who told me in confession, "Go,
go and wet yourself, [shower] don't think of it, go and
take a walk, it's asinine." I don't think when I have
a sexual desire it makes me a pig. I was called pig
for so long in my life, but I don't think that anymore.
It's just physical, it's like a mechanism, but I still go
to confession, because in my prayer life I want to be
pure before God, but pure, what is pure? But I know
I want to please God, I know if I went to God and tell
him, God it happened to me again but I don't want it
but it's here it's like a need. Only one time at confession when I said I come to confession but I don't think
I can feel guilty, the priest said, "Then why do you
confess it." A Jesuit Father I met on a retreat told me,
"But everybody masturbates." Another priest said,
"How low can you fall?" This damn Catholic Church,
I've met wonderful priests speaking of God's love, but
the last priest wasn't one of them.

Quite a number of the women discussed how priests dealt with
the issue of masturbation. There was a wide variance in the priests'
responses. Officially the Catholic Church, as Sipe indicates, main-
tains its abhorrence for masturbation. Empirical research was studied for a report to the Catholic Theological Society of America. The
findings in the report on masturbation (although mainly positive
findings were quoted) led to an indecisive conclusion that "no ethical position is compelled by the empirical data." I will continue to

include data collected on the impact of priests' advice and counseling with regard to masturbation as it appears in the transcriptions.

Very few women spoke about fantasy. Kate said she had a lot of sexual thoughts and feelings, mostly for the parents of the children she taught, or for the priests. She said,

> I would fantasize sometimes but not a lot. I just figured it wasn't part of my life, it wasn't going to be part of my life. It made me happy to feel sexual feelings. I didn't think it was wrong or anything. I just thought it wasn't going to be part of my life. I got a tremendous amount of pleasure out of masturbation, and a tremendous amount of guilt. I thought I'd discovered something nobody else ever knew. I never talked about it. I kept thinking, how can you stand to sin? For this I'm going to go to hell - I don't think so! This isn't separating me from God! I confessed it when I was in my 20s, when I was in the convent, never when I was a kid. I don't know what made me confess it. I felt like it had been a secret and I was really no longer ashamed of it when I confessed it. I still felt it was not right to do, but I wasn't afraid anymore and so that made it okay to talk about it. I only confessed it once, to a wonderful priest who I thought would not judge me, or condemn me at all. He didn't. He said that he was a double sinner, which was really sweet. When I entered I stopped masturbating the whole time I was in formation. But then when I started teaching I began again, that's when I felt really guilty. I used to say well I'm not with a partner or anything but I could satisfy myself, which was real nice. Women in my order were real comfortable talking about feelings and

sexuality. I don't know if this was part of my leaving but I was real comfortable talking about masturbation and sexual relationships, having intercourse. It wasn't a taboo subject anymore. I just felt way more comfortable with sex because I was a nun, isn't that weird? In the context of religious life, it was something I grew to appreciate even more and respect more.

The very word "masturbation" elicited discomfort for many of the women. Lisa was one of them. Her memories from childhood experiences were so clear, one can easily understand her reluctance to accept the connotations of sin her adult world would later put on this experience to sully the pleasure of her memories.

When I think of masturbation, it equals sin. Oh yes, I do hate that word. I remember when I was seven or eight years old, I must have been experiencing orgasm, I did not know what to call it. I would hold my crotch and jump up and down and I would get these wonderfully pleasurable feelings that I now know must have been orgasms. At the time I had no idea what I was doing. It wasn't like direct manipulation to my clitoris or anything, it was kind of a general feeling that just filled my entire body. It was an orgasmic feeling almost in its purity that's the only way I can describe it. I was experiencing it as a child and I felt it from the tip of my toes to the top of my head. The orgasms I have now are pleasurable and they're wonderful but, my memory of what that feeling was like as a young child, I have not experienced as an adult. All that I can think of is that it was pure pleasure without any guilt. Something changed; I don't know when it changed, when I began to feel guilt. Throughout my teenage years I definitely masturbated, I remember feeling guilty about it. I can't imagine speaking to my mother about it, but I remember her saying to me "If you can't decide if something is a sin or not, just confess it, say to the priest, I think I committed a sin against the 6th Commandment" [thou shalt not kill]. I think about the repertoire of my conversation with the priest in confession, Father, I disobeyed my mother, I talked back, and I think I committed a sin against the 6th commandment. The priest would always say "If you're not sure then it's not a sin." I always felt that covered it. When I was in the convent I came to the point where I knew it was not wrong. I remember talking to a priest about masturbation and he just set my mind at ease about it. It was like "It's a very natural thing, go for it, take care of yourself, no big deal." I remember feeling very nervous talking to him about it, but it was like "This is natural-what's the big deal?"

Lisa's story illustrates beautifully the innocent experimentation of the child and the misinterpretation without true knowledge of the parent. Of interest here is how her mother counseled her to confess a sin against such an inappropriate commandment. Yet reflecting back to historical evidence that masturbation ultimately equaled death, the mother may simply have been passing on misinformation in her own interpretation. As important as the mother's comments were, perhaps of more alarm was the reaction of the priest when she attempted to confess the "sin." No information was offered to clarify the child's true concerns. However, later in life she still felt compelled to "test the waters" to see what the official thinking would be. Significantly she says "He set my mind at ease about it," even though she had just said she had come to the point of knowing it was not wrong, the implication here being that she still felt on some level that it was a bad thing to do.

Margaret, already traumatized by incest, found the experience impacted her self-pleasuring also. I asked did the incest reduce her natural tendencies to touch herself? She replied "Oh sure, sure" I continued to ask if she had recovered and how this impacted her masturbation presently? She grimaced. I asked, "You don't like that word?"

> You know what, I used to do that as a kid because
> there used to be some stress relief, if nothing else, in
> that. I always felt so guilty afterwards. I used to think
> this is a terrible thing to do. I never even understood
> why I wanted to do it. I would do it and wonder why.
> As a little kid I'd been so used to being stimulated,
> I can see that now. In high school I used to do that
> very infrequently, maybe twice a year. In the convent
> for seven years I didn't do it but five times because it
> was still, to me, something that was very wrong. Also
> nobody said it was okay. I think maybe if someone
> had said this was normal and okay, I still would prob-
> ably not have believed them, but it would not have been
> such a bad thing. I don't know at what point in my life
> it became okay. I never felt right about it. I remember
> when I was in therapy they asked me "What do you do
> when you masturbate?" I said, "I never do that." I think
> it was never anything I felt good about, even as an adult.
> I would wonder if it was worth all the guilt afterwards.
> I think it was also a reminder of being a kid; it was just
> one more thing, so I hated that part of it too.

Margaret remained extremely conflicted when her self-plea-suring was concerned. She was, however, open to talk about it and felt she could explore the issue with friends. This should help overcome the last vestiges of fear and guilt whose genesis lies in the incest she suffered as a four-year-old. That experience was compounded by a sex negative punitive religion.

Lua Xochitl had lived a life of self-imposed chastity for 30 years, 12 of those years as a professed nun. She denied ever having had sexual contact with a male or a female nor had she ever attempted self-pleasure. This lady enthralled me for four hours with her life history and future plans. A major milestone in her life was the first time she ever masturbated. However, she paints a picture with words to describe the significance,

> I went to Catholic School. My entertainment in school came from sports and the Glee Club, but in terms of pleasuring myself, absolutely not. Very Catholic, very Christian, very fucked up! It takes a long time to unlearn those lies and that behavior. What is Christianity? It's a lot of guilt a lot of fear and a tad of love. I was 18 years old and a very naive innocent girl. I was raised with the energy of faith and I believed in the church and the Christ and definitely in Mary. When I entered religious life I entered with that innocence and that faith. I had such a load of fear that I probably cut off my body from my neck down, slowly, myself, and when I went into the convent it was probably blessed and sanctified. When I think of my sexuality as a young maiden, it was pretty much dormant. From 1955 to 1968 I was pretty much dead from the neck down, my body was dormant. My intellect was juiced in the classroom; I was a natural teacher. When people ask me why I stayed so long in the convent I have to say because of the teaching. In '68 I went on a weekend workshop. That was the weekend when all the institutions in my life were shattered. That's church, Christianity, the government. That's family,

the presidency, that's everything. What's remarkable for me is that I felt totally good about it. This weekend was the beginning of the unlearning of the lie. What happened that weekend was that people who were much more knowledgeable and aware of what was happening on the planet and in society were holding up the contradictions to us. Part of the weekend dealt with sexuality and connecting how sexual repression then makes for an oppressive society in which we live. By the winter of '68, I was sleeping with nothing on, no night coif or gown. I remember the first time I felt my own body with my own hands. I remember as I've gone back to that moment laying on my bed and saying a prayer to the mother and I said, "Help me to know my body, help me to have joy in my body," and I began to masturbate. Just to feel my body, just to feel my hands on my body, I had never done that in my whole life, I was 31 years old. It was wonderful, it was a coming home, and I remember not addressing the mother as Virgin Mary any more but Earth Mother. I later found out in saying Earth Mother that I was connecting to my indigenous roots because that's how indigenous people in this country speak to the Mother. I orgasmed and my whole body vibrated, I had no recollection of ever feeling that before, other than when I would see the colors of flowers. When I was very little I would see the oranges and reds of flowers and my panties would get wet, and I'd get punished for it. There was a real fear of bodily pleasure. That message was very well inculcated. When I masturbated for the first time, what came back to me was a flash of that little girl who would see flowers, purples and oranges and reds and get wet. I must have masturbated all night long. It was wonderful. Also, what I think I felt was the power, all mine for myself and on my behalf. I didn't need anyone else to do it for me. That was quite something because I had a very negative self-image. I do remember that at one point, leading myself up to orgasm, I hesitated before I came and stopped and I saw the light. I realize now as I go back to that moment that I was unknowingly taking myself into a shamanic space, where you go between the worlds. It was quite something. I would take myself up to peak, not peak and just hang there. I would see images of water and yoni and then I'd see the light. I would do that sometimes 20 times a night before finally allowing myself to orgasm. I think what probably happened was that I had become politically conscious, plus the experience of being sexually my own self-pleasurer. There was no way anyone was going to get anywhere with that one. I said fuck them all, this is my body and I'm claiming it. I knew that when I masturbated I went into a place of great joy, ecstasy, and I had been taught that when you know the Christ and when you meditate that some of the saints had ecstasy, like Teresa of Avila. I thought, she must have masturbated and we've never been told, maybe she did. I wonder what Mary was doing at the Annunciation? Hey, I really do believe women at that time were wiser with their bodies, that's my feeling. I think Mary knew her body really well, that's certainly not what I was told and it's certainly not what's held up to the Latina young woman. She is the Virgin, she is docile, she is submissive; fuck that shit she knew her body!

Lua Xochitl was the second woman to mention Teresa of Avila in a sexual, spiritual capacity. Elizabeth showed me a picture of Teresa's face, and said this to her was a representation of spiritual, sexual ecstasy. She said she believed that it was truly possible to achieve the same level of physical pleasure on a mystical plane.

The majority of women waited to be asked about their masturbatory history, and often displayed discomfort with the topic. In some cases I waited until close to the end of the interview before asking about this to see if the topic would be addressed spontaneously; it was not. This was the one area most women avoided. Caroline's story is representative of those who received repressive messages in a religious setting. Her story has its own twist, which adds a new element to an already interesting life.

> I never masturbated before going to the convent, no. I know I was so closed down and all the messages we were ever given were always negative. I remember going to Senior Retreat and we had a question box. One of the questions must have been on sexual arousal because the priest said in a very rough voice, "All right now listen up, I'm going to answer this question. I will answer it once so pay attention because I am not going to speak to this subject again." Then again I thought, "Oh my God, are we even supposed to hear this?" He went through this very clinical account of what sexual arousal was and I thought "Well who wants that anyway?" It was always something that someone else did. If you wanted to be good you could never do this, this sex thing is in another realm. So it was like I was scared to death. I didn't know what the "it" was, but I knew I wasn't going to do it. The older I got the more I felt like I was strange and different. It's like you're supposed to know this, other people do

this, yet it was like fogginess. The first time I masturbated was in the convent. I read a book and there was something in it about masturbation and I thought I'd try it. I was stoned, and it was very powerful and it took me someplace else. But the next day I was scared, I thought I'd done something wrong. I did get over that but it took me a long time. It's interesting in the context of being with a partner it's easier, but it's always out of synchrony and if there's an inkling of getting turned on I need to smoke dope. So there's all this conflict going on because I don't want to smoke dope but I want to be sexual. I still think there's a shame that I still can't get to that place. I feel, as hard as I've worked I'm still blocked. I wonder what would our sexual expression be in our society if there were no should's or should not's?

As previously mentioned, these are very complex stories. Caroline experienced conflicts on various levels throughout her life. Her love map was forever imprinted at this stage of her life when she needed dope in order to be sexual with herself for the first time and reach orgasm. As noted in Chapter Six this pattern remained a source of conflict for her. To explain the significance of a love map it will help to understand concept. A lovemap was originated by John Money to assist a discussion of why people like what they enjoy sexually and erotically. According to Money, it is "a developmental representation or template in the mind and in the brain depicting the idealized lover and the idealized program of sexual and erotic activity projected in imagery or actually engaged in with that lover."

According to Money, the word *lovemap* was first used in 1980 in an article entitled: *"Pairbonding and Limerence."* Before this time, as he states, Money began to talk about lovemaps, in precursory form, with his students in lectures.

Money describes the formation of an individual's lovemap as similar to the acquirement of a native language, in that it bears the mark of his or her own unique individuality, similar to an accent in a spoken language. A lovemap is usually quite specific as to details of the physiognomy, build, race, and color of the ideal lover, not to mention temperament, manner, etc. Since its inception, the concept of "love maps," applied to interpersonal relationships, has found apt acceptance and is frequently referenced in love / relationship / sexual-evolution theory books; as for example in Wilson and McLaughlin's 2001 *The Science of Love*.

In "Gay, Straight, and In-Between: The Sexology of Erotic Orientation," Money (1988: 127-128) suggests that love is like a Rorschach (ink blot) test, where if projections (shaped by a body/mind's lovemap) on the other are mutual, pair-bonding occurs, typically in a courtship phase of mating.

Mary simply dismissed the subject of masturbation with one sentence when she said, "I'm not a person who's done a lot sexually with masturbation or anything. It just didn't appeal to me, or given me any charge. I know it does for some people." She did not deny ever masturbating, but by the tone of her voice and the set of her body language I knew not to proceed with the questioning. This topic made her extremely uncomfortable.

Hilary said,

> So far as sexuality is concerned I don't remember
> anything but old childish things. I don't remember
> anything about masturbation; anything about anything
> except my mother kept saying I was a late bloomer as
> far as developing. I wasn't nearly aware of anything
> when I went in the convent. I turned 18 the day after I
> went in.

Sophia told me that she had no sexual awareness until after she got married. She was married to the same man for 25 years and had never masturbated. To her knowledge, her husband did not masturbate either. It was after her husband's death two years ago that she began to explore the area of self-pleasuring at the encouragement of a male friend. I asked initially about her early experience and she told me, "No never. It never occurred to me. I must have been naive or something, no, no, but I've been learning and I've been reading." I asked for clarification, because she was a very sensuous woman in her dress and her physical appearance, "Let me understand, you had never in your life, up until two years ago ever self-pleasured?" She answered,

> No, ah, ah, never. I just didn't need it. Why should I? After my husband died, a friend took me to an adult shop. Well; looking at those vibrators in the store, I was just shocked. I'd honestly never seen anything like that. When I was married we never discussed anything like that, I don't think I even knew how or even thought of it as something people did, never.

Stephanie, a quietly spoken mother of two teenagers, had been a nun for 10 years. She left her community and married within three years. She had no sexual experience prior to entering. She denied knowledge of masturbation until after she entered. In response to the question, "Did you ever self-pleasure?" she said,

> Once when I was a postulant I did, but not a lot. I worried that it was sinful and I shouldn't be doing it and shouldn't be thinking of this area so I just stuffed it, stuffed it all away. I didn't look at it and every time I felt like it I stuffed it deeper. I was 18 or 19 and in the next 10 years I thought of it but I didn't do it because I thought it would lead me out [of the convent]. I didn't want to disappoint anyone and so I didn't want to even toy with anything that might lead me out the door. So I just shoved it away.

June entered the convent at age 16, she left after less than a year and was married by 18. She never had any experience of masturbation until after she married. There was a period in her early marriage when she masturbated often but felt very guilty because she thought it detracted from the normal relations with her husband and therefore stopped all self-pleasuring. She thinks in retrospect that her feeling was that it was wrong to have personal sexual gratification apart from her husband.

Pamela responded to my question about self-pleasure with an emphatic,

> No, I never have, I don't know how to do it, but sometimes if I take an afternoon nap I'll have an orgasm, a physical feeling. I don't do anything, don't touch myself or anything, it just happens. I don't do anything. I just fall asleep and then Oh God, it's so exciting, and it's wonderful. Sometimes in the morning I'll dream and then it will happen, I guess that's what an orgasm is, this great sensation.

An interesting footnote to this segment is Pamela's suggestion for herself, that she should perhaps visit a clinic, the reason being, "Charles has tried to do everything with me and nothing works. He's tried but nothing works for me." I asked if she thought she continued to be anxious about sexuality. Her answer to my question was, "I don't know. Now I want more of a sexual life. [She told me previously they have "sex" two or three times a week but that she does not always orgasm]. "I never thought of that before. I want to learn more about sex. I read a lot about things and Charles will ask what I'm reading and I wonder, yes I need to learn about having orgasms and stuff."

The implication I read into this statement was twofold; (1) Pamela defers her sexual needs to her husband and (2) Pamela isn't really sure if she is indeed climaxing. I feel self-pleasuring will be a very important component to her understanding her own needs and reaching the levels of sexual maturity and personal pleasure she seeks. A final comment from Pamela will I'm sure speak for many when she said,

Having grown up in the Catholic Church, all the bad things they say about sex that I don't believe, must be inside of me. Yes it's still there, but it makes me pissed off. After all these years it makes me pissed off and I want to learn more about sex and I want to look into sexuality classes so that I can be more of a sexual person.

Alison spoke in chapter 6 about her expectations of those who take vows of chastity and a promise of celibacy to live up to those promises by denial of all sexual acts. I asked her how she understood her own self-pleasuring in the context of what she had just said. She answered,

I don't know, I don't know. I didn't see any conflict at the time, nor do I now but I expect my priests to keep their vow of celibacy and my sister to keep their vow of chastity. So maybe I'm confused as to what entails keeping it. Did I break my vow by self-pleasuring? Would I have been breaking it if I had gone off and had intercourse with a man? Did I break it when I masturbated? Where's the line, is there a line? Is it black, is it white, is it gray, and every shade inbetween? If religious life has any value, what is the value of religious life? If religious life is still bound up in taking vows of Poverty, Chastity and Obedience, and if that's the core of religious life, then I'm still black and white on those issues.

The confusion Alison expresses had no conclusion. Although she admits to masturbating on a regular basis she now sees a conflict when it comes to avowed celibates acting out their sexuality. She does not define masturbation as a sex act however.

In answer to the question "Do you think your Catholic education affected your view of sexuality positively, negatively, fearfully or not at all?" The responses were:

VALUE	N = 38	N = 37	N=37
	BEFORE %	DURING %	AFTER %
Positively	18%	27%	35%
Negatively	37%	21%	19%
Not at all	24%	19%	11%
	21%	33%	35%

Chapter Eight
Girls to Women: Reflections

The meaning of life lies within us. The beginning of the search for truth lies in each person's story. To truly hear one another is to respect one another.

— Pat and Barbara, *No Turning Back*

In this last chapter of their stories, my subjects are back in the society they attempted to leave. For the majority, the transition in their careers was uneventful; their sex lives, however, have followed a more varied path.

There were similarities in life choices for example, most of the women continued in the same career as they held in the convent. The majority remained in teaching, from elementary through university level. There were several therapists or other members of the helping professions. One was a lawyer. Those who no longer practiced their Catholic religion did however remain spiritual, although some struggled to find a new route to express it. What was clear was that sexuality was not taken for granted. It was a subject for enquiry and curiosity. When they were asked to think about sexuality in view of their religious experience, they all felt comfortable with their decision to leave the convent. Those for whom sexuality was still a source of struggle expressed no wish to return to a religious life. I think this was due to the fact that overall it was obedience not chastity which had been their primary motive for leaving. However, no one expressed regret at having made the decision to enter religious life.

For Mary, Ursula and Caroline, sexuality remained a challenge, one about which they continued to ask questions and search
for answers. Mary had yet to experience either self-pleasure or a
sexual initiation with male or female. Ursula struggled to identify
her sexuality and in fact could not decide conclusively if she was
lesbian, straight or bisexual. Caroline was in personal conflict on a
very basic level because her sexual turn on and ability to climax was
tied to the use of marijuana, a habit she did not want to continue,
but without which she could not achieve orgasm. Ruth and Stephanie took two years after leaving their communities before meeting
their prospective spouses and marrying. Stephanie had children immediately. Ruth had none. As will be related, Ruth was prepared
to remain single; she had such a hard time meeting "Mr. Right."
Maria, Miriam, Helen, Marian and Pamela all married priests or
brothers, and had established these relationships to some varying
degree whilst in their communities. Hazel, June, Sophia, Margaret,
Pamela, Stephanie, and Kathleen all married and had children soon
after leaving the convent. Grace and Elizabeth claimed they were
very happily married without children of their own. Lisa, Virginia,
Hilary, and Rachael lived with their lovers. Sara had a child and
lived with the father. Ione was fully out as a lesbian. She had a
female lover but lived alone. Lois came out as lesbian many years
ago; however, in our interview she alluded to the fact that bisexual
would probably be a better classification. Lois was attempting to
establish a relationship with a woman, but did not preclude the option of being sexual with a man in the future. Kate identified as bisexual. She had her female lover but lived alone. Lua Xochitl was
travelling the world after having had several male lovers but never
marrying. Clare married and had a child that died; she discovered
her husband to be a bigamist, had her marriage annulled and lived
alone. Those who left the convent the latest (later than 30 years
old) had no children. They apparently had not used contraception;
they said "It just didn't happen" (they did not conceive).

After Ursula retired from her job at 62 she began to work on
her sexual issues. The denial of her sexuality and the mental chaos
it caused throughout her life continued unabated until addressed in

therapy and biofeedback workshops. She had not experienced any worry-free sexual acts, either self-pleasuring or with either gender partner. Self-identifying as lesbian caused her inner turmoil due in part to its being contrary to her religious belief system. Being unable to control her sexual urges was a constant source of inner struggle and had been tremendously painful.

> When I see the path I have walked since my retirement to face up to myself, my psychological journey to face all those inner pressures, it has been very hard. I now understand it was because I couldn't face all the pressures of my history. When I retired twelve years ago, I couldn't run away from myself any more. The fact that I had been an abused child, the rejection of this homosexuality [her lesbian tendencies], I had horrible pressure [psychological]. So I went through three different treatments and there has been a healing, a great healing. I can say I look at sex today very differently. As far as others are concerned I understand their desire perfectly, it's me that I have a problem with, and because basically I was told my sexuality was bad.

She said the healing had allowed her to recognize that she enjoys being held by a man; but thinks it would still be difficult to be spiritually and physically joined to men. However, that is a big change from having only fantasized about women. She claimed that her despondency came from a need for a mother's love. This need for nurturing by the mother had been a very common theme in other interviews. Although many of the women stated that their fathers were a great influence on their sexuality and personal formation as women, those deprived of their mothers' love seemed to have had great difficulty recovering from their loss. Some had indeed not accomplished this and even in their later years, felt the pain. I reminded Ursula that nobody had ever given her permission to honor her sexuality. She responded, "I feel despair about the masturbation thing, because it's done alone without a partner. I can't do it with a woman because I'm fighting the homosexual issue." She asked, "Is this deviant?" We conversed for a moment on the irrepressible need for sexual outlet and she admitted she did not feel 75 years old in her sexuality, and on consideration I must agree. Perhaps an adolescent could identify with the confusion described here. Ursula attended Mass and was a daily communicant. She was however adamant in her condemnation for what she called "those damn self-righteous Catholics." She said she understood why the Churches were empty and why people do not practice their religion. "I hate the word practice, I do not practice my religion, I love to go to Church. God understands me, damn it, he understands I am not a piece of wood!"

Mary had likewise done a lot of personal growth work and had a desire for sexual fulfillment. She had yet to meet a man with whom she felt comfortable being sexual, but even more importantly had not achieved sexual fulfillment in self-pleasure. She believed if there were any unremembered child sexual abuse in her past, then the memory of it would surface if she had sex with a man. I feel, in this case, perhaps a clinical sexologist, working with a surrogate could be helpful to guide her through this experience. As stated in Chapter Six, no therapy was given to assist her with body image concerns following her mastectomy. Her confusion and reticence to be fully sexual could be linked to her lack of personal acceptance, fear of rejection and also fear of opening up her unconscious mind to the possibility of child molestation. Mary is still a practicing Catholic and had her business office in the convent where she used to live. This appears important in that she hadn't broken free of the past even to the extent of "moving out" physically.

Hilary had a number of experiences since her departure from the convent. She talked about dating a man whom she thought was absolutely fabulous and he turned out to be a great "philanderer." However, she was still "crazy about him" even though her friends warned her against the relationship. She said,

He just made my body tingle; it didn't matter that he was a philanderer. I even made myself not see him. It was like mortifying yourself [as we used to do] in the convent, when you wouldn't eat something you'd want to eat, until I really realized what a jerk he was.

Hilary was still looking for the passionate relationship in her life equal to the memory of her first love for the priest.

I haven't personally hit on the guy who wants to make a huge effort over me except the person I'm with and his effort hasn't worked really well. I don't know if in real life you keep working on finding someone because you could go your whole life and not hit the right person or hit the right person who's wrong.

Hilary, the woman who had been sexually exploited by both a priest "friend" and her therapist, had a variety of experiences following her departure from the convent. For instance, she dated a younger man; he was in his early 30s and she was 42. She told me that they had sex and he thought it was great. He called her up and wanted to marry her. At that time she toyed with the idea of getting married and having a family but decided he was too young and turned him down. She wasn't feeling a great emotional pull although "he was a gorgeous man." Another man she dated, when she was on a temporary split from her live in-lover, turned out to be a transvestite.

So I have this relationship with a man who has a few fetishes. He liked to wear women's clothes, diapers, and children's clothes. And I said to myself, this is interesting. I'm an open person, and I did have sex with him, it wasn't bad. It was a little thing that he wanted me to wear the man's clothes and I think I did once. It was nothing bad, it was like someone who had a foot fetish

and wanted to pet your foot, so what? I went to a couple of transsexual meetings and there were transsexuals
there and others, it was interesting to me. So I feel like
I'm an open person. After a while it got boring because
it was all so self-absorbed. But it was very interesting. So since then, about 15 years ago, nothing else has
happened. I'm still with the same man, sex isn't all that
important; I have too many other distractions.

Hilary taught in a parochial school and did not articulate her
feelings on the subject of religion or God at that point in her life.
Her demeanor was one of acceptance, if a little fraught and overwhelmed. She didn't judge any of the experiences she had in a
negative way, nor did she address the men who had taken advantage of her in an angry fashion. It was just put down to experience
and she was matter-of-fact about it.

Lua Xochitl had a most interesting life since her departure
from the convent. She followed a pagan religion and was a self-
described "trusted and loved crone." Before I met this woman I
was intrigued by her energy which was apparent even over the telephone. She exuded vitality and joy, mysticism and common sense.
The feeling of being part of a sisterhood was profound when speaking to her both in person and on the telephone. Her initial sexual
awakening with a man occurred in a Cuban rebel training camp.
The couple was very much in love and they intended to marry.
"We were going to be married. I went back to Cuba a second time
but political changes happened in Haiti and he had to go back. We
couldn't marry." I asked if she had ever wanted children.

No. Well, I wanted them earlier in my life but I
became a teacher for 15 years. The first time I made
love with Carlos in Cuba he asked me about the convent. He said "Are you sorry that you lost 14 years of
your life?" I said "No, I didn't lose 14 years of my life,
I know this and this and this and my only regret is that

I'll never have children." I was only 32, I just thought
it was over for me, and he said to me, "You and I have
children all over the world and we are making a better
world for them." I think he came into my life to help
me never feel that I was barren and I've never felt that
I was less because I'd never had children.

At 60 years she had embarked upon a world trip to follow
her ancestral heritage from its place of origin in Spain back to the
United States, traveling first to New Zealand and then to Europe.
Her only contacts were at the first stop, after that she planned to
"trust in the Mother" to find her places to stay. Her sexual life had
progressed also from that early romantic beginning. She fell in
love with a much younger man and, when that relationship ended,
went to Brazil to get away and at the time was in acute depression.
There she met a couple and they became good friends. One evening, when the wife was away, the man declared his love for Lua.
She said that at first she could not even imagine a relationship.
However, after a while she saw that the feelings were becoming
mutual and to keep her integrity towards her "sister" [the wife] she
left Brazil. She never married, but did have one long-term intimate
relationship with a man; one that she said was her only truly intimate experience. As an example that progress was taking place
throughout the years she told me that she just "turned on to a Euro-
American" man for the first time last year. "And that's because
I've grown, I stopped relating to people according to color a long
time ago." I said to her, "your evolution has been phenomenal" and
she answered,

Hasn't it? What it was for me was coming home to
my body, sexually and spiritually. As I'm talking to
you, that's what I understand. When I remember that
first time masturbating and taking myself to peaks,
some place in my mind there was knowledge that

woman has always known this. The spiritual, sexual
part of myself came together. The political, spiritual
self became wedded later. But I've never told the story
before to understand what happened there. So when I
had my first sexual experience with a man there was a
sense of spiritual as well, orgasmically I can't tell you
it was that great, but that part of me that felt inferior
was just put aside to be looked at much later.

I asked if she felt women who had been in convents were less
likely to take their sexuality for granted. She answered,

No they don't, and also when we understand it as spirit
also and spirit is in the body, it's the only thing that
matters. The vibration of spirituality and sexuality
are so mirroring of each other. When I would look
back at that time I understood. That's why I had no
expectations for men to do it for me. That's why I
went through a period of my life where it was okay for
me to teach men how to make love, they couldn't be
expected to know, how could they?

Lua Xochitl was a vibrant, sexual woman, full of spirituality in
her pagan rites and in her vitality for life. Her anger and dismay at
the Catholic Church had ebbed. She used to feel that she wanted to
bomb a church before she died; now, that feeling had gone because
she believed the Church to be dying all by itself!

Lois was representative of the feminist influence so prevalent at the time the subjects were making the greatest transitions,
in the 1960s and 70s. She spoke confidently and forcefully for
over two hours and told me about her life in what appeared to be
minute detail. Yet she made a brief reference to an abortion as a
young woman, after she had left the convent. This major incident
was not referred to again and I felt she assiduously avoided the
subject throughout the interview. Her reason for entering was the

prospect of becoming a doctor on the African missions and serving the world in an adventurous fashion. She masterfully flowed with seemingly in-depth analyses of herself, answering questions without actually giving very much away. She was politically aware prior to entering and became extremely political during her two and a half years in the convent, and was eventually asked to leave. Once again, as in Grace's story, I heard the convent referred to as a commune, bearing all the hallmarks of 60s and 70s thinking. Lois had taken a copy of the Communist Manifesto with her to the convent in her trunk, and was considered a radical and very outspoken. After she left the convent and went back to college she had bouts of severe depression with thoughts of suicide. She said she had no vision of the future and added, "I knew I didn't want to get married." Eventually her life stabilized. As described previously her sexuality found expression first in a romantic slow relationship and later with multiple partners of both sexes. However, she knew she wanted to go to graduate school and, when the time came for her to do that, she was quite prepared for the end of her relationship. This became a pattern for her; one of beginning an academic project and putting her sexuality on hold until that was completed. She explained it this way:

> That's really how I live my life. Even now I decided not to have an affair until I finished my book. I put personal ads out last November and I got two answers to the ads. But then I got my book contract and thought I don't want to call someone and say I can't start a relationship until April when I get my book done, so I didn't bother. So now I'm thinking of going out again, and I went on a weekend camping trip and met this woman there. She calls me up out of the blue and propositions me; this was the day I was supposed to make my phone call for a sex date. So she's telling me that she's free and she's bi-curious, and she's telling me about her sex life and I said "I don't know."

217

I had all this illness and pain in my 30's and 40's, I felt as if I was 70 then. I wasn't open to sex because I was in so much physical pain, and now I said, here I am an old lady in my 50s and I'm really horny and I want to date. I feel as if I have this 50-year-old body, who's going to think of me as a sex object? She said "Well I do, I want to have sex with you." So I have a date next week. I've always found it really easy to talk about sex. I think this is really interesting because my mother gave her mother information about sex. My mother went through nursing school and so knew a lot more about her body than her mother and so ended up telling her about it and then my sisters and I told my mother about sex. It was very strange, it was like I was this really clean slate, it's like I was asexual and then - [she paused for thought, then continued] - I have a theory. I think there are two approaches to sex. One is intellectual and the other is gonadal. Some people say "Oh I don't know, I got myself in so much trouble with this guy and ended up in bed with him." To me it was always so calculating. For instance I would leave my birth control pills on the dresser so that if my date came to my room to get my jacket he would see the pills and it was intentional to let him know I wanted sex. I don't know if it was my first lover who told me I needed experience, or if it was my own need for experience. I think it's a great way to meet people, to connect with them. I really took it that I'd rather get to know you through sex than have conversation. My attitude changed somewhat when I became more professional and when my health problems began. I don't

intellectualize when I'm in an experience but before it
I can plan it and know I just want the sex and we don't
have to get married or anything. I went through a lot
of change in my life, I've had sex with 60 men in my
life, and I quit having sex when I was 29. The way I
see it, to me I'm liberated, right, we're talking about
the 70s, right? To me the men I had sex with saw
me as a slut in terms of "Oh yes I believe in women's
lib." They believed all this but in the end I was not
the woman you marry, I was not the woman you date
[I understood this to mean there was no real relationships with these men, they were simply sex partners
with no commitment. On reflection she was angry
at the men.] Oh yes they had their talk down but in
the end they saw me as a slut. They were really lousy
lovers. Now I really want an orgasm if I'm going to
be involved in sex with somebody. If the man has
an orgasm and I don't, I get really angry. Especially
back then I didn't say anything. I was just stewing.
Then I realized I'd had sex with a number of men and
they orgasmed and I didn't, I wished I'd taken their
money for it. I really felt for all they were saying that
the vibes worked that I was a slut. I thought the more
sex I'm having the more pissed I'm getting, and where
am I going to meet someone who thinks about it like
I do. So I quit having sex. I thought I'd figure it out,
why I'm constantly getting charged up and constantly
being disappointed. I began to read lesbian literature
and wondered why am I only giving this to men? I'm
discriminating against women. So I again intellectualized it and decided to come out. I've never heard

a coming out story like that. I explored this with
my friends. I was having sex with a lot of different
women and there were a couple of awkward situations
where people would say, "Well who are you going to
take home?" A little jealousy thing. I really have a
great deal of comfort about sexuality. At one stage I
was so comfortable I would sometimes rather have sex
with someone than go out to dinner. It seemed like an
equal choice to me.

Lois asked me if I'd heard similar stories from other former
nuns and, when I answered "no," she continued,

I think that's really passive. My thought is this is my
universe. I'm going to jump into this universe and
find out what's in here and how do I manipulate it. My
imagery about sex is that it's a giant swimming pool,
and we're all in it. There's the kid's part and there's
the pedophiles that are in with the kids and swimming
where they shouldn't be, and there's all these other
people swimming around together and touching each
other for a while before swimming on. Or you can be
asexual and stay on the side not touching anyone. I
was on the sideline, probably had my back turned
toward the pool [before entering]. Then I felt like
"yes now I want to jump in." Of course I did have that
period of chosen celibacy, that's really unusual.

In conclusion she told me she could not be monogamous because "the world deserves me." She said she was disillusioned by
the double standard of the Catholic Church and no longer practiced.

After Ione left the convent she attempted to have relationships
with men on several occasions. However, eventually she acknowl-

edged her lesbianism. Her reference to life, in her case, convent life, as a swimming pool was reminiscent of Lois. She concluded her interview with,

> I guess when I look at my history, what I keep striving for is the integration of the spiritual and the sexual life, and that is what I feel I've been moving towards all these years. Recovering from the sexual abuse and then deciding not to be a sister, and not to be celibate anymore and then understanding myself as a lesbian. My personal philosophy, how I see sexuality is, I think sexuality for me needs to be in the context of a loving relationship, in a committed relationship with another person. I just can't do it just to have sex, I don't feel moral judgment on other people who do, it's just the way I'm made. A lot of the women I was in with have left; a lot of the visionary types have left. So around the time when I left, and after I left, was a big exodus. I think it's because the order isn't changing fast enough and those people get tired. I guess as I see myself now, I still have a stronger sex drive than most of the women I know. At this time in my life I think I'm trying to be more integrated, more out as a lesbian and to continue in my ministry work that I'm doing. I think sexuality is a subject that a lot of people at least in my circle are a bit intimidated and fearful of, and I feel like I'm more willing to talk about it than most of the people in my group. Although I feel very successful in my work life and my education, I feel a little bit behind in my relationship skills, so I feel like that's a challenge for me now. When I talk to other lesbians I realize, when we were teenagers like a lot of the kids I teach, they're

dating and going through all that stuff at 17 and 18 what I'm going through at 35. What they're learning now, I'm learning now. In this area, I'm a little bit of a late bloomer. I feel as if I'm in the reverse of a lot of my friends who got married early, they're going to workshops and finding their spirituality and I feel as if I did that, I'm more like in the reverse. One of the reasons I left was that I wanted to be sexual. The struggle with myself to try and remain celibate started to seem somewhat ridiculous. The sexual experience was also part of the spiritual experience; I saw it as integrated. But I also started to feel like the convent was trying to close me in a little bit, not just sexually but to really become who I am, the convent started to feel as if it was closing in on me. People would say, you don't seem like a nun. I wonder if the convent becomes too small a fish pond or a swimming pool for those women who leave, I think some of them develop and grow and some of it is because of the environment of the convent and then they almost outgrow the convent, you know? As I said before, when I went to dinner I would be sitting with missionaries, and therapists and people who had their doctorates in history, educators, doctors, and people in the medical profession. It was fascinating. Someone got back from Africa and wanted to talk about the social conditions in Africa. I get the feeling that they just become too big for the swimming pool, and the convent starts to seem limiting. Of the women who left, less than half left because they wanted to be in a relationship. A lot of them left because they were tired of answering for the church. They could no longer stay because they felt it was repressive, they found it to be an oppressor of people. At least the way they talk to me about it, not a lot of them left because they wanted to be in a relationship. A friend of mine just left in January and her reason was because she wanted to be in a relationship. Some of the nuns said to her, "Some of the women have relationships and stay, why don't you just stay?" But she couldn't do that, so she left. I probably left because I needed to grow in other ways. I had grown a lot intellectually, academically, spiritually, and emotionally. Because I had gone through recovery from the sexual abuse my depression that I'd suffered from for many years lifted, I had much more energy. I think my next growth path was an intimate relationship, and I couldn't do that in the convent because when you fall in love with someone you want to be sexual with him or her. I thought, this is ridiculous that I'm trying to stop this being sexual just because I have this vow and I think falling in love and being sexual is a holy thing. So that was the cutting edge for me personally, it was to test the waters in an intimate relationship. The convent I would say was the place where I healed. The sisters taught me that life could be different than the life I grew up in. The joy and a curiosity about life and growing, the world seemed to open way up.

Sara expressed a certain empathy with Ione when it came to her feelings about supporting a Church, which felt repressive to her. In fact Sara was quite a lot stronger in her feelings when she spoke about her experience on the African mission.

It was really transforming. It shattered any worldview that I had. It just put me back to square one
and it scared me out of my mind. All my symbols
were gone. We had to look at life in a very basic way
and rethink things from the bottom up, [re-think] the
Church that I was a part of. It was the first time to
cover your head and wear a veil and stuff. That was
never a part of what I wanted, we never wore habits or
anything. It was very oppressive of the native cultures,
yet there was tremendous work being done to educate
people and help them along, there was something very
primary that was being destroyed and had been destroyed over time. I was so alienated from the structure that I was a part of that it was very, very difficult.
The missionaries would go out to the outlying Churches that were just communities of people. I remember
I went to the Easter service with an Irish missionary
priest. We went up into the hills to this one tribe that
was so inbred they couldn't even build a house that
would stand up; they were all desperately retarded and
so were isolated from the rest because the other tribes
didn't want to deal with them. This priest would go up
there and help build houses and do things for them. He
would perform the midnight Easter services for them,
lighting the fire and all that. People made instruments
from cans and stones, they sang their own songs. The
babies were being nursed, people were being baptized,
the sky was black, there was a full moon and there
were thousands of stars and the ritual was so real. I
knew what was happening in a way that I never tuned
into before. I never understood the rituals the way I
did in Africa. You just have this conflict of the church

224

constantly destroying their symbols, so what do you
do? That set up such a conflict in me, it was such a
culture shock, it was almost as much a culture shock
coming back as it was experiencing it and if I'd had my
druthers, I would have headed back to Africa.

It became evident as my interviews progressed that there was a great deal of curiosity and continued questioning among the group, around sex and intimacy issues. Of course, it is difficult to assess or compare my findings to the general public. I began asking the question; "Do you think the slow development of your sexuality has led to a prolonging of your sexual curiosity?" The answer was invariably "yes." Several of the women had virtually no sexual experience prior to leaving their communities and once they became sexual their curiosity and interest had not waned in the subsequent years as testified by their autobiographies.

Ruth was in the convent for 13 years and when she went home to tell her parents she was leaving, her mother told her that her life now had no value. Her photograph was on the mantle with her brother a priest; they were the success story of the family. Ruth had no sexual experience up to this time. The convent did an aptitude test on her and the results came out highest for wife and mother and lowest for teacher/nun. She said this astonished her. She had remained a teacher for many years following her departure from the convent, but found eventually her heart wasn't in it and finally decided to leave teaching and became a massage therapist, and loves it. When she left the convent she tried to meet men in a variety of the usual places. Dances proved fruitless, she disliked bars and friends introduced her to men she made no connection with. Eventually she applied to a dating agency. She had a few dates through this service but none worked out until they sent her the name of John, the man who was to become her husband. He had been married before and therefore needed to get an annulment. She said,

It was cute. I wanted someone tall, dark and handsome and I got a small, fat and blond one, who looked
just like me. We just had a very, very good time. We
married in June and he died the following August, not
that year, the following year. It was very pleasurable
and exciting. We had a very playful time. We played
in every room in the house, in the car, everywhere.
John used to say the Lord kept me on ice until he came
along. He said, "You were slow to get started but now
I can't keep up with you." At the end of the homily at
John's funeral I stood there and kind of grinned and
said, at this moment I feel the same kind of feelings
that I had when I had sex with John. Well my girlfriend said she'd never heard me say the word sex in
the whole of my life, which I never did! There was a
pause and a bit of giggling. Then I said, "I am totally
satisfied, but if I could get more I'd take it." Then
everyone in the church broke up and laughed. It's
not that I'm not sexual, because I am. I have a good
time. I used to tell John I'm my father's child, not my
mother's. Because my mother's idea of sex was just to
have kids and that was it, but my father was hot to trot.

A measure of Ruth's sexual growth came when she told me
that John once shared with her that when he was married to his
first wife he would always have to look at *Playboy* magazines to
"take care of himself" after they had made love. Ruth wanted to
know what was it in the *Playboy* magazines that really turned him
on, because she wanted to learn how to do it. She said she had told
her husband, "You know my background. You will have to be my
teacher. If I had to do it again I would still choose to do it, even
knowing it was going to be as short. There was an urgency in ev-

erything we did." Ruth mourned her lost love, and she moved on. In the ensuing years following the death of John she had friends with whom she became sexual.

> There's one friend who all I need to do is lift up the
> phone and say come over and he would love it. I know
> I don't want a permanent relationship with him and
> we've talked about that. There's another friend who
> I've known 11 years. He married four years ago but
> we slept together many, many times. He asked me to
> live with him but I didn't want to give up my house.
> Then he wanted me to buy this little island with him;
> we went to visit it. It was very romantic, it sounds like
> a phenomenal fantasy but it wouldn't have worked. He
> asked me to marry him, but he is an alcoholic, and I
> couldn't share my life with a bottle. We had a lot of
> fun and it was very playful but we both agreed that
> once one of us was in a committed relationship, our
> relationship had to stop. And when I say something's
> going to stop, it's going to stop. I get on really well
> with his wife, and she knows of our past and she said
> thanks. I have taken care of myself. I know I'm a
> very sexual being and I know when to say no. I've
> had a lot of support.

Ruth had done a lot of therapy, where she was able to address and deal with the abuses in her childhood. "Those types of things have really helped me in my life." Five years after John died, her doctor convinced her to go to an intimacy workshop and from there she learned a lot about sexual freedom. I asked Ruth if she could reflect and compare herself now to those early days.

> Oh I'm an absolutely different being, total freedom,
> total freedom. You know and even in the process in
> the past few years I know there has been more change

> and more change, and I know there is more coming. I
> also know I will re-marry, I don't know who he is, I
> haven't met him yet. I'm very content, but when I meet
> him I know I'll marry. I'm 58 years old and having
> fun. When I left the convent my brother said "you've
> got a lot of catching up to do." I told him recently I've
> caught up with you and gone way beyond you, because
> I think I had experienced an intensity in life that was
> so powerful.

Virginia joyously ran around her office telling everyone she loved oral sex. She also told me sex was so important to her she strung flashing Christmas lights around her bed and left them there to celebrate her sexuality. She was 50 years old before her first experience with a man and now looks upon her relationship with great enthusiasm and exuberance. She told me she was more interested, more playful, more intense than her partner, which we agreed was probably due to the fact that she was still processing a new experience. After being a devout nun for so many years her spirituality was lost and she was in transition searching for an alternative source. In her own words she said,

> I don't have resolution to that, it's really hard for me
> and I've done everything I can imagine to find it. I
> really wonder if it can even happen because I don't
> think I even believe in God. The place that I best find
> myself besides being a Catholic, for whom it didn't
> work, is a Buddhist. It influences me a lot.

While she was still in the convent Virginia searched for many years to find her way back to the spirituality she once had; her search continues. She was not alone in feeling that coming to terms with her sexuality was somehow entwined with her spirituality. She rejoices in the former while she seeks the latter. This is a common theme expressed in a variety of ways by many contributors.

Ruth spoke briefly about attending intimacy workshops. Lisa, unknown to Ruth and on the opposite coast, also attended these workshops. A long time into our interview after sharing some intimate details of her relationship with her friend within the convent Lisa told me,

> God, I've never ever told anyone these things before, I must feel really free to talk. I've never ever talked about it before; you know I don't even know that I would be able to be this open with you if I had not experienced these workshops. No way, I would never have shared these things with you, that is just a realization. That workshop just said, hey this is your humanity, this is who you are, this is okay, it's not wrong to be like this with another human being whether it is a man or a woman. Thank you, thank you for that because it was love, it wasn't using, it was love. I can understand people who are gay. God, our society is so screwed up about that. I'm proud, I'm proud that I had the courage to do what I did at the times when there were so many restrictions about not doing it. My God, I'm a damn courageous woman! I'm a damn good woman! Sex is indomitable unless you castrate yourself, unless you rip that part of you out.

This statement said two things. First is the growth that was evidenced by both Lisa and Ruth in attending these workshops in order to explore and gain knowledge about their own sexuality. They are not alone in this search; most of the women had been in some form of therapy and all were most eager to explore the question of their sexual growth. Second, it is testament as to the usefulness of this methodology for eliciting personal feelings and insights.

Sophia was a virgin until her wedding night and her 28-year marriage was monogamous. There was no history of self-pleasure because she felt it was not necessary when she had a partner. As far as she was aware, her husband never self-pleasured either. Although theirs was a very traditional marriage she had always considered herself a very sexually open woman. She said,

> I have gay men friends, for the opera, shopping things like that. I've always had gay friends. I like to be around gay men, I feel real comfortable. I have lesbian friends, in fact I have one friend at the moment who was lesbian and then got married. Her husband died and she's openly gay now and we're good friends. It's not a problem. My brother and his lady friend say, we love to be around you because we just never know what to expect. I'm very comfortable with anybody's sexuality, anybody's race, it doesn't bother me.

In the two years since her husband's death her life and home have been transformed. One of her gay friends took her to a sex shop and helped her buy toys and condoms. She laughed and said,

> I never practiced birth control but lost a lot of pregnancies. Now I'm buying all this stuff. I bought the *Joy of Sex* and lots of other books because he told me it would be good for me. He's a great friend. When my husband died I didn't date or go out much. I had my gay friends and my girlfriends. There were one or two attempts by men but I thought it was rude so soon after my husband's death. One man asked me out to dinner and I told him I'd have to ask my son. My son and his roommates got dressed up and waited to see this guy before I went out.

This last comment points to Sophia's traditional views and practices, (obtaining her son's approval before she went out on her first date). Yet at the time of our interview she was dating a much younger man and said she had a lot of fun with him (sexually). She is openly vivacious, sexual, and very happy. At the time the

Church refused to allow her to marry her late husband. She told the priest to "go to hell" and only goes to Church to support her friends and family by attending services.

Kate's life-story was one of major change, with the exception of her job. When she left the convent after 30 years she continued her career, but she said,

> Now I never pray, never go to Church and my friend
> the priest, I loved when I was in the convent, can't un-
> derstand it. It used to mean so much to me, and now
> I just don't think about it. I don't know, I guess I'm
> over that, too. I did it; it's finished. It's not that I don't
> like God; it's that I don't have any reason to deferaver
> to God, I don't think I'm mad or upset. My life is very
> full and being religious at all is just not viable at all
> now. I may go back, but not right now. My relation-
> ship with God was always close even when I was a
> child. I was in such distress because of my Dad. Isn't
> that amazing? So it really ties back to my Dad and al-
> coholism and so it's been a long relationship. So being
> in love with God filled a big space in my life.

Since Kate left the convent she had made attempts to meet people through dating agencies with no success. Her priest friend was leaving his order but she felt this was not a viable relationship because she felt he was insecure. Since she had now established her bi-sexuality her options are wider. She said,

> I see myself open and I love people in general and
> now I'm open to lots of people. I'm lots more relation-
> ship oriented. I think lots more things are going to
> happen to me. I tend to still be passive--just as I said
> that--things are going to *happen* to me. I need to make
> things happen for me.

231

One from the group who left the convent after a short time was June. She went back home after one year in the convent and married her old boyfriend within another year. She was a virgin until her wedding night and said she owes her positive feeling about sexuality to her husband. She had six children in eight years because birth control was not allowed in any form for practicing Catholics. Her brother who was a priest "would not give permission" for her to use contraception and so she rationalized,

> If it's evil to stop conception, it's also evil to have so
> many children you can't look after them. That's how I
> made my decision. It caused great anguish at the time,
> but it also allowed me to be more open sexually with
> my husband, every contact was not a cause for fear of
> getting pregnant. How can you be open to sex when
> you're scared to death of getting pregnant?

Because June was so young and inexperienced when she married, her sexual growth took place within the marriage. She said sexuality had grown in importance over the years. Her voracious reading habit had given her a lot of food for fantasy. The fantasy she was most attached to involves bondage and rape. This leads her to quite considerable conflict in her relationship with her husband. She had not shared this fantasy with him but finds it difficult to turn on sexually without the stimulus of her fantasy. This made her feel guilty because she felt it detracted from her intimate relationship with her husband. This fantasy also had a mystical quality for her, one that she was in the process of trying to understand. She told me the fantasy causes her some distress, since her mysticism and spirituality are entwined with her sexuality. She denied ever having been sexually assaulted, and repeated that the genesis of the fantasy was in the books she read. June did not say, nor did I ask, if the male in her fantasies was a God-like figure. This would have been an important question since all of us were potential brides of Christ with daily reminders about keeping our virginity and chastity pure for our only lover. I am reminded of the holy cards I received from my fellow sisters on my clothing day (the day one receives the habit). One inscription read, "This *Love* is *Being showered* on you Frances, *prove* yourself *Worthy* of it. *Do* all for *the Glory* of *God*-your *Beloved* and *future Spouse*." Another read, "And looking up they saw no man there but only Jesus." Finally, "Jesus Christ is mine and I am His." All the messages, both explicit and implicit during formation are to see God and Jesus Christ as lover on a spiritual level. It was possible that some of the stimulation for her fantasy could have been formed in the convent. A young impressionable 16-year-old, a voracious reader all her life but sexually naive and repressed may form sexual ideation from gazing at images of the crucified Christ for many hours. Later in life perhaps this experience could explain the fantasy of the bondage scene.

June was very much involved with the Church and actively supported her husband in becoming a Deacon. There was some conflict here because she felt she was instrumental in her husband's success. She worked harder in the course, scored higher than he did yet it was her husband who put on the robes of office and she cannot. With a little laugh she recalls ribbing the priests while she was helping her husband, "I straighten the vestments and say, see what you celibates are missing; you have nobody to dress you." She strongly believes priests should be allowed to marry. She was independently involved in an organizational role in a new parish, and finds her spirituality growing as well as her sexuality.

Hazel, the wonderful storyteller, remains devoutly Catholic and also thoroughly focused on learning more about herself on every level. She expressed real pleasure in having a forum to examine her past sexual growth. Today she and her husband are going through more changes as they adapt to her husband's health problems. She was very aware of the impact on their sexuality of this illness and was attentive to finding ways to overcome those issues. Sexuality was still important to her, as was her devotion to Catholicism and her personal spirituality.

Stephanie was 28 when she left the convent after being there for 10 years. She said she didn't want to have a relationship immediately upon leaving the convent. It was a year after leaving before her first relationship. Sexuality, she said, was never a big deal for her, and she was a self-described conservative person. Yet when she left the convent she remembered a conversation she had with her mother about sex.

> I remember having a conversation with my Mom about it because she felt you shouldn't have a sexual relationship before you were married. I remember saying, Mom I'm 29 years old, this is stupid. Who cares if I'm married or not married? The only thing that matters now at least to me is if I had a child out of wedlock. Not because it was moral but how would I take care of the child, I wasn't making enough money to do it all.

I asked Stephanie if she felt that the man she married courted her, or did she go out looking for a partner?

> Definitely courted, I was afraid to be aggressive. No, not so much afraid, I was uncomfortable with being aggressive and I still am. That's the way I was trained sexually, that's the way I was brought up. I'm still uncomfortable with that. Watching my daughter's generation they will call boys and I think that's great but some little part of me isn't comfortable with it happening too much. I guess that's from my past.

I asked, "Do you regret the restrictions placed upon you when you look back?" She responded, "I think there is probably a happy balance between the two and I would have preferred to have walked that line rather than the completely free flowing." I asked if she could take a look at herself now and try to imagine what her life would have been like without those restraints; a very difficult question,

> I probably would have been--um--it's hard to say, I'm a shy person naturally anyway, and I don't know why I'm shy. I don't know if it's the way I'm made or the way I was trained. So I don't know that I would have been any less restricted anyway. I don't know why I was that way, there are so many factors that made me the way I am; maybe I would still have been fearful anyway. I think I probably thought I'd never have children. I never planned to have children because from being twelve I wanted to be a sister and when that didn't work out, I didn't have a plan. I was open to it but I didn't think I needed to rush out and find someone and have children. Although by the time I was about 33 I thought if I don't meet someone by the time I'm 35, maybe I'll adopt a child because I felt I wanted children by then but not initially. I was in a vacuum for a while. When I first saw the man I married I thought, "Phew he's a handsome guy," and he is still a very good-looking man, not so young anymore but he's cute. Then as I got to know him a little more, I thought this man is a real pompous ass. He's very in charge and very confident, and he irritated me. I remember talking to Mom about him, she was interested in getting me married off so that I was squared away so she could relax, but I told her he's a pompous ass and I'm really uncomfortable with him. We were acquaintances for a couple of years, we would see each other occasionally and then he called me and asked

me out to a play and I said okay. I went just because
I wanted to see the play. Then I got to know him on a
more personal basis and I realized he was a very good
man, and he is a very good man. It gradually, very
gradually, grew to be love and wanting to have his
children, take care of him and do the family thing. It
came together once we got to that point.

She added a sardonic comment of "Boring, right?" as an end
to this statement. I wanted to know what she felt about her sexuality today, and so therefore asked her what she felt.

It's dull, it's very dull and it's like we are so busy
there's no time to enjoy each other. It's like it's a little
corner stuffed somewhere. Even if I had time for it,
it's not something I would choose first, I'd much rather
go put my feet in the ocean, bake in the sun, or read
a good book. It's not a large part of my life anymore,
it was for a long time, I'd say until seven or eight
years ago. My husband is a really intense man, he's
a workaholic, he's gone all the time. I feel he doesn't
have time to do enough pausing to spend time with me
and I probably resent that. I feel like he's always rushing in and rushing out. I don't know if he cares if I'm
even there as long as the food is there and the clothes
are washed and the house is clean. I know he would
deny all that and he would say, "That's not true, you're
number one," but that's how I feel and that colors our
sex life. I don't want to be intimate with someone
who doesn't have time for me so I've just lost interest.
Certainly I watch TV or a movie and see a cute hunky
little guy on there, or see some cute little butts at a
game or something and thought I wouldn't mind pat-

ting their little butts. Of course I wouldn't do it in real
life, but I sat there and fantasized about it. I still have
all those feelings, but not for my husband.

Stephanie denied ever contemplating an affair. "No, I wouldn't
do that, and not because it's immoral but because it's hurtful. I
wouldn't hurt myself and I wouldn't hurt him or my kids, it would
be damaging to everybody." At this point I asked Stephanie how
she dealt with her sexual feelings since she told me that she did not
self-pleasure often, and she said,

It's not a big deal, I put it away; it's not the important
thing in my life; my kids are, and now they are getting
to the point where they will be going off on their own
and that will be a big issue for me. What does Mom do
with Mom when they are off doing their own thing. I
think I felt, once I had children, I was a real person and
now they're going off and does that mean I'm not going
to be a real person? I don't know what to do about that,
I have to do a whole lot of exploring around that.

Stephanie still considers herself a Catholic, though she describes herself more as a Christian.

I certainly have the basic philosophy, I think I'm
Christian. I don't care what the Pope says, I honor
him as a good man, but I don't do everything he tells
me. It is difficult to raise my children in a Catholic environment that I don't agree with at least in this area.
It's not like it was for me, there probably is no religion
like that anymore. I'm really down on institutional-
ized religions. I don't think that's what Jesus meant to
do in the first place.

Another long-term married woman was Alison; she and her husband have had twenty-five years of marriage. She entered the convent at 18 years and stayed for 11 years. Alison met her husband at the wedding of a friend of hers before she left the convent. She didn't see him again for a year after her departure from community. However, after their next meeting in the summer, they married within a year. The reason Alison gave for avoiding intercourse prior to marriage was fear of pregnancy. She became pregnant almost immediately after her wedding but this pregnancy failed. She went on to have three live children in quick succession. When she thought she was pregnant again four months after the birth of their third child her husband had a vasectomy. They are both active, devout Catholics and she justifies the decision to have the sterilization as it made no sense to keep having babies one after the other. She said she knows they should be excommunicated but they still continue in their religious practices undaunted. "The rule didn't make sense. I didn't feel the Vatican or the Pope had any business making that decision for me."

Alison and her husband have always been steadfastly monogamous. She had a hysterectomy at 40 years and breast cancer six years ago. The chemotherapy affected her sexual drive somewhat. However, she still felt herself to be a sexual woman. She wishes they could be more sexual but felt confident that they have a very good sex life, "It's never been just sex for us, it's always been making love and is very special."

It is astonishing to consider the power that could repress such strong, independent women as this group proved to be. It was a power which was so much stronger for so long than their understanding of their sex drive. The following stories will illustrate that it was, on occasion, a corrupt power, which the women were fully aware of. Yet while some women attempted to live their own vows of chastity, priests who should have been bound by equally strong vows perpetrated abuses at worst and at best simply ignored their vows.

The next contributor to this Chapter is somewhat different from the rest. She was asked to leave her community, not as in Lois's case for being an outspoken radical but because she "blew the whistle" on the misconduct of priests and seminarians in the parish where she worked. The focus for me in this story was to evaluate how a woman dedicated to her religious life, with no intention of leaving, was impacted by her own desire for honesty and the need to protect her integrity. Rachael had been a nun for 13 years when she became embroiled in a situation which was to change her life trajectory.

> I was working in quite a traditional setting doing counseling and teaching. At that time we were still being assigned to our jobs and I got what was supposed to be the plum assignment. One of the women who had been a council member in our community, which is almost a lifelong deal, her brother and this priest were classmates, and the two men and this woman went to Catholic university together, so there's a long, long history. One of my first shocking introductions to any kind of sexuality was when a priest was sent to our parish to live and for counseling so that he could go back and work, a relative of the pastor. The reason I knew about this is that I was on the parish council and I had approximately one third of my meals with the priests every week, so knew everything that was going on. It was mentioned at one of the planning meetings that he had been arrested for soliciting in one of the neighboring towns and that he had been in a psychiatric clinic. You know I wasn't getting this so I asked if the man was selling drugs, why is he going to live half a block from a Catholic girl's high school? And they looked at me like I was very innocent. It was so funny as the pastor explained in great detail to me that the man was homosexual

and the girls were in no danger. There was always a
lot of discussion about married clergy and married
religious. I guess another of my enlightenments came
when I was asked to deliver a package to another parish out of town. The pastor said I want you to know
that this is Saturday, and when you get there, and he
mentioned the name of the priest, his wife and child
will probably be there because they stay at the rectory
every weekend. He didn't want me to say some stupid
thing. I worked in the parish for four years. There
was more and more sexual activity among people that
I was aware of. I don't know when it started but the
two priests that I worked with were dating and apparently the pastor also because shortly after I left, he left
and was married. One of the women from a religious
community that was in the school came down and I
mentioned to the priests that she was going to be coming. The guys said I know so and so will be here in
a month. I said who's so and so? Oh that's her lover,
and sure enough the guy was living in the rectory in a
month. This was very common knowledge.

It transpired that this couple followed each other around in
their religious houses. I asked if they remained in religious life.

This particular couple left. I know others that did
stay and it was a real awakening for me during those
years. It wasn't something I considered for myself,
maybe because I never met anybody, I don't know.
I didn't have much time. I was doing so much and
religious life and work life were so important to me I
couldn't see that anything else could be included. One
of your questions was, would it have made any differ-

ence to you if you could have been sexual and stayed in the convent? No. The reason I left the community was, well, I didn't have any problem with people having these personal sexual relationships. That was their own decision. But I was responsible for training seminarians and I was responsible to have them visit people and have different groups do social activities, religious classes, scripture discussion, this sort of thing. I had them for a couple of years. Everything seemed to be going reasonably well and then we had a switch. Some went to another parish to work and we got some more. A couple I had known for a long time in the parish were very helpful and I had them do extra work with the seminarians which they volunteered to do. One day they called me up and asked if I would go over to see them, they had a problem they would like to discuss with me. They wanted to know if they really had to have sex with the new guy? I was absolutely horrified, because it was not a real consensual agreement. These guys were using their position and taking advantage of people. They were young clerics in their 20s; the ones that we got at that point were all college graduates.

I asked Rachael if they were trying to coerce both the men and the women into sex.

It was both. One of them was going and having sex separately with both and playing them off against each other. In other cases, it was just one person. There were about half a dozen people involved in this. It was just too much for me. I didn't know how to handle it; I did not know how to approach the pastor. We were literally the first parish to have the students, experimental situation. I was trying to figure out what I was going to do when one of these guys came to me and told me he'd heard about the people coming to me and wanted to know if I was upset. I told him I was more than upset, that these young men were here as a representative of the Church to nurture these people's lives not to take advantage of them and use their position to abuse them. I told them, "If you want to have a personal relationship with someone, that's different." Well he didn't see it that way and that's not what his confessor told him. Then I found out that these guys all had the same confessor and they were having relations with him. It was beyond me. So I decided the best thing that I could do was go back to the community with this. It was a very bad mistake. I went back to the community to the Sister who had been my work supervisor who had got me the job and who was the woman I mentioned previously who was close with the pastor. Anyway that was just before she was elected the Superior General of the community. I told her I really needed some help in dealing with this but I knew it couldn't go on. She accused me of lying and that I was trying to destroy the seminary and destroy the Church, and that if I didn't recant what I'd said she was going to throw me out of the community. I had no choice. So I said fine, I'll just have to sign my papers because it's true, I can't say it's not. Something has to be done; it can't be allowed to go on. So I signed my papers that day and that was that. I don't know what happened but the pastor left town soon after that and the people were not willing to continue

the training program because there was nobody there
to do it and then it went into more of a diocesan-wide
program for all of the seminarians. I'm sure it went
on and I know very well in view of all the things that
have come to light in the diocese of this city that it
continued and that it wasn't just limited to that small
area. I have always been very sorry that I didn't do
anything to stop it. I mean I didn't know what to do at
that time. At that point I left the community and went
to work in social services in the city and have been
there ever since; that was in 1968. I was 32 years old.
This was a real shock, I had absolutely no plan, but
I had no choice. As I speak to people now they say,
"But you had rights." What did we know about rights
back then, come on? We didn't have any rights, nobody thought about rights. It was very, very difficult. I
had some very low periods and I still do. I was able to
resolve that and got on with my life.

A seminarian that she worked with for a while developed a very
strong relationship with her and they became lovers. He was from
the same seminary as the priests in her previous story and was still
a practicing priest. She continued with her story with these words.

He told me he had been lucky because he had been
assigned to the confessor from the previous group
and, after he made a move on him he had asked to be
reassigned to a new confessor. He was ordained and
we were still seeing each other; we were very close. I
don't know why he got ordained because he always
talked about leaving but that was his thing, not mine.
I went to his parish one day for something and the
assistant pastor's girlfriend was there, and she said

something about my friend's girlfriend, and it wasn't
me. I questioned him and I found out that he was also
having relations with the other assistant. That he had
lied to me about his confessor also, because it was the
same man and he said he learned from this confessor
that it was okay to tell people whatever you wanted to.
That was that, off I went. Now with hindsight and maturity if there is this problem I don't want anything to
do with it. This was my first experience and I thought
I don't need someone like this, for anything. That was
the end of that. Later he married someone else and
I haven't seen or heard of him for years. Afterwards
I wondered how I could have been so stupid after all
that went on, how could I have even talked with someone from there?

I asked for clarification if she felt that this was an isolated incident in one seminary with one unscrupulous confessor. She told
me, "I know that there have been some similar, more isolated incidents in smaller areas. There's no way of knowing how widespread
this is." Now this incident has been behind her for many years and
she got on with her life. I asked her how she saw her sexuality
had changed over the years since she left the convent and stopped
socializing with men of the Church. She continued,

I dated a few people, I was not really interested in
developing a relationship and having children; I have
never seen that as my role in life. It seems interesting
and pleasurable but not something I want to do. I met
my partner 20 years ago through someone at work.

For a year he asked her to go to lunch until she asked outright
if he wanted lunch or a date. He wanted a date and so they began
to see each other. They developed a close friendship. They decided that they would live together and share everything but neither

244

wanted to get married and have children. She explained,

> In the beginning we had a sexual relationship, on and
> off I enjoyed it, like every other couple it's up and
> down. It's hard to answer a question how often do you
> have sex? Because it varies, sometimes we'd have lots
> and sometimes little. Then about 15 years ago we did
> some experimental group-sex.

They stayed at a motel that was used almost exclusively by
nudists and swingers, and they met someone they knew who invited them into a playroom. They went to the room and enjoyed it,
and went back a few times. She said she found it exciting, but the
AIDS scare curtailed their participation. She continued,

> Maybe about 10 years ago, our lifestyles got very ac-
> tive. We really took stock of our lives and we elimi-
> nated a lot of things. I said I really have to see what
> I want to include in my life. I suggested many things
> that we should give up and one of them was sex, for
> time and energy. I loved it but I don't know, it was
> just time and energy; when I got home it was just too
> much and it became just another chore. It was not
> essential to our relationship. So we decided to do that
> and we have been in this celibate relationship for about
> 10 years and it's worked very well for us. There may
> be a time when that will change but we're not looking
> at it right now. We were happy when we were having
> sexual relations and we're happy now. I miss it oc-
> casionally, sure. If I really thought it was something
> essential, for him or for me, I would resume it. So that
> is where I am in my life.

I was curious to know if she engaged in similar methods to sublimate her sexuality as she had done when she entered the convent. She answered,

> No, I don't think so because I don't see sexuality as
> sex alone, I see it as sensuality and really your whole
> being and I don't feel that it's gone. I masturbate,
> but not very often. All my life if I was going to do
> something I set my mind on it and that's the way it
> was going to be. I think that's the way I do each day,
> and whether I'm sick or have a headache, this is what
> I'm going to accomplish this day. It wasn't as if I
> decided I was giving it up because I didn't like it. It
> was simply that my life was overcrowded and at that
> point I couldn't give up going to work or any of the
> other demands and sex to me was something that was
> expendable. It took time and energy. It wasn't the ce-
> ment that held our relationship together.

Rachael's story is significant in that she was the only one who was forced to leave in this fashion. Although while in the convent she would not engage in sexual relationships with clerics, she did so once out. She made no reference to this contradiction. Her sexual practices also are deserving of mention, namely being open to group sex, to living out of wedlock amongst other things. She was able to make the transitions in her life with a lot of calculation. Maintaining her integrity was integral to her decisions. Given the huge blow her expulsion from the community dealt her life plan, it was a great credit to her flexibility that she was able to make such a success out of her life. At no point in our interview did she express any regrets apart from disappointment at the ill treatment by her superior and her involvement with the seminarian.

Elizabeth also spoke about sexuality of priests and nuns as being a widespread issue and she learned about this because several years into her career in the convent she was chosen to be a leader in her community and went away to school to prepare for the job. She met a man who became a very good friend.

> We talked a lot, we shared a lot, we gave each other back rubs, I was into learning massage at the time but there was nothing sexual, nothing overtly sexual even though the energy probably was, there was nothing overtly so. I got close to other men and women there but we never did anything sexual. One of the women actually had a friend come visit and they were lesbians, she left her community and moved in with this woman. Another nun fell in love with a brother from Australia and they're still friends and they're still in their communities so I had a lot of experience at that time. Then I came back and was working in my new position and I got really sick; things were difficult from then until I left the community eight years later. I really feel it was my body rebelling. I had been repressing parts of me, including sexuality, enthusiasm, joy. My body finally gave out. I did a lot of spiritual direction at the time, I did a lot of retreats for priests and nuns, I was kind of surprised that every priest and brother that I ever worked with on retreat or spiritual direction had sexual relations, every one of them. Some long term, some occasional. Only a couple of women did, and I worked more with women than men. Every man did that, I think that was really interesting. What's this about celibacy, what's the Church really doing to these men?

I wanted to know if this was any specific area of the priest-hood, for example diocesan priests only or missionary priests. She answered,

> Orders and diocesan both, some missionaries. I
> worked with so many. There were a lot more homosex-
> uals among the diocesan priests and in this one group
> of brothers. Most of those in community had some
> needs met by being in community, their personal, not
> sexual needs. I think that for men, the preservation
> of the species is just so strong that they are a lot more
> sexual. I still work with men and I think every man
> that I work with has relations with someone other
> than his wife. Isn't that interesting? They don't all
> act on it. I'm thinking of one client who always has
> another woman and in the guise of spirituality. It's not
> sexual, but most of the others have been. I just find
> men different from women. Women are often satisfied
> with closeness and cuddling, but men have that drive
> so strong. That's been my experience anyway. This
> is an important point. When I was doing spirituality
> for a center at a university, one of the guys who was
> in the group had a friend who was a novice master in
> another state, who he wanted me to meet because he
> said we were so much alike. So he did finally come
> to visit and we had an immediate connection. It was
> really powerful. We shared all the same interests, all
> the experiences. He was doing the same job as me and
> had gone through the same training a year ahead of
> me. We grew to be really good friends, even though
> he was in another state and I was here. He decided
> the next year to take sabbatical the next year to do his

Master's and wanted me to fly to his state and drive out with him. I couldn't do that. But the next year he came out for my birthday and we went to dinner. He said he'd been working with his spiritual director and decided he'd done everything in his life except make love with a woman. Finally with the help of the Spiritual Director he had decided that this was the time. I told him, "Well it's not my time because I'm choosing to stay in my community." He said, "Oh I'm choosing to stay in community too, but this is what I want and I want you to be the woman." I said, "No way, but I'll still be your friend." He in fact did have an affair with this woman on the same program, which was clearly his next level. I felt really betrayed. How could he do that? I wanted to keep it at the level of friendship. In fact he became the stimulus to make me take a good look at myself and decide whether this is really what I want for the rest of my life. That's finally when I left. I did a lot of work with my spiritual director and my doctor; he told me "The environment you're allergic to may be the community." I took one year's leave of absence. With the help of my Spiritual Director I got well. Meanwhile, my friend the priest before he left the priesthood, before he said anything to his community, married a woman. It was really ugly. Then he left his community. I left my community during winter Solstice '88 and met the man I married in May. I dated him for a couple of years. We were sexual before we married.

In retrospect Elizabeth regretted not taking the opportunity to be sexual with the priest. However she pointed out that it would have been impossible given her senior position within the order.

When I pointed out the conflict in the situation she responded, "It was, [a conflict] and it wasn't. The conflict was felt in my body but my head was very clear. Because I had made my choice, I had made my vows." Elizabeth became very sick in her years at University. The illness presented as allergies and progressed until,

> I was curled up in bed; I thought I had flu. I went
> home at the end of that year quite sick and they called
> it environmental allergies to all sorts of things. I went
> from being very healthy, real capable, to wanting to
> sleep a lot. I felt rejected a lot because of the changes
> in me. One of my friends said, "I don't even know
> you anymore." That's how sick I was. I probably had
> it for five or six years. Then I took my year off and
> felt a lot better. I went back to Formation work. It
> began in the year of my 39th birthday, so it happened
> when I was 40. I talked to my Spiritual Director who
> was a Jesuit. I told him, "I'm happy in community;
> they really love me, I really love being here, I have no
> reason to leave." Finally, he said "Remember the story
> of Abraham. God didn't call him from something but
> for something, and so it was on blind faith." I thought
> that maybe God does have something in store for me
> and, if so, then I'd better be off. Maybe it's the envi-
> ronment I'm in that I'm allergic to, so I left. Then I got
> well. I didn't take the whole year and when I wrote
> my letter I said, "I made my vows until death and in
> many ways I've died." I'd been so sick that I felt like
> I'd died, so I left for health I'd say. My husband is
> great. Going in the convent the week after I turned 18
> I didn't have much experience of the world and he is
> very grounded. I carry more of the spiritual for him.
> He's not religious at all.

When she left, she wondered how she would support herself and what had all the training in spiritual life prepared her for. She was burned out on teaching but what she found was that,

> People are hungry for God. I still feel like a Formation director. I have groups of women who come and I teach spirituality in all religions and all modalities, so I'm still doing my work. It's my personal love and I'm very satisfied now. I don't feel like my time in religious life held me back from growing. It stifled a little bit of my growth, but I feel very fulfilled. Very few of my friends are truly fulfilled with who they are and what they're doing, but I truly am. A lot of my clients say they are not happy they are still searching.

I asked if she now sees a sexual and spiritual connection. As stated earlier in Lua Xochtl's story, Elizabeth showed me a picture of Teresa of Avila to illuminate her profound reply. "To me they really are part of the same. I look at that picture of St. Teresa and doesn't that look like sexual ecstasy as well a spiritual ecstasy? In a lot of my experience it's the same, just a wonderful gift that God's given us." I asked if she ever regretted staying so long in her community. She answered,

> No, I was ready when I was ready. If I had just gone to college and then got married, I wouldn't have the richness of life that I've had. I'd probably be a very straight woman. Right now I'd say my spirituality is not a Church thing at all. It's beyond it. When I left, an ex-priest came to me and told me that when he left the priesthood a woman came to him in an unthreatening way and offered herself for him to explore his sexuality with. And he said I just want to make the same offer to you, and I did and it was wonderful. He said "I have to be careful because I'm falling in love

> with you. You have so much passion." So much more
> than the woman he was going to marry, who had never
> been in a convent. I didn't like it when we stopped but
> I met Luke soon after.

The last piece of insight is that she reiterates her free spirited attitude, that she wouldn't follow the rules if she thought they were stupid, and that most of the other women she knew, who left, were like her.

Sara was the single respondent to this study who entered a missionary order, and as such can attest from personal experience what Elizabeth told me from anecdotal evidence.

> I think my experience of being attracted to people
> there [in Africa] is important. I mean the missionar-
> ies are desperate. I could have had a date every night.
> The Irish missionaries particularly were just very
> attentive, "come to the seminary, come to dinner, rock
> climbing, and mountain climbing." It was just fun you
> know in that way, just sick. I don't think there's a celi-
> bate missionary over there! I don't in any way blame
> anybody because it's just so different. It's the comfort
> you need to survive over there for any length of time.
> I wasn't sexual myself although I had the opportunity.
> I just didn't see myself as a sexual person. I wanted
> adventure more than that. I didn't take up any op-
> portunities and they were there very easily but I think
> I was in such culture shock. Then I got malaria and
> you're a pariah for a while after that. I found myself
> being flattered by the attention that I hadn't had, and
> feeling very desirable, but finding that people were
> seeking comfort for the wrong reasons. They were
> seeking the alternative, not the structured Church.

Sara left the convent after being a missionary nun for 12 years and becoming disenchanted by the life as well as facing the prospect of not being allowed to attend law school. She denied any sexual involvement within the convent although she had ample opportunity while on the mission. Once she left the convent she attended law school and dated occasionally but made no real connection. She became aware of "the old biological time clock ticking" and began to think that she didn't want to spend the rest of her life alone.

The loneliness issue came out at that time and the issue of having a child. I thought I wasn't together enough to have one. I wanted it in terms of a relationship. After law school I just had fun. You know you have this kind of an ideal image of the exact person you'd like to meet and the magic of the whole thing. A friend of mine told me about this man who was working in her firm and said she thought we'd really hit it off. I said, "Tell me about him," and she said, "Well, he's married." So I said, "Oh, I don't want to meet him." Well, she set up a situation where we would bump into each other. We did, and if I could have painted a picture of somebody that really would have gotten my rocks off this was the person. He was immediately attracted to me in the same way. It was like soul mates meeting in time, but he was recently married. His wife was living in another city. I didn't believe such a person existed, and that he should feel the same was just incredible. We had a three and a half year extremely lively erotic relationship and just very connected.

I asked Sara if that was her first sexual relationship and she hesitated for a moment before deciding to edit her story by refusing to give me details of her first sexual encounter. She made no further reference to that subject. Her story continued with the lover that she had enjoyed so much, yet knowing it wasn't going anywhere because,

> I felt guilty about his wife. I'm sure he felt guilty but it didn't stop him. It was the most incredible sex and sexual experience I've ever had. Maybe it was because it was my first prime partner. That could wear off quickly, but we could talk about anything, we did everything. We liked similar things and it was just incredible. Then his wife became pregnant and I said, "That's it" [she ended the relationship]. And then I met my current partner.

This person still holds a lot of her loyalty, for one thing because he was the father of her child. However, at the same time she felt as if it was an abusive relationship and she had been turned off and felt that she had to put a stop to the manipulation she felt. Sara concluded,

> I want someone who's there for me. I want a full relationship, not just get my rocks off. He said I was just not sexual but that's not true. You go through the question and wonder, "Am I?" But no, I want more and so I just stopped being intimate with him just because it was so much a part of the abusive relationship. He would get what he wanted and then he's out the door and down the road. I just had to stop that in my life. It was like a fix. I really wanted it in my life but I didn't want it on the terms I'd have to get it with him. Now there's just no opportunity, time or people, I'm kind of stuck for a while.

CHAPTER NINE
EPILOGUE: LIBERATION -
THE JOURNEY CONTINUES

If this belief from Heaven be sent
If such be Nature's holy plan,
Have I not reason to lament
What man has made of man?

— Wordsworth

onclusions drawn from this research, I trust, will be a trib-
ute to the women generous enough to give their time and
their life stories to help further knowledge of sexuality as
it relates to former religious women. Additionally, their understanding of the role spirituality played in their sexual development
has been enlightening to me as I hope it will be to others.

They are complex stories, sharing many commonalities but at
the same time each with its own individual characteristics. I was
looking for common themes of attitudes among a group of women
who voluntarily committed themselves to life-long celibacy and
asceticism, and then made the transition back into secular life. On
a fundamental level I found, that from childhood on, there was a
consistent and widespread attempt to repress sexuality. From that
followed my main conclusion, namely that one of the most cohe-
sive bonds between all of the participants was the irrepressibility
of their sexuality.

A common theme in all the life histories was the childhood
message (occasionally subtle, mostly adamant) that sex was some-

thing to be avoided, or even stronger. Sex was wrong and bad. It was to be feared. It was (and still is for some) a source of shame, fear and guilt, or a combination of all three. When reporting on shame and guilt surrounding sexuality, the data shows:

SHAME	N = 46	N = 44	N = 44
	BEFORE %	DURING %	AFTER %
YES	61%	48%	25%
GUILT	N = 42	N = 42	N = 42
	BEFORE %	DURING %	AFTER %
YES	50%	52%	36%

Comparative data from Ellison/Zilbergeld (1994), when self reporting on their feelings following masturbation, showed that 21% of Catholic women experienced shame and guilt equally. This compares to 15% of the general population of non-Catholic women who shared these feelings. Since my data found that one-third continued to feel guilt and 25% felt shame around sexuality (not specifically masturbation), I construed there to be an indication that some of the old lessons were still being heard. In my sample, masturbation was a sexual release, used infrequently by most that admitted to it at all. Self-pleasure was the area the majority of women still had difficulty with at the time of our interviews. The average age of first masturbatory experience from the wider data was 16 years. Frequency was on average, once a month or less. In the area of sexual repression leading to sexual expression, I would say for the above women, the repression began to ebb in the years they were in the convent. Vestiges of the old thinking were evident from Lisa and Stephanie when conflict and confusion was expressed around the area of masturbation and vows of chastity. Significant in this was that both women deferred to priests for permission around this personal practice, and did not discuss it or look for support for their own sexuality from other women.

In the stories there was no reference to fantasies before or during their entry to the convent. After they left, three women spoke about this topic. June talked about her bondage fantasy, which she was very attached to and had no understanding of except she felt it had a mystical quality. Stephanie admitted to some fantasy around the young men she saw on the television or the football field. Kathleen felt that she made her fantasy come true. In her fantasy God told her she could marry her beloved friend in a spiritual union. For this woman, sexuality and spirituality were totally entwined and she absolutely believed in the authenticity of the service she went through, which made her Laird's spiritual wife. It brought her great happiness and peace in the marriage that was so unfulfilling for her. In the questionnaire data, in all areas of sexual activity listed, there was a consistent increase in the numbers of women who fantasized as they transitioned into and out of religious life.

When asked, how important was/is sex to you? The scale was, (1) Very important (2) Important (3) Slightly important (4) Not at all important. The responses were as recorded in the following table, showing a considerable increase in the importance of sexuality in their lives:

	BEFORE %	DURING %	AFTER %
1	18%	16%	41%
2	11%	29%	43%
3	42%	32%	12%
4	29%	23%	4%

When asked about sexual satisfaction and curiosity I wanted to understand their feelings relative to their perception of most women their age. I asked, was/is your perception that you are: (1) Very much above average (2) About average (3) Somewhat below average (4) Very much below average. The responses illustrated a steady increase in their perception of growth in those areas. The tables below show an increase in number from before they entered to currently:

SATISFACTION	BEFORE %	DURING %	AFTER %
1	11%	9%	24%
2	20%	20%	43%
3	29%	28%	20%
4	40%	43%	13%

CURIOSITY	BEFORE %	DURING %	AFTER %
1	10%	11%	22%
2	47%	49%	65%
3	13%	21%	11%
4	30%	19%	2%

A good indication of change and sexual growth throughout the transitions was indicated from the answers to the question asking if clergy should be allowed to marry:

	BEFORE %	DURING %	AFTER %
YES	53%	86%	98%

All the questions with Before, During and After data, show an increase in number toward a more liberal, sexual tolerance.

The data showed the minimum age for entering the convent was 16 years old, the average age being 19 years. Of the interview group, only two women admitted to any consensual sexual experience prior to entering. Both were self-described child prostitutes although only one actually prostituted herself as a teenager for money. Marian was sexually active but did not permit penis-vagina penetration until after she married. All of the other participants denied being sexually active prior to entering, although most had dated in high school. Information in the wider data showed age for first heterosexual intercourse as:

AGE	N = 49	PERCENT
≤ 4	1	2%
15 – 20	5	10%
21 – 29	11	22%
30 – 39	22	46%
40 – 49	4	8%
Never	6	12%

Range = 4 – 47   Mean = 30

Average age for first *same sex* experience was 27 years. Proximity and availability of partners probably explains this same sex figure. Nine respondents had their first experience prior to entering and seven whilst in the convent. When asked if they were aware of sexual activity within the convent, 44% knew of activity among fellow Sisters, 54% with clergy, and 36% with lay people. Again, data from the questionnaire showed four women admitting to having had their first heterosexual intercourse while in the convent. One woman had two partners and another had ten partners.

Very few had any informed sexual knowledge prior to entering their communities. Caroline's story of the retreat priest exhorting them to refrain from French kissing was more typical of this group experience. The fact that Caroline did not know what French kissing was, was also an accurate glimpse into the sexual development more common to this group. In the general data, when asked if sexuality played a part in their decision to enter the convent 50% said it did, with 76% seeing it as an escape from sexuality. Escape from sexuality and dysfunctional, alcoholic homes predominated as the reasons given to enter religious life. The life demonstrated by the nuns to these young women was independent, respectful, peaceful and ordered. They felt empowered and had life choices and options not available to them should they have remained in their family of origin, where female role models were, in their opinion, disrespected and disempowered. A fundamental influence in most cases was silence around sexual subjects. Silence, coupled with power of parents and priests, seems to have been a negative force in most cases. When I began this study, I anticipated finding the influence of fathers to be paramount in the suppression of sexuality in the life history of the subjects. Although in some cases this was true, as in Helen's and Sophia's stories, fathers were memorable for their alcoholism and physical abuses in the worst cases, yet overall, did not appear to have had traumatic effects on the women. Ruth, June, Miriam, Marian, Virginia, Pamela, Hilary, Ursula, Ione, Kathleen and Maria, expressed stories of lasting pain experienced by them because of neglect or cruelty perpetrated by their mothers. Mothers appeared to be very much more prevalent as negative forces on these women, leaving life-long scars of painful criticism and perceived neglect. I am reminded of Louisa May Alcott's words, "What *do* girls do who haven't any mothers to help them through their troubles?" Girls such as Ursula, Caroline and Kathleen were representatives of one end of the spectrum. These were women who spent their lives searching for their mother's love and always wondering why they were not worthy of it. Undoubtedly, a major force in these women's lives was their longing for a mother's love. Lua Xochil's motherless infancy and childhood represented this forcefully. For many, the affection and attention given to them by their nun teachers was the greatest force in their decision to enter the convents. The kindness and devotion of these women predominated in the narratives.

There was such a high incidence of perceived abuse and alcoholism in this group that I had to look at the reason why I neglected to address the issue in my questionnaire, and neglected to anticipate its prevalence in the interviews. I came to the conclusion that silence and prohibition around sexual subjects was such a part of my own background that it was an unconscious denial and suppression on my part to avoid a forbidden topic. Further, the image of the perfect family, where the children were expected to portray to the world "their best face" was I think, endemic to this type of background, thus enabling the abuses to continue with impunity. This behavior was amply illustrated in Chapter Four, particularly in Margaret's story. She was the victim of incest by her brothers and friends from the age of four. On entering the convent she said she was very lonely because she had a mental image that she came from the perfect family. It took a long time before she saw how dysfunctional that thinking was. I have had numerous conversations with therapists all around the country who have, and still are, working with religious men and women. Their anecdotal reports, together with new empirical data from Chibnall, Wolf and Duckro , plus other reports from abused nuns, convinces me that the subject has only just begun to be addressed and much more work needs to be done in this area. This group of women had done a lot of work on their own issues and continued to search for answers. As Pamela said, "After growing up in the Catholic Church, all the bad things they say about sex, that I don't believe, must be still inside me. After all these years it makes me pissed off and I want to learn more about sex, so that I can be more of a sexual person."

When they entered religious life, all but two of the young women continued in the same pattern as their family of origin, namely that of an autocratic, patriarchal environment. Silence was the defined way of dealing with sexual issues in their childhood and this method was continued in the convent. Personal friendships were strictly prohibited and any interaction on a one-to-one basis was denied. The formation period was when the young women were totally isolated from family and the outside world. The result for many was dependency, servility and subjugation, particularly with regard to their sexuality that was never allowed free expression. The exception to this group was Sara. She entered after Vatican II and had very different novitiate experiences from that of the majority. However, she was expected to follow the rule of chastity, and did so. All of the women repressed their sexuality to some degree whilst they were in the convent.

To overcome dependency and sexual silence is never easy, especially in a world where the Superior's powers are maximal and the subordinate's power is minimal, and the required response to every order is complete obedience. Very often the result is rebellion or a childlike, blind obedience. Rebellion in this group took the form of physical illness. As stated in Chapter Five, depression, general physical illness, anorexia and allergies were amongst those reported. Understanding the root cause of these conditions appears to have evaded both Sister and Superiors. None of those who had been in counseling told me that they had been advised to express their sexuality. Two had been in some way molested by their priest therapists and yet remained in their orders for some time afterwards. They did not tell me that they felt they had received the message that being sexual was healthy or permitted. In some way the opposite message was given, and it left the women feeling confused and guilty.

The 1960's saw many social upheavals. Of particular importance to this group was Vatican II which demanded more personal accountability from every member of the community. At the same time the feminist movement was further demanding women to claim their full place in society. Several women referred to this fact during their stories when they said they entered in order to love more, not less, and to devote their lives to a higher calling. They told me that they would have joined the Peace Corps had it been available to them. By entering religious life they thought they could devote themselves to a higher standard, because women they saw at home were not honored, and nuns were. A truth, for all but Ursula, was that the convent was a safe nurturing place. With very few exceptions they had only positive things to say about their Sisters and their communities. Even those who had experienced severe illness so described their time within their communities.

The struggle to stay in religious life while at the same time honoring their integrity and enjoying an open relationship became very complicated for at least one subject. Maria tried to live *The Third Way* (described in Chapter 6) which was an alternative to strict monasticism. Sipe discusses *The Third Way* in depth, along with the philosophy behind it, and attributes the founding of this philosophy to Dr. Eugene Kennedy, a former priest. In a telephone interview on April 8.1998, Dr. Kennedy told me that he had written articles for different magazines in the 1960s and 70s, articulating his belief that human relationships were more important than any structure. He felt that many religious men and women today tried to live this "high order," deepening their personal relationships while working together within the Church. He said,

> I don't believe the Third Way is viable for most people…In 1966 or 1970, I observed it and I interpreted it, but never proposed it. I have always supported healthy relationships whether between priests and nuns or anyone else. It is much better to have healthy relationships.

Given the prevalence in my study of relationships between nuns and religious men, many were practicing *The Third Way* even though they did not label their actions as such. Others had covert sexual relationships. Some women rationalized that as long as they weren't genitally sexual it was acceptable behavior. Only one of these women did not adamantly assure me that no genital sex took place. This self-editing is in itself interesting. Those women who had same-sex relationships also avoided genital contact. They fulfilled their sexual needs with kissing, cuddling and breast play. In some cases they had developed enough of a sense of independence as to be able to take full responsibility without making any excuses or giving an explanation other than that was what they had done. They felt no guilt or conflict. Grace and Kate are in this category and were fully sexual whilst still under vows. The group who were sexual within the convent, but left in order to be fully, i.e. genitally sexual (their definition), is a lot larger. Marian, Miriam, Maria, Helen, Hilary, Pamela, Virginia, and Ione stated the fact that they needed to leave in order to have the freedom to express themselves sexually.

Apart from Ione, who discovered her lesbian tendencies in her early years in religious life, all those who were sexual during their time in community began these relationships after they had been in for an average of 10 years. All held their relationships to be very special and retained in their memories with great warmth and delight. Only in Maria's story did I detect some feelings of the relationship within the convent being somewhat one-sided. She was giving pleasure to her priest friend, whilst receiving little sexual pleasure in return. This disparity appears to have continued to some degree throughout their lives outside of religious life.

For most of those women who left, married and had children, their sexual progression appears to have been in response to the needs and coaching of their husbands. Reports often included such statements as, "he taught me," "he showed me," and "I learned from him," amongst many others. Pamela was an interesting case in that she married a man 12 years her junior who was a religious brother, yet he gave her sexual self-help books and was able to teach her. Stephanie was the only member of the group to express boredom in her sex life, and this was mainly due to the inattention of her husband. She displayed a healthy fantasy life, even though she rarely acted upon it with self-pleasure. The remainder of the married women with children expressed great interest in sex.

The struggle to merge sexuality and spirituality is a phenomenon particularly experienced by Catholic religious men and women. Few other religions require this sacrifice. Reflectively, the majority of this group did not declare a devout love of God as their primary reason for entering religious life. However, they did find religious life sufficiently fulfilling to subjugate the full expression of their sexuality for, in some cases, as many as 30 years. The average stay for this group was 13 years. Those who remained in religious life beyond the novitiate, and took vows, saw the legitimate outlet of their sexuality to be in their work. Those who only experienced their postulancy and part of the novitiate said that prayer and work occupied them totally. All of those who stayed for many years stated their work was their passion. As Maria said it was where they "were juiced." This, combined with strict discipline, was designed to control sexual urges. Lua Xochitl said sexual energy went into cleaning floors and scrubbing and polishing and teaching school. Maria spoke of getting some subliminal sexual pleasure by being on good friendly terms with her male students. This was in her early days in the convent before she met the priest she was to fall in love with. Spirituality became conflicted, as they became more sexually aware. The very anchor that was holding them to religious life began to slip. The old message that sexuality was bad and dirty and can easily be repressed, worked for a time, using the tools they had learned in their youth. Then they grew up in the convent and found sexuality within themselves, and for themselves. Many spoke of the safe haven the convent provided for them. It gave them time to think in a sex-free environment, if that was what they chose. They began to question the suppression. Sara particularly argued the case for more sexual education with her Formation Directors. It appeared that the need to freely express that part of themselves that could be called sexual became relentless. When Lua Xochitl discovered self-pleasure it opened up her sexual world. The others discovered their suppressed sexuality by meeting someone who ignited it.

Ursula, whose life struggle had been to merge her sexuality with her spirituality, continued that struggle. I realized from our opening prayer together and the candles she burned as we spoke, the incredible depth to this woman's pain and the need to express her story. I hope, in the reading of this work, she finds a little enlightenment and insight brought about by shared repression and pain of other participants. However, she had spent the past 15 years nurturing herself, and is at a point where she is beginning to accept her body, and not see herself as "dirt of a pig" for honoring the beauty and the mystery of her nature. She sees God as a loving and personal entity and, at 75 years old, very clearly illustrates how we as human beings bring terrible dishonor to ourselves when we do not claim our bodies, honor and accept our sexuality. Because Catholic young people grew up with the message sex is bad and in opposition to the good, which was spiritual, attempting to merge the two in a healthy lifestyle was very difficult for some. I believe for a majority of the populace on this planet, sexuality is integral to our spiritual nature and is as important a component in making up a whole person. Because of fragmenting at such an early age, many people have had to spend the rest of their lives trying to put the pieces back together again.

I expected celibacy to be the vow that most women, who held sexuality to be very important to them, would claim as being the one with which they had most conflict. Although the freedom to be sexual was the reason most actually left, the vow most objected to, was obedience. In fact, this was the universal reason for leaving. Some began to say chastity and then changed it to obedience. It took a while for me to realize the reason behind this. Poverty, Chastity and Obedience are the three vows taken. If the nun is truly "Obedient," all the others are controlled. To maintain their integrity, they had to confess each transgression, and being sexual was defined by the majority as a transgression. Maintaining their own sense of integrity was an issue stated in almost every interview. Mary, in her letter to Rome requesting release from her vows, cited her issues with celibacy as her reason for leaving. Yet she qualified that when she told me she really could not live the rule of obedience. On a wider level, all wanted to make decisions for themselves, keep their own money, live where they wanted and with whom they wanted. Sara actually said celibacy was her greatest conflict, and reason for leaving, and in mid-sentence changed it to obedience.

I anticipated that a majority of the sample would have remained as practicing Catholics, with all that that title entailed. This was not the case. Of those who identified as Catholic, all have separated to some degree from the dictates of the Church, particularly where it concerned contraception. In the general data, almost 100% agreed with a woman's right to control conception. All of those practicing Catholics had some degree of concern about the organization of current Church practices. The majority did not identify with what they thought was out-of-touch-Papal control. Again, the majority had broken away from strict observances of the Church, yet had maintained a deep and residing personal spirituality. These women expressed their spiritual growth as a continuing journey, one that they were still very active in researching. Many expressed concerns that the Catholic Church remains exclusively male-driven with only a minor role for women within its structure. Of those who related this male control to include sexual education, it was done so in angry terms. Ursula's words about Catholic education around sexuality still echo in my mind when she said, "I should circle this one with red blood! So many are still twisted because of that stinky education." I heard enough confusion and pain to agree with her. Those women such as June, who saw herself helping her husband achieve the Deacon's position and then having to accept the role of "dresser" and helpmate, are very justifiably angry at the inappropriate high-handedness of the Church. However, they submit because there is no alternative. Therefore, although there were representatives of the modern Catholic woman among the participants of this study, the majority had denounced the Church of their childhood on most levels. If participating at all, then it was on a modified version of their own choosing and with a great deal of their own variations. Most of those modifications were surrounding the impact of the Church's teaching on sexuality and personal marital relations, where they felt the Church had no place.

Sexual patterning is clearly shown to have changed dramatically in most cases during the transitions. Furthermore, those changes appear to be continuing. A case in point here is Grace's story. When I met this woman I was at the point of choosing my doctoral topic. Grace self defined as heterosexual having had one sexual relationship with a priest and no same sex relationship up to that time; she was 55 years old and had been out of the convent for five years. At that point in her life she had begun her first love affair with a woman and was totally open to the fact that she would probably self define as bisexual from then on. The striking point of this story is the open attitude of a woman this age, with such a background. This is one major trait common to the majority of the group. Open-minded and non-judgmental would be how I would describe them. In some sense it is a phenomenon best described by Grace when she said: "I just felt way more comfortable with sex because I was a nun, wasn't that weird?" Lua Xochitl said something similar when speaking about her experience at the weekend workshop which so changed her life. She found the nuns to be far more sexually open and avant-garde than the general populace at that workshop. I felt surprised and honored that so many trusted me with their stories and were willing to speak as candidly as they did on the issue of their sexuality. This is a highly educated group of women with the data showing 86% having attended graduate school. It had been a serious concern to me, given the retrospective quality of this research, that incidents may have been remembered that could have caused discomfort for the women. This was not the case. The emotional strength of this group has been extraordinary.

This has not been a purely intellectual pursuit. It began as such, a means to an end, that of earning a Ph.D. But it became much more. This is a work from my heart. The findings of this research have changed my own life-long perceptions of women who were nuns. These life histories have been extraordinary, given the religious background the women came from. The sexual development has been truly impressive.

In conclusion, I feel very sincerely that women generally and globally need to recognize, nurture and honor themselves to achieve wholeness. No part of that humanity can we afford to ignore or dishonor. Spirituality and sexuality are conjoined for many people in order for them to be fully human, and we must find peace and honor in both. There are of course some dedicated men and women for whom a celibate, ascetic life is fulfilling; historically they have always been amongst us. How those people honor their sexuality would be the topic of another book. However, as has been illustrated very clearly from the narratives, the practice in any system of taking young women (or men) from a childhood of indoctrination and expecting them to make lifelong commitments and vows of cebebacy in their early 20's is wrong. Keeping women in such blatantly subservient roles has literally degraded both them and the institution. Their place at the feet of men is an outrage in any century but surely should be totally unacceptable in the 21st Century. Why then does it continue?

I saw a recent program on Oprah where she interviewed young nuns in their convent. The site of those young (and old) faces continuing the saga of the past left me feeling disheartened. The dreams of Vatican II have been repressed; the windows slammed shut, the breath of fresh air suffocated;

A testimony to the power of the penises up to the Pope!

BIBLIOGRAPHY

---- (1996) The Growth and Decline of the Population of Catholic Nuns Cross-Nationally, 1960-1990: A Case of Secularization as Social Structure Change.

Ardolino, E. (Producer). *Sister Act.* Touchstone Films, 1992. (Film).

Armstrong, K. (1981). *Through The Narrow Gate.* New York: St. Martin's Press.

Armstrong, K. (1983). *Beginning the World: A Former Nun's Memoir of Her Painful but Triumphant Journey into Life.* New York: St. Martin's Press.

Baldwin, M. (1950). *I Leap over the Wall: Contrasts and Impressions after Twenty-Eight Years in a Convent.* New York: Rinehart & Co.

Balucelli, R. (1975). The Decision for Celibacy. *Theological Studies. 36* pp. 219-242.

Barromeo, M. C. (Ed., 1967). *The New Nuns.* New York: The New American Library, Inc.

Bernstein, M. (1976). *The Nuns: A Firsthand Report.* Philadelphia: Lippincott.

Bokenkotter, T. (1990). *A Concise History of the Catholic Church.* New York: Doubleday.

Brown, G. (1981). *The New Celibacy.* New York: Ballantine.

Brown, P. (1988). *The Body and Society: Men, Women and Sexual Renunciation in Early Christianity*. New York: Columbia University Press.

Bullough, V. L. (1976). *Sexual Variance in Society and History*. Chicago: University of Chicago Press.

Calianni, J. F. (Ed., 1968). *Married Priests and Married Nuns*. New York: McGraw-Hill.

Catholic Theological Society of America (1977). *Human Sexuality. New Directions in American Catholic Thought*. New York: Paulist Press.

Chibnall, J. T., Wolf, A., & Duckro, P. N. (1996). A National Survey of the Sexual Trauma Experiences of Catholic Nuns. In Press. Expected publication date, Dec. 1998: *Review of Religious Research*.

---- *Review of Religious Research. May/June 1998. 57 (3)* (1998). Women Religious and Sexual Trauma.

Chittister, J. (1995). *The Fire in These Ashes: A Spirituality of Contemporary Religious Life*. Kansas: Shead and Ward.

Chittister, J., Campbell, S., Collins, M., Johann, E., & Putnam, J. (1977). *Climb Along The Cutting Edge: An Analysis of Change in Religious Life*. New York: Paulist Press.

Clark, K. (1982). *An Experience of Celibacy: Creative Reflections on Intimacy, Loneliness, Sexuality and Commitment*. Notre Dame, IN: Ave Maria Press.

Craine, R. (1997). *Hildegard, Prophet of Cosmic Christ*. New York: Crossroad Publishing Co.

Curb, R., & Manahan, N. (Ed., 1985). *Lesbian Nuns: Breaking Silence*. Florida: Naiad Press.

Daly, M. (1973). *Beyond God The Father.* Boston: Beacon Press.

Daly, M. (1985). *The Church and the Second Sex.* Boston: Beacon Press.

DeMartino, M. F. (1979). *Human Autoerotic Practices: Studies on Masturbation.* New York: Human Sciences Press.

Diderot, D. (1972). Translated by Tancock, L. *The Nun.* London: Penguin Books.

Doehring, C. (1993). *Internal Desecration: Traumatization and Representations of God.* New York: University Press of America.

Dolan, S. A., Meier, M.M., & Dill, C. A. (1993). The Changing Image of Catholic Women. *Journal of Religion and Health, 32 (2),* pp. 91-106.

Ebaugh, H. R., Lorence, J. and Saltzman-Chafetz J. (1993). The growth and decline of Catholic religious orders of women worldwide: The impact of women's opportunity structures. *Journal for the Scientific Study of Religion; 32 (1)* pp. 68-75.

Ebaugh, H. R. (1977). *Out of the Cloister: A Study of Organizational Dilemmas.* Austin: University of Texas Press.

Elizonado, V., & Greinacher, N. (1980). *Women In a Men's Church.* New York: Seabury Press.

Eller, C. (1993). *Living in the Lap of The Goddess: The Feminist Spirituality Movement of America.* New York: Crossroads.

Ellison, C., & Zilbergeld, B. (1994). *Sexuality of Women: A Survey of 2,632 Women* (Unpublished data)

Evasdaughter, E. N. (1996). *Catholic Girlhood Narratives: The Church and Self-Denial.* Boston: Northeastern University Press.

271

Fahey, A. (1982). *Female Asceticism in the Catholic Church: A Case Study of Nuns in Ireland in the Nineteenth Century.* A Dissertation. University of Illinois.

Ferraro, B., & Hussey, P. (1990). *No Turning Back: Two Nuns' Battle with the Vatican over Women's Right to Choose.* New York: Poseidon Press.

Fisher, D. (1980). Priest-nun marriages happier than average. *National Catholic Reporter*, January 18.

Flaherty, A. M. (1992). *Woman Why Do You Weep? Spirituality for Survivors of Childhood Sexual Abuse.* New Jersey: Paulist Press.

Frein, G. (Ed., 1968). *Celibacy: The Necessary Option.* New York: Herder & Herder.

Friedan, B. (1963). *The Feminine Mystique.* New York: Norton.

Fox, M. (Ed., 1987). *Hildegard of Bingen. Book of Divine Works.* New Mexico: Bear & Co.

Fox, T. C. (1995). *Sexuality and Catholicism.* New York: George Braziller.

Garibaldi-Rogers G. C. (1996). *Poverty, Chastity, and Change: Lives of Contemporary American Nuns.* New York: Simon & Schuster Macmillan.

Gergen, K.J., & Gergen, M.M. (1983). *Narrative of the Self. Anthology Studies in Social Identity*. New York: Prager.

Goergen, D. (1974). *The Sexual Celibate.* New York: Seabury Press.

Goldenberg, N. R. (1979). *The Changing of The Gods: Feminism and the End of Traditional Religions.* Boston: Beacon Press.

Gonsalves, H. J. (1996). *The Experiences of Catholic Religious Women Following The Organizational Changes Of Vatican II.* A dissertation. Massachusetts School of Professional Psychology.

Green, R. M. (Ed., 1992). *Religion and Sexual Health: Ethical, Theological and Clinical Perspectives.* Massachusetts: Kluwer Academic Publishers.

Greer, G. (1970). *The Female Eunuch.* New York: McGraw-Hill.

Griffin, S. (1978). *Women & Nature: The Roaring Inside Her.* New York: Harper & Row.

Groeschel, B. J. (1985). *The Courage to be Chaste.* New York: Paulist Press.

Haeberle, E. J. (1983). *The Sex Atlas.* New York: Continuum Publishing Co.

Harrington, M. (1995). *Hail Mary? The Struggle for Ultimate Womanhood in Catholicism.* London: Routledge.

Harrison, V. (1986). *Changing Habits. A Memoir of the Society of the Sacred Heart.* New York: Doubleday.

Hendricks, G. (1995, September) Whatever Happened to Sister Jane? *America. 173(6),* p. 17.

Henry, S. (1994). *The Deep Divide: Why American Women Resist Equality.* New York: Macmillan.

Hite, S. (1976). *The Hite Report: A Nationwide Study on Female Sexuality.* New York: MacMillan Publishing Co.

Hooper, J. (February, 1998). Masturbation's Mid-life Revival: Hands Solo. *Men's Journal. 7(1)* p. 89.

Hulme K. (1956). *The Nun Story.* Boston: Little, Brown and Co.

Jarvis, W. (1984). *Mother Seten's Sisters of Charity*. A Dissertation. Columbia University.

Jewison, N. (Producer). *Agnes of God.* Columbia Pictures, 1985. (Film)

Kane, T. (1993). *A Subtle Revolution: Significant Changes in the Lives of Roman Catholic Nuns in the Last Half of the Twentieth Century. (Sisters of Mercy).* A Masters Thesis. Sarah Lawrence College.

Keane, P. (1975). Sexuality in the Lives of Celibates and Virgins. *Review for Religious. 34(2)*

Kelly. G. L. (1966). *Female Masturbation.* California: Banner Books.

Kinsey, A. C., Pomeroy, W. B. and Martin, C, E. (1948). *Sexual Behavior in the Human Male.* Philadelphia: W. B. Saunders Company

Kinsey, A. C., Pomeroy, W. B., Martin, C. E. and Gebhard, P. H. (1953). *Sexual Behavior in the Human Female.* New York: Pocket Books.

Kraft, W. F. (1979). *Sexual Dimensions of the Celibate Life.* Kansas City, KS: Andrews and McMeel.

Lachman, B. (1993). *The Journal of Hildegard of Bingen.* New York: Bell Tower.

Liftin, A. I. (1985). *Structural Change in U.S. Catholic Women's Orders After 1967: Placing Religious Innovation in Sociological Context.* Ph.D. dissertation. Columbia University.

Lightfoot-Klein, H. (1989). *Prisoners of Ritual. An Odyssey into Female Genital Circumcision in Africa.* New York: Harrington Press.

Lowenstein, J.G. (1996). Sister Severia. World Press Review, June. 43 (6)

Lund, C. (July 1979). Should Women Leave a Sexist Church? *U.S. Catholic.* pp.37-40.

MacAllister, R. J. (1986). *Living the Vows: The Emotional Conflict of Celibate Religious.* San Francisco: Harper & Row.

Marcus, K. M., & Francis, J. J. (1975). *Masturbation from Infancy to Senescence.* New York: International Universities Press.

Masters, R.E. L. (1967). *Sexual Self-Stimulation.* Los Angeles: Sherbourne Press.

Masters, W. H., & Johnson, V. E. (1966). *Human Sexual Response.* Boston: Little Brown.

McAdams, D.P., & Ochberg, L. (Eds., 1988). *Psychobiography and Life Narratives.* Durham and London: Duke University Press.

McNamara, J. K. (1996). *Sisters In Arms: Catholic Nuns Through Two Millennia.* London: Harvard University Press.

Michael, R. T., Gagnon, J. H., Laumann, E. O., & Kolata, G. (1994). *Sex in America: A Definitive Survey.* Boston: Little, Brown & Co.

Miller, S. (1985). *The Shame Experience.* London: The Analytic Press.

Millett, B. (Ed., 1982). *Hali Meidhad: Early English Text Society # 284.* London: Oxford University Press.

Money, J. (1986). *Love Maps: Clinical Concepts of Sexual/Erotic Health and Pathology, Paraphilia, and Gender Transposition in*

Childhood, Adolescence, and Maturity. New York: Prometheus Books.

Murphy, M. (1987). *How Catholic Women Have Changed.* Kansas City, MO: Sheed & Ward.

Murphy, P I. (1983). *La Popessa. The controversial Biography of Sister Pascalina, the Most Powerful Woman in Vatican History.* New York: Warner Books.

Murry, M. (1994), *The Law of the Father? Feminism & Patriarchy.* London: Routledge.

National Catholic Reporter. (1996) 32 (22) (March 29). Order apologizes for abuse. p. 7.

Nevid, J. S., Fichner-Rathus, L., Rathus, S.A. (1995). *Human Sexuality in a World of Diversity.* Boston: Allyn and Bacon.

Newman, B. (1987). *Sister of Wisdom. St. Hildegard, Theology of the Feminine.* Los Angeles: University of CA. Press.

Newman, J. (1994). *Going In.* London: Penguin Books.

Ohanneson, J. (1980). *Women: Survivors of the Church.* Minneapolis, MN: Winston Press.

Pomeroy, S. B. (1975). *Goddesses, Whores, Wives & Slaves: Women in Classical Antiquity.* New York: Schocken Book.

Quinn, S. (1988). *A Mind of Her Own: The Life of Karen Horney.* New York: Addison-Wesley.

Ranke-Heinemann, U. (1991). *Eunuchs For The Kingdom Of Heaven: Women Sexuality, and the Catholic Church.* New York: Penguin Books.

Ritter, K. Y., O'Neill, C. W. (1996). *Righteous Religion. Unmasking the Illusions of Fundamentalism and Authoritarian Catholicism.* New York: Haworth Pastoral Press.

Rosenwald, G. C., Ochberg, R. L. (Eds., 1992). *Storied Lives. The Cultural Politics Of Self Understanding.* London: Yale University Press.

Ruether, R. (Ed., 1974). *Religion and Sexism: Images of Woman in the Jewish and Christian Traditions.* New York: Simon & Schuster.

Sanday, P. R. (1981). *Female Power & Male Dominance: On the Origins of Sexual Inequality.* New York: Cambridge University Press.

San Giovanni, L. (1977). *Ex-Nuns: A Study of Emergent Role Passage.* New Jersey: Ablex Publishing Corporation.

Making, A (1978). *Ex-Nuns: The Cultural Politics of Self Understanding.* Norwood, New .Jersey: Ablex Publishing Co.

Schwarz, K. A. (1996). *Female Psychosexual Development and Women's Relationship with the Institutional Roman Catholic Church in the United States: A Feminist Psychoanalytic Investigation.* Ph.D. dissertation. Alameda, California: School of Professional Psychology.

Sergio, L. (1975). *Jesus and Women: An Exciting Discovery of What He Offered Her.* Virginia: EPM Publications Inc.

Sipe, A. W. R. (1990). *A Secret World: Sexuality and the Search for Celibacy.* New York: Bruner.

Sipe, A. W. R. (1996). *Celibacy: A Way of Loving, Living and Serving.* Missouri: Triumph Books.

Szasz, T. S. (1970). *The Manufacture of Madness.* New York: Harper & Row.

Szews, G. R. Convent memories: good, bad and secret stuff. (October 12, 1990). *National Catholic Reporter.* p.15.

Thomas, G. (1986). *Desire and Denial: Celibacy and the Church.* Boston: Little, Brown & Co.

Webster's College Dictionary. (1991). New York: Random House, Inc.

Welldon, E. V. (1998). *Mother, Madonna, Whore: The Idealization and Degradation of Motherhood.* New York: Guildford Press.

Wilson, M. BVM. (April 1995). Breaking Open the Silence – Healing the woundedness. *Salt Magazine*

Wise, R. (Producer). *Sound of Music.* C.B.S. Fox, 1965. (Film).

Wong M. G. (1983). *Nun: A memoir.* New York: Harcourt Brace Jovanovich.

Zimmermann, F. (Producer). *The Nun story.* Warner Bros., 1959. (Film).

8541507R00153

Made in the USA
San Bernardino, CA
12 February 2014